CORPORATE HUMAN RESOURCES DEVELOPMENT

CORPORATE HUMAN RESOURCES DEVELOPMENT

A Management Tool

Leonard Nadler, Ed.D.

Professor of Adult Education and Human Resource Development
Department of Education
School of Education and Human Development
The George Washington University

American Society for Training and Development
Madison, Wisconsin

 VAN NOSTRAND REINHOLD COMPANY
NEW YORK CINCINNATI ATLANTA DALLAS SAN FRANCISCO
         LONDON   TORONTO MELBOURNE

Van Nostrand Reinhold Company Regional Offices:
New York   Cincinnati   Atlanta   Dallas   San Francisco

Van Nostrand Reinhold Company International Offices:
London   Toronto   Melbourne

Copyright © 1980 by the American Society for Training and Development

Library of Congress Catalog Card Number: 79-24839
ISBN: 0-442-25624-8

All rights reserved. No part of this work covered by the copyright hereon may be reproduced or used in any form or by any means—graphic, electronic, or mechanical, including photocopying, recording, taping, or information storage and retrieval systems—without permission of the publisher and the American Society for Training and Development.

Manufactured in the United States of America

Published by Van Nostrand Reinhold Company
135 West 50th Street, New York, N.Y. 10020
and
American Society for Training and Development
P.O. Box 5307, Madison, Wisconsin 53705

Published simultaneously in Canada by Van Nostrand Reinhold Ltd.

15 14 13 12 11 10 9 8 7 6 5 4 3 2 1

Library of Congress Cataloging in Publication Data

Nadler, Leonard.
    Corporate human resources development.

  (Van Nostrand Reinhold/American Society for Training and Development Series)
    Includes index.
    1. Employees, Training of.   2. Personnel management.
I. Title.   II. Title: Human resources development.
HF5549.5.T7N28   658.31′24   79-24839
ISBN 0-442-25624-8

Van Nostrand Reinhold/American Society for Training and Development Series

Selecting and Developing Media for Instruction, by *Ronald H. Anderson*
Test Construction for Training Evaluation, by *Charles C. Denova*
The Guidebook for International Trainers in Business and Industry, by *Vincent A. Miller*
Corporate Human Resources Development, by *Leonard Nadler*

Preface

Since there has been a virtual explosion of books for managers, one may well ask, "Why another?" A review of books available for managers rapidly indicates an absence of material related to human resource development (HRD). As a result, too many managers have been ill equipped to handle a major area of their responsibility.

Since the late 1960s, I have been conducting workshops, making speeches, and generally communicating with managers about HRD. When asked for printed material, I have had to resort to my own writings, which were directed toward HRD practitioners. Obviously, the focus for practitioners would not be the same as for managers. Hence, the need for a book written expressly for managers.

Corporate Human Resources Development does not attempt to provide managers with an in-depth study of the HRD field, its antecedents, and all the current issues. Managers do not need to become experts in this area of operations, but they do need to know enough about it in order to make the necessary managerial decisions.

Increasingly, managers are making decisions about people rather than about the physical and financial resources of their organizations. Although people have always been important, there is a new understanding of the need to consider people in all managerial decisions. A significant number of people-related decisions are in the area of HRD.

Chapter 1 presents an overview of the field of HRD and some definitions. These are important, for many people are rushing into the area of human resources as it gains in popularity. Each group brings its own definitions, or rapidly develops new ones, without any thought to what has previously evolved. Thus, they tend to use the terms very loosely, which inhibits effective communication.

The distinct separation of learning into training, education, and development is more than a semantic exercise. In fact, the distinction is crucial if HRD is to make a necessary and important contribution to an organization. In Chapter 2, the reader will find specific applications and examples. The major focus is on employee HRD, but, as the reader will note, organizations frequently provide HRD for nonemployees.

As the HRD function grows, more employees within the organization are identified as HRD practitioners or specialists. We have moved far beyond the "stand-up instructor" into activities requiring more preparation of the HRD people and a higher level of sophistication and specialization. The reader will find, in Chapter 3, a way of looking at the people doing HRD in terms of their roles. This provides a model that has value for staffing decisions required of managers.

The HRD function cannot exist without appropriate physical and financial resources. What is appropriate? Chapter 4 highlights the financial aspect in terms of policies and practices that apply to HRD. The reader may be surprised at the various alternatives that are possible and the implications for managers.

Managers need not know much about how learning takes place, but they should be familiar with some of the major trends and terminology. The material in Chapter 5 will facilitate communication with the HRD people by exploring some of the so-called jargon. Each field has its specialized vocabulary, and the words are not defined in the dictionary. In this chapter, the manager will become familiar with some of the words and concepts, as well as be helped to recognize some of the trends in the field.

Evaluation is a problem in almost any endeavor. There are various processes and models, and Chapter 6 presents a helpful way to look at the task of evaluation. There is specific emphasis on the relationship of the manager to the evaluation process. The model and process are related to the earlier material on the concepts of HRD, which emphasizes that a lack of concept can impede effective evaluation. The reader will readily identify how the application of the HRD distinction among training, education, and development can lead to more specific and useful evaluations.

HRD is essentially a management tool within the organization, and therefore requires organizational support. In Chapter 7, a model for providing such support is outlined, as well as specific managerial behaviors that are required if the support system is to be effective.

The HRD function is directly related to many aspects of organizational life, and Chapter 8 offers material related to power, placement of HRD, ethics, unions, and other factors that are too often overlooked. The value of HRD to the organization—and to the individuals in it, are explored with indications of how HRD can and should relate to nonclassroom activities. There is also additional material on nonemployee HRD, including customers.

There is an ongoing debate about the relationship of organizations to social issues. In the HRD function, this debate becomes sharply focused and requires the constant attention of managers. Chapter 9 provides some background on what organizations have done in relation to the disadvantaged, minority groups, and community relations. The role of the government is related to the kinds of decisions managers need to make about HRD.

The closing chapter provides a broader picture by examining the international and multinational aspects of HRD. Hardly a day passes without some reaffirmation of the principle of interdependency in this world. Large organizations are constantly confronted with international factors, and an increasing number of small companies are feeling the impact of foreign investment in the United States and the effect of human-resources policies in other countries.

One of the problems I confronted in writing this book was the ever-present consideration of sex. Does one use *he* when referring to a manager? *he/she? h/she?* Attempts to depersonalize by extensively using *it* do little to facilitate understanding. Thus, herein, *he* is used generically to signify a person of either sex. Where the sex of the individual is relevant to the example or issue, this is so stated.

It is impossible to list all of the people who have helped to bring this book into existence. However, some note should be made of the efforts of my long-time friend and professional colleague, Robert Craig. As director of publications for the American Society for Training and Development, he saw the need for this book and encouraged me to develop the necessary outline. He also made the important contacts with the publisher that resulted in this volume.

Most of the help came from the innumerable managers with whom we have worked in organizations, in public seminars, in consulting relationships, and in formal and informal contacts. The reader may wonder about the use of *we* and therefore I should note that without the emotional support of my wife, Zeace, and the professional insights she provided, this book would have missed its mark. She kept it from being pedantic. Her insightful comments at each stage of its development were crucial.

LEONARD NADLER

Contents

PREFACE vii

1. What is Human Resource Development? 1

   Human Resources 2
      Human Resource Development (HRD) 2
      Human Resource Utilization (HRU) 3
      Human Resource Environment (HRE) 3
      Areas of Controversy 3
   Defining Human Resource Development 4
      Organized 5
      For a Definite Time Period 5
      The Possibility of Behavioral Change 6
   HRD and the Organization 7
   Managers Make Decisions About HRD 8
      Should We Have HRD Programs? 8
      Who Should Attend HRD Activities? 10
      How Much Should We Spend? 11
      Should We Set Aside Space For Classrooms? 12
      Should Supervisors Be Instructors? 13

Benefits to the Organization 14
   Increased Productivity 14
   Internal Mobility of the Workforce 16
   Employee Satisfaction 17
   Organizational Goals 18
   Quality of Work Life 19
   Human Resources to Match Other Resources 20
Conclusion 21

2. Activity Areas of HRD   22

Overall Concept 22
Training 23
Education 24
Development 25
Not for Employees Only 26
   Customers 26
   Related Companies 28
   Franchise Operations 28
   Families of Employees 29
   Cooperative Programs 29
   Absence of Development 30
Reasons for Training 30
   Deficiency in Performance 30
   New Products and Processes 31
   New Policies 33
Reasons for Education 34
   Workforce Planning 34
   Preparing Replacements 35
   Career Planning 35
Reasons for Development 37
   Unforeseen Organizational Change 38
   Sensitive to New Movements 39
Conclusion 39

3. Staffing for HRD   41

Roles and the Human Resource Developer 42
   Learning Specialist 43
   Administrator 46
   Consultant 51
   Applying the Role Concepts to the Organization 55
Staffing Practices 58
   Categories of HRD People 60
Resources for Staffing HRD Activities 64
   Internal and External Staffing 64
Conclusion 71

4.	**Providing Physical and Financial Resources**	**72**
	How Much Should We Spend on HRD?	72
	Budget Item	73
	Cost Center	75
	Profit Center	76
	Variations	78
	Facilities	78
	Space	78
	Equipment	79
	Supplies	80
	Internal	81
	External	83
	Internal and External	85
	Financial Policies	86
	What Are the Policies Related to HRD?	86
	Record Keeping	86
	Human Resource Accounting	88
	Training	89
	Education	89
	Development	90
	Cost Systems	91
	Cost-Benefit Comparison	91
	Front-end Approach	92
	Conclusion	93
5.	**Instructional Strategies for HRD**	**94**
	Some Concepts	95
	Models	95
	Curriculum	96
	Learning Theories	97
	Some Commonly Used Strategies	97
	Group Learning	98
	Individual Learning	99
	Trends	101
	Behavioral Science	101
	Organizational Development	102
	Transactional Analysis	102
	Assessment Centers	104
	Behavior Modeling	105
	Self-Directed Learning	106
	Conclusion	107
6.	**Evaluating the HRD Effort**	**108**
	The Manager and Evaluation	109
	Concepts of Evaluation	110

Planning for Evaluation — 110
What About Objectives? — 113
Evaluation Elements — 115
   Data Gathering — 116
   Analysis — 117
   Feedback — 118
The HRD Concept — 120
   Training — 120
   Education — 121
   Development — 123
Conclusion — 123

7. Organizational Support for HRD — 124

Concept of Support Systems — 125
   The HRD Concept — 125
Organization Involvement — 126
   Time — 126
   Financial Resources — 127
   Participation — 128
   Training Committee — 129
Pre-Training — 129
   Selection of Trainees — 130
   Determining Objectives — 131
   Evaluation — 131
   Confer with Prospective Trainees — 131
   Arrange for Work Coverage — 132
   Review Material and Course Content — 132
   Notification of Trainees — 133
Training — 133
   Avoid Interruption — 134
   Maintain Contact — 134
   Participate in Selected Sessions — 136
   Attend Closing Ceremonies — 137
Job Linkage — 138
   Re-entry Ritual — 138
   Review Goals — 139
   Provide for Evaluation — 139
   Provide the Opportunity for Trainee to Apply New Learning — 141
   Provide for Sharing with Peers — 141
   Provide Compensation — 142
Follow-up — 142
   Reports from Trainees — 142
   Identification of New Needs — 143
   Additional Materials — 144
Conclusion — 144

8. HRD and the Organization — 145

- HRD and Power — 145
    - Programs of Skills and Knowledge — 146
    - Programs for Minorities — 147
    - OD and Power — 148
    - Confront Power Implications — 149
- Placement of HRD — 149
    - To Whom Should HRD Report? — 149
    - Centralized or Decentralized? — 150
- Ethics and Responsibility — 152
    - Do We Have the Right? — 152
    - Responsibility — 153
- Unions — 154
    - Linkages — 156
    - Creating a Dialogue — 157
- HRD for Non-Employees — 158
    - Prior to Hire — 158
    - Meetings — 159
    - Customers — 160
- Conclusion — 161

9. Social Issues and HRD — 162

- Disadvantaged — 162
    - Legislation — 163
    - Corporate Actions — 163
- Changing Workforce — 164
    - Workforce Projections — 164
    - Non-Americans — 165
    - Minorities — 167
    - Implications for HRD — 168
- Community Relations — 169
    - Utilization of Facilities — 170
    - Supporting Community Learning Programs — 171
    - Career Education — 172
- Economic Conditions — 174
- Government Role — 175
    - Legislation — 175
    - National Norms — 176
- Recognition for Non-Collegiate Study — 177
    - What is Academic? — 177
    - Cautions — 177
- Conclusion — 178

10. International and Multi-national Aspects of HRD — 179

- Paid Study Leave — 180
    - Legislation — 180

International Labor Organization	181
It Can Happen Here	182
IFTDO	182
Levy System	183
Operating Abroad	184
School Systems and Degrees	184
Expectations of Host Countries	185
Going and Coming	187
Job Assignment	187
International Meetings	190
Conclusion	191
Bibliography	**193**
Index	**195**

CORPORATE HUMAN RESOURCES DEVELOPMENT

1 What is Human Resource Development?

From their first basic course in business administration to their most recent learning experience, managers are constantly reminded of resources: physical, financial, and human. Successful managers who have never been to school very rapidly learn the need to focus on these three resources. Until a short while ago, human resources received the least amount of attention, unless there was a behavioral science component in the business administration program. Currently, an increasing number of units in graduate business administration programs are devoted to organizational behavior. In addition, we have seen an increase in the numbers of books and articles seeking to alert managers to the need for focusing attention on "the human side of management." The concern over human resources became so pervasive in the mid-1970's that the field virtually exploded into a variety of specializations concerned with human resources. "Personnel" is no longer an adequate term to describe what is happening in the field.

This chapter presents a general overview of some human resource concerns and how they relate to the concepts discussed later. Issues will be discussed briefly in this chapter, and then expressed in more depth and detail in the following chapters. The intent here is to get some terms defined so the reader can focus on the concepts rather than the semantics.

2 CORPORATE HUMAN RESOURCES DEVELOPMENT

This book was written for managers in all organizations—public and private, profit and non-profit. Throughout, examples will be cited from the wide variety of organizations that have made contributions to the human resource area. There are managers who have made the trip from the private sector into government through public service leaves granted by their organizations, and one of their more significant findings is how similar managerial behavior in government is to that in many large U.S. organizations.

HUMAN RESOURCES

The major focus of this book is on the relationship of managers to human resources, and, more specifically, to human resource development (HRD). This term will be explained in more detail in the next chapter, but it is essential that we briefly explore it here, particularly in relation to the various kinds of human resource activities which have emerged.

There is still no agreement on the terms used in grappling with the whole concept of human resources, and there are many reasons for this. For one, there is no single undergraduate degree in the field, as yet. Therefore, people in the field of human resources come from a variety of disciplines and each brings along his own terminology and concepts. Even at the graduate level there is insufficient distinction among the fields, although programs in HRD are now emerging.

At the time of this writing, it is possible to see the clarification of three major areas of human resources, as shown in Figure 1-1.

Human Resource Development (HRD)

This area is the major focus of the book, but it is sufficient to say here only that HRD is concerned with providing learning experiences for people.

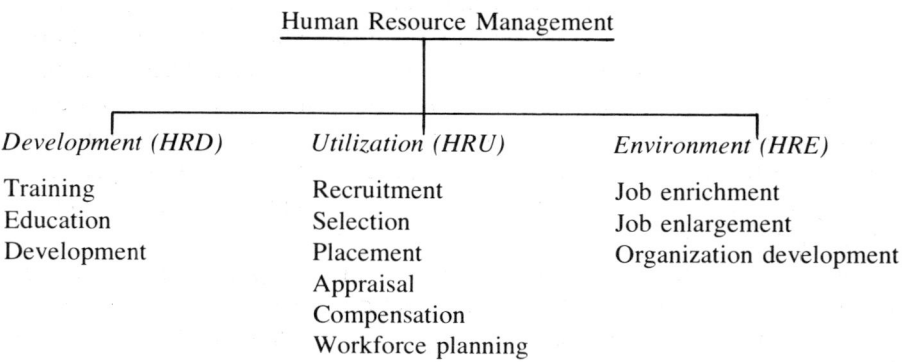

Figure 1-1.

Human Resource Utilization (HRU)

These are obviously the traditional functions of the Personnel Department. They are still needed, and they are very important. Without attention to these activities, few organizations could continue to function, particularly if they are labor intensive rather than capital intensive. In all organizations, HRU is an important activity.

Human Resource Environment (HRE)

This is the newest of the three areas of specialization. Before 1970, one would have been hard pressed to find many organizations with any significant numbers of people involved in any of these areas. Some leading organizations utilized external consultants, but even these organizations seldom considered having a unit devoted to HRE. Increased concern over the quality of work life has contributed to underscoring the necessity for an organization to have people who are concerned with HRE.

Areas of Controversy

At present, and for some time into the future, we can expect to find controversy in organizations capable of producing guerrilla warfare. It is much like the in-company conflicts which were part of the technological boom of the 1960's. Each unit of the company felt that what it was inventing, producing, or marketing was the prime activity of the company. Managers were devoting inordinate amounts of time to reconciling conflicts among various units. This is what is happening in human resources. There are boundary problems as organizations struggle for appropriate placement of some activities.

Workforce planning. Where does this belong? Traditionally, this has been the function of the HRU people. They are the ones who should be in contact with the upper levels of management to know the long-range planning and the human resources needed to staff the future operations of the organization. Yet, the HRE people also want part of this action, for the kinds of people to be recruited and selected will have a direct impact on identifying the appropriate environmental factors. The HRD people, if they think it through, should stay out of this conflict. Once plans have been agreed upon, the HRD people have a contribution to make in providing the learning experiences to produce the desired workforce, identified through the appropriate planning techniques.

Counseling. An outgrowth of concern over the quality of work life, as well as the quality of life outside of work, has led to the growth of what is called career planning or career development. When applied to those who are around the age of 40 it is called mid-career planning or mid-career change. It arises from a variety of sources, including dissatisfaction with the nature and routine of work (environment) or with the present job or future possibilities (utilization). Meanwhile, the HRD people are moving into this field and contributing to the confusion.

Industrial relations. This used to be a well-defined area concerned with union negotiations. Slowly, it broadened into areas concerned with both environment and utilization. With increased talk of worker sabbaticals, it now overlaps with development. But it is none of these, which is why it has purposely not been included in Figure 1-1. At this time, it is not possible to say whether it can be subsumed under any of the three areas, or whether it is a fourth area. In looking at organizations, it becomes apparent that the relationship and placement of the industrial relations (IR) function is more dependent upon history and personalities (both labor and management) than any other concerns.

"Who is in charge here?" This is the major controversy. A new designation of Human Resource Management or Human Resource Administration is emerging on the scene. Some universities already offer degrees in the field, though the behaviors and competency for such a position are far from clear. For many years, we can expect the management position in human resources to be filled on a basis that has little relationship to prior preparation. There are some organizations that have purposely chosen *not* to fill the position with anybody coming from HRD, HRE, or HRU! Rather, they choose a general manager or plant manager and rotate that person through the HRM position. A common title is Vice President for Human Resources.

DEFINING HUMAN RESOURCE DEVELOPMENT

To begin with, let us avoid the use of the word "training." HRD is not synonymous with training, yet it has its origins in that term. When the American Society of Training Directors was formed in 1942, the term "Training Director" was in common usage and was adequate for that period. As time passed and the field began to grow in broader directions, the name of the organization was changed to reflect this, and it became the American Society for Training and Development.

The movement, during the early 1970's, toward human resource development reflects more than a cosmetic change. It reveals significant conceptual changes. In the U.S., in the 1960's, the term was associated with the efforts of the Department of Labor concerning the disadvantaged. Even then, however, there were those who could see broader implications. Fortunately, the Department of Labor ceased using the term and there are probably few who remember that part of its history.

HRD is not new. It is our understanding of the term that is new—or rather, *was* new, since today, increasing numbers of people and organizations are using the HRD term. What we now need is a very clear definition of the term, before we can explore how management relates to HRD.

The term "human resources development" means those learning experiences which are organized, for a specified time, and designed to bring about the possibility of behavioral change.

The term "learning experience" refers to purposeful or intentional learning, not incidental learning. Although many of us learn constantly from the incidental learning experiences that flood our lives (from TV, newspapers, discussions with friends, having an accident), HRD is concerned with the learning experiences which meet identified criteria. Below, the components of our definition of HRD are examined separately.

Organized

The learning experience must have some form of organization. This does not mean that it is only formal. On-the-job learning is certainly organized, or else it is likely to fail. However, it is a non-formal learning experience. Formal usually means taking place in a classroom learning situation, along with other learners. Using a teaching machine, with only one learner at a time, is organized, but is commonly classified as non-formal. The distinction between formal and non-formal is still being explored and it is important to our discussion to emphasize that organized learning includes both.

There has been an increased interest in self-directed learning, and some of the best work in this field has been done by Allen Tough and Malcolm Knowles. If there is an actual increase in self-directed learning, as Tough and Knowles predict, we will see more non-formal learning situations. These will still be organized and will need the support of the regular HRD function.

For a Definite Time Period

The necessity for a time period helps to clarify both purposeful learning and the organized aspect of the learning. The learner and the organization must set aside specific periods of time for the learning experience. Learning never stops, but there is the need for terminal points at which the learner and the organization can assess what learning has taken place and its relationship to performance.

It is important for the learner and the organization to know when a learning experience starts and when it is completed. Think of your own experience. You are scheduled to attend a "management retreat." This is usually held away from the office (sometimes called "off-the-ranch"). Before you go, you need to know how long you will be gone and make the necessary arrangements. A manager's time is important and this prior preparation is essential. Tasks or meetings must be covered, since others in the organization may be relying on your presence. They will need to know how long you will be absent.

As a manager, you also want to know where your people are. This does not mean a constant tracking operation, unless that is your style of management (if so, you have other problems we cannot address here). Still, an organization cannot be run without some mechanism for the manager to know where people are. The manager doesn't have to know where the people are every minute, but he should not have to hit the panic button because they are away without some prior plan for coverage. Any plan is dependent upon the definite time period allocated for the learning experience.

The Possibility of Behavioral Change

When somebody offers you a learning program that guarantees behavioral change, become extremely cautious. You can find programs that guarantee learning takes place, but that is very different.

Later in this book we will discuss evaluation: what can you expect from HRD and how you will know if programs have met objectives. Learning is sometimes defined not only as the acquisition of new behavioral patterns (through skills, attitudes, and knowledge) but also as the utilization of this new behavior. Knowing and doing are not always the same. Helping people learn is not always easy, but in most cases, it is possible. Helping people change their behavior is much more difficult.

The emphasis on the word "possible" is an important caution. There are times when HRD people promise too much, and managers expect too much in the way of behavioral change. All your HRD people can offer is that, as a result of the learning experience, the learner *may* change. Whether the change actually takes place or not is related to many factors over which you have much more control than do your HRD people.

You can have the HRD people conduct programs on safety, but if managers and supervisors do not reinforce this behavior, it rapidly disappears. Take the case of wearing safety goggles. The HRD program may have given all the statistics about eye accidents, indicated the types of safety goggles available in the plant, described how and when to wear them, and even provided each person with his own pair of goggles. Then, a manager or supervisor visits the line. In the course of the visit, the manager is told, "In this area, everybody is to wear safety goggles." The manager responds by saying, "But I am only going to be here about half an hour, and I am only going to observe—I won't be going near the machines." In essence, the manager is conveying the message to the worker that safety goggles really aren't necessary all the time, and each person can choose when to wear or not wear them. Managerial behavior on-site can wipe out a good deal, if not all, of the learned behavior in the HRD program.

Another example comes from a sales force of a clothing manufacturer that had asked to have a program on "Using Behavioral Science in Selling" designed. Working with the internal HRD people, such a program was drawn up. During the design process, it was identified that consulting behaviors (described in detail later) were highly appropriate for the kind of selling that management said was wanted. A program was designed, and then conducted. Several managers were involved in developing the program and all gave their approval and support—or appeared to do so. About three months after the program, the internal HRD people followed up, and despite all the apparent support from the managers about the salesman as a consultant, the message some of the managers were still giving their salespeople was, "Don't consult—sell!" These managers were effectively contradicting the learning, and the cost of the program for their subordinates was a total loss to the company.

You, as a manager, must go beyond lip service. You must support such programs by your own actions.

HRD AND THE ORGANIZATION

HRD is generally found in larger organizations, and there are some identifiable reasons for this, though any organization—no matter what the size—actually provides some kind of HRD. For a particular organization, the HRD program may be insignificant in terms of the organization's overall budget. One may not even be able to find HRD in the table of organization, company phone book, or other observable documents.

Even in a small organization, however, somebody is providing learning experiences for new employees. It may be a very brief on-the-job experience, the coaching of one employee by another, or a supervisor telling an employee to read the manual that came with some newly arrived equipment.

No matter what the size of your organization, if you look around you will probably discover more HRD in operation than you realized existed. Some HRD activities are conducted without a specific managerial decision, or even without the knowledge of management. Even these clandestine HRD operations can contribute to the success of your organization.

Larger organizations tend to have much more going on in the way of HRD. There are usually individuals and units identified as having this responsibility. This practice has served to broaden the gap in human resources between large and small organizations. The smaller ones need HRD to become more effective and more competitive, but they are the organizations least likely to allocate sparse resources to HRD. Instead, the small organization relies on recruitment (HRU) of those who have received the benefits of HRD in large organizations. Or, the small organization tends to bridge the gap by other means which usually force them to hover near the survival level and to rely on less well-prepared members of the workforce.

To overcome this problem, during the late 1960's and early 1970's, the

Congress authorized a program entitled the State Technical Assistance Act. It was administered by the Department of Commerce and was designed to provide HRD for small companies, particularly in technical areas. During its brief existence, many small companies took advantage of the program. Unfortunately, the legislation was allowed to expire and it has been suggested that it was because of lack of political pressure by small business people. As a result, we are back to the previous situation, with large companies improving their workforce and productivity through HRD programs, and small companies relying on other approaches, which force them to lag behind.

MANAGERS MAKE DECISIONS ABOUT HRD

All managers are constantly making decisions about human resources, and most managers are making decisions in the realm of HRD. When a manager chooses *not* to make a decision about HRD, this constitutes a decision *against* HRD! In the absence of some positive decisions by managers, little will be happening in HRD in that organization.

Managers are paid to make decisions, and some of these are made explicitly while others are implicit. Richard III, we are told, thought he was only making an observation when he cried out, "Will nobody rid me of this priest?" It was taken as a decision by his subordinates and the deed was done: the priest was assassinated.

In more recent times, it has been suggested that part of the tragedy of Watergate was this kind of implicit decision-making. It may not have been any direct decision by the then President Nixon, or even some of those around him, though some have been found guilty in the courts for issuing illegal orders. Of more significance is the climate of the organization which leaders produce through their implied decisions, or lack thereof.

HRD is an area with which many managers are not sufficiently familiar, and that is one of the reasons for this book's existence. Few of us wish to tread through unfamiliar corporate mazes. Rather, many managers will focus their attention and decision-making on familiar areas. From the outside, it may seem that the manager has delegated this function to some other level of the organization as a sound managerial practice. More frequently, a manager will avoid decision-making about HRD so as to avoid the necessity for professing ignorance or only slight familiarity with this area of organizational operations.

Let us look generally at some of the decision-making areas in which managers should be involved.

Should We Have HRD Programs?

The literature in the HRD field tells us that programs are designed and provided based upon specific and identified needs. There are those who contend that HRD programs should only be provided by organizations when there are problems to be solved for which HRD is an appropriate response. Generally speaking, this is true, but it is much too sterile and unrealistic to work as a hard-and-fast rule.

Decisions about HRD programs are reflections of the philosophy and practices of managers. HRD is a response, and it will reflect the kinds of questions managers ask as they move toward decision-making. If managers do not ask questions, those responsible for HRD will try to function in terms of the kinds of questions they *think* the managers would ask. The pitfalls in this vacuum are obvious.

There is an initial decision about HRD which managers must make. Should there be any HRD programs at all? This will definitely relate to the philosophy of management concerning the workforce, as tempered by the availability of physical and financial resources.

Managers of small organizations, with extremely limited resources, try to meet their needs for skilled workers by having high entry level requirements. Such managers look for workers, at all levels, who can be employed and functioning at a high level immediately, with no need for any HRD activity.

This is a short-sighted approach and usually results in labor costs being even more expensive. We know that the more learning experiences an individual has, the more he wants. The small employer cannot provide these, and it should be no surprise that the employee therefore chooses to move to another organization.

Even if turnover does not become a factor, it looms on the horizon. In times of a tight labor market, such as we had in the first half of the 1970's, small organizations benefit from the lay-offs by large organizations of highly skilled workers, including middle managers. When the labor market loosens up and jobs become more plentiful, it is the small organization that loses out in the competition for the available workforce.

Assuming that a worker finds a small organization which meets his financial and emotional needs, does this mean that HRD will not be a factor? Highly unlikely. As technology changes, internal organizational relationships change. As changes take place, there is usually the need for some kind of learning experience. The employee may feel the need strongly enough to identify and pay for the learning experience out of his own resources. More likely, he will endeavor to find employment with an organization which can meet those needs. The small organization, then, is once again faced with finding a replacement from the external workforce. It is a constant process which plagues managers of small organizations, and one with which they have received too little assistance.

It should not be assumed that managers in large organizations have no human resource problems. Obviously they do, but the tendency in large organizations is to hire specialists to assist the manager. Historically, that is what happened to the area labeled as the personnel function. As organizations became larger and management more specialized, the tendency was to move all human resource decision-making into one unit, called the Personnel Division or some similar designation. In hindsight, we can see that the result was to withdraw from managers some of the decision-making and any real concern for the HRU functions.

The same history is being repeated with HRD, but with one difference. HRD is still new enough, as an organizational unit, to avoid the isolation which causes non-HRD managers to say "Do it for me, not with me." A well balanced HRD unit is beneficial to any organization, if it is the result of sound and continuing management decisions. The unit should not merely function on the strength of the personality and drive of the manager of the HRD function.

Who Should Attend HRD Activities?

The obvious answer to this question is *those who need the learning experience*. But this is not always the case. Ruth Salinger, of the U. S. Civil Service Commission, found that managers were unclear as to the contribution to HRD to increased productivity. Given this lack of clarity, it is no wonder that managers leave too much decision-making to the HRD staff. Selecting the correct person to take part in the learning experience is more than a matter of determining who needs it. The decision must also reflect the plans of management for the employee, the type of work being done, and the unit in which it will be performed.

An example of this comes from a multi-national company which provided extensive learning experiences for those of its employees who would be working overseas (outside the U.S.). It was obvious to this company (and others) that a good employee could be ruined by being sent to a foreign assignment with inadequate preparation. As it was a large organization, and many people were being sent on overseas assignments, the company had developed a specialized HRD unit with the capability for providing these necessary in-house programs.

Suddenly, the unit was advised that it was going to be shut down! This was traumatic for the HRD people, as well as for the employees in the pipeline (in the process of being assigned to the learning programs or currently enrolled). Actually, the decision was not sudden. For over half a year, top management had been discussing the need for a change in policy. This organization, like many in the international field, was moving toward staffing its overseas managerial positions with people from the particular country, rather than continuing to send personnel from the U.S. Feeling the need for some secrecy until the decision was final, nothing had been communicated to the HRD unit, which was still geared up for a large effort.

In this instance, with the need for secrecy, there was a possible explanation. Yet, it appears that top management was too security conscious. During the period of their decision-making, they continued to approve increasing expenditures for an operation that they were planning to terminate. They preserved their secret, but gave a message to the organization: *Who would be next?* Which other part of the organization is under discussion with the thought of closing it down or curtailing its operations?

It is not easy to reach a decision on how to handle such a situation as the one described above, but who promised that management would be easy?

On a day-to-day basis, management decisions on who should attend HRD activities will be shared at various levels of the organization. Managers may rely on the HRD people to suggest who should participate, but the final decision must still rest with the managers of the employees who will be attending.

Selecting and approving attendance of specific employees is only part of the involvement of management. The way in which the management decision is conveyed will also communicate a great deal about who should attend. If there has been a management decision to send somebody to an HRD program as some form of reward, the manager should not try to obfuscate by calling it something else. Most people in the organization are wise enough to recognize this situation, and if a manager does not acknowledge the action, doubts will be created about the selection of other participants. When managers select people for HRD programs, the reasons should be stated in such a manner that there is no doubt about the intention.

Unfortunately, there are other areas of ambiguity. These arise most frequently when managers are not fully informed of the basis or need for the learning experience. Then, the management decision may be made on the basis of who can be spared; in other words, who could the unit do without for the time the program will take? There are situations in which managers will assign employees to an HRD program as a form of punishment; no direct behavioral change is expected, except that the employee may have to miss the regular car pool, or the usual lunch companions. The HRD program thus becomes something to avoid. Clearly, this is a waste of the organization's resources, but it does happen.

The selection of those who should attend is an important decision, and one in which each manager should make sure he is involved.

How Much Should We Spend?

It would be helpful if managers could be given some kind of rationale about the limits of expenditures for HRD. At present, all we can do is pose some questions:

- What percent of the payroll should be spent on HRD?
- How many hours, per employee average, should be made available for HRD?

- What portion of the profit should be allocated for HRD?
- What kinds of problems can HRD solve?

It is almost impossible to give managers any clear answers to these questions, and these are by no means all the questions that could be asked. Many of these questions involve the philosophical base from which management is proceeding.

One study, conducted by The Conference Board, indicated that one in eight employees had participated in HRD experiences in the previous year. This was a study conducted among 600 companies representing 7500 of the largest employers in the U.S. For that year, these companies reported spending about $2 billion. Generally, we do not have sufficient data in the U.S. to enable managers to make any comparisons among organizations, but the total expenditure for *all* employees is probably much higher.

In Great Britain, as in some other countries where the government is much more involved in the HRD picture, it is possible to begin gathering the necessary data. Applying this to the U.S. becomes almost impossible, as we must make allowances for the cultural, philosophical, and economic factors which are so difficult to quantify.

In Japan, the emphasis is on developing internal HRD facilities, rather than relying on the school system. Each major organization has its own company schools which teach theory and skills, usually related only to the company and its products and equipment. The regular school system could not possibly meet the needs of the major Japanese companies, and is not expected to. Compare this with the U.S., where our thrust has been to attempt to bridge the gap between school and work.

Managers are responsible for allocating and utilizing the financial resources of the organization. Yet, at this time, there are insufficient criteria available to help managers make these decisions as related to HRD. This contributes to the kind of fighting and grandiose promises which are, regrettably, a hallmark of some HRD programs.

Should We Set Aside Space For Classrooms?

Managers make decisions about physical facilities, and this includes those requested for HRD purposes. These decisions are extremely crucial, for once they are made, they are costly to reverse. An initial decision can have much more far-reaching implications than originally expected.

The management decision can range from agreeing to provide a single room for HRD activities to the $100 million facility of Xerox at Leesburg, Virginia. No matter what the facility, some kind of decision has to be made at some level of management. Once the physical facility is established, there can be many other implications.

If space is set aside for classrooms, the tendency will be to use classrooms. But what if the approach of the HRD people is to have the learning take place as close to the job as possible? Or, what if the plan is to emphasize individualized instruction, which requires a different facility than a classroom? The word "classroom" does not do justice to the possibilities within that confined space; for instance, the seats may be fixed or movable, and there may be provisions for audio-visual presentations.

These are areas about which managers must make decisions. Of course, they rely on their HRD people to make recommendations, but these should be carefully scrutinized, for they represent the philosophy of the HRD unit as much as its physical needs. Managers should be sure that the physical facilities they are authorizing are consistent with the philosophy and practice of the organization.

Space for HRD can be provided in other ways. The budget can be made available so the HRD unit can rent space or use external conference facilities. This is a common practice, as evidence by the increase in the number of such facilities available.

Where the organization is heavily engaged in production operations, the HRD staff may request that the learning facility be as close to the operations area as possible. This is based on sound principles of learning and is certainly a desirable situation. This may mean, however, that a line supervisor must be prepared to give up space which might otherwise by used for production. To avoid conflict, management should examine this closely and then make a positive and open decision. To force the HRD unit and the line supervisor to "fight it out" may prove very costly to management at a later date.

Should Supervisors Be Instructors?

This question is often asked, and is a misleading one. Instruction is already a crucial element of a supervisor's job. However, not all supervisors agree with this, and it is important for managers to clarify this part of the supervisor's responsibility. As with any similar management decision, if the supervisor is to be an instructor, management must be sure that there are the appropriate rewards and recognition for this behavior.

There are some obvious examples of how supervisors function as instructors. There is the case where the supervisor must work with each new employee until the employee has reached a suitable level of performance. There is no question but that the supervisor does this through instruction. The conflict arises when the organization does little or nothing to prepare the supervisor for this function. If the supervisor does not feel comfortable serving as an instructor, then it is unlikely that he will give valuable time to being an instructor, even when his services are needed desperately. The HRD unit can help the supervisor acquire the necessary skills to instruct, but without firm management support, it is doubtful the skills will be utilized.

In some situations, the supervisor may not do the actual instruction, but instead, he will rely on a carefully selected subordinate. In one major auto company, they have assigned a "utility-man" (or woman) for this function. The supervisor, with the approval and support of management, can take an employee off production and use him to instruct new employees or experienced employees who need some additional instruction. The union has concurred in this assignment and the rate of pay for this work has been mutually established. When there is no need for instruction, the utility-man may either fill in on the production line or do other work as assigned by the supervisor. Such an arrangement cannot succeed unless management has approved it, and, as in this case, reinforced it through the process of union negotiation.

If the supervisor is to be used as an instructor, management must make adequate provisions. Usually, supervisors are rewarded for production, service, or whatever the output of the unit. Management must build in the necessary reward and support for supervisory behavior based on instruction, as well as giving orders. Managers have to find ways to communicate to supervisors that instructing is not non-productive time, but is necessary if production and quality are to be maintained.

BENEFITS TO THE ORGANIZATION

Managers can use HRD in many ways to benefit the organization. The specifics will vary from organization to organization, but there are some general areas which can be discussed.

Increased Productivity

Particularly in a manufacturing organization, productivity is the crucial element which can spell the difference between profit and loss, survival and collapse. Productivity should not be confused with production. It is possible to increase production by overtime, by hiring additional workers, or by procuring additional equipment. Productivity means bringing about the desired increase in production, not by adding to the workforce or the equipment, but through the greater efficiency of both.

For some managers, this distinction may be difficult to determine. In service situations, where measurement of output is difficult (if not impossible), the concept of productivity has less meaning. For other managers, the concept may have been forgotten or may have received less attention in light of other priorities. It is agreed, however, that without a constant increase in worker productivity, a company (and a nation) will have difficulty competing in our industrial world.

To clarify this distinction, let us take an example. If an employee is producing eight widgets in an eight hour period, that is production. If the goal is to increase production, the work day can be lengthened to ten hours and the worker will be expected to produce ten widgets. (As a sidelight, productivity actually goes down, for with labor cost at time-and-a-half, the unit cost of those additional two widgets is higher than the cost of the first eight.) Productivity would dictate that a manager try to find ways to have the employee produce ten widgets in the eight hours. In the past, this was usually accomplished by some kind of speed-up, and the techniques that were used made industrial horror stories. Production might have been increased, and there might have even been some temporary gains in productivity, but the manager usually paid for these gains in other ways—through lowered employee morale and trust, an increase in rejects, breakdowns in equipment and machinery, and provoking the employees to form stronger unions.

When production was tied to machine operation, a manager could obtain equipment that would work faster, thereby forcing the employee to work faster. The famous Charlie Chaplin film, *Modern Times,* depicted how ludicrous and counterproductive this could be.

This does not mean that a manager cannot increase productivity, but it does tell us that other means should be sought.

Organizations that are competing on the international market are very familiar with the productivity concept. Managers in such companies are constantly comparing the productivity of their own workers with that of the workers in the countries with which they are competing. Within the U.S., the term is much more a part of the vocabulary of economists than of managers.

One factor contributing to either a loss of productivity, or to only negligible gains, is the assumption that a worker, once skilled, remains at a skill level. When workers do repetitive functions, they tend to lose some of their skills. Doing the same tasks over and over will not necessarily increase skill level and related productivity, but rather will result in "stale" performance, which lowers productivity.

At first reading, this may seem to be contradictory. After all, the more one does a task, the better one should become at it. Let us take a non-organization-oriented task in which most of us are involved: driving a car. After many years of driving, do you tend to repeat many of your actions without much concern or thought? As long as you do not have accidents (or near misses), you just keep on driving even if your techniques are not what they were in earlier years. The confrontation comes when you try to back-park, in just the three steps that you used when you were more expert at back-parking. Now, when faced with this need for back-parking, you may exhibit avoidance behavior by going around the block to find another space which does not require this maneuver. Faced with the need to perform (i.e., to park the car), the maneuver may take much longer and involve a good deal of curb scraping and bumper contact. Likewise, an employee may have lost some of his skills that were previously at a high level. The employee is now accomplishing the same task, but with diminished efficiency and a resultant higher cost to the organization. This is an area where a manager can use HRD very effectively.

The benefits of HRD for management are not limited to the area of productivity. Some jobs are difficult to measure. For example, in a managerial job, the element of productivity is not as significant. HRD will not help the manager measure his job, or any job. However, if used carefully, HRD programs can contribute to improving some observable elements of job performance. One example is in the area of communications. If it is identified that some members of the organization can benefit from a learning experience in written communications, the HRD people can organize and deliver such a program. At the end, it should be possible to identify how written communications have improved, though there is no productivity measure available for quantifying this change in behavior.

Internal Mobility of the Workforce

We have a society in which external movement in the workforce is an accepted way of life. Some people are employed right out of school and remain with the same employer for their entire work life. In our economic society, this is the exception rather than the rule. In some other parts of the world, it is just the opposite: one worker can spend an entire work life with the same employer (Japan is an outstanding example of this). Given frequent changes in employment in the U.S., we research and gather statistics and other data relative to these external workforce changes.

Much less has been researched and is known about internal mobility; that is, movement within the same organization. There are many reasons for an organization to want to reduce turnover and keep the same people working for the organization for long periods of time, and this is another area where HRD and HRU must work together through activities such as career planning.

One reason for people leaving an organization where they are functioning well is the lack of opportunity for internal movement. This is sometimes confused with a lack of opportunity for promotion, but not all internal movement is promotion (though, generally speaking, that is the major thrust). At higher levels of the organization, there is usually some kind of replacement schedule which is designed to bring about the orderly replacement of executives and managers. It is generally recognized that without some plan, the organization will find itself woefully short of needed leadership because of retirements, deaths, resignations, and other forms of attrition in the workforce. Once we leave the upper levels of the organization, it is often much more difficult to ascertain any plans for orderly movement of people through the organization.

There are organizations that do have good internal mobility plans (sometimes called career development or career pathing), but they are too few in number. As a manager, you should look at your organization and find out if such a plan exists. If it does, how is it working, and how do the various human resource activities relate to the plan? If your organization does not have such a plan, it is important to determine what you are losing in its absence.

When the economy is expanding (as it was in the 1960's), there is a great deal of room for growth and internal mobility. When conditions are not so rosy, are you likely to lose significant people from your organization because they do not see any place to go? Why should they stay with your organization when there is no expansion, and therefore, perhaps, no movement for them? Part of your workforce will not want to move, and that is fine. People who are supervisors or managers tend to seek movement, which may be one reason they achieved that kind of job in the first place.

Have you identified your best people? Do you want to keep them? Then what plans do you and other managers in your organization have for keeping these people: More pay is the usual response, and it is a good one. But it is not sufficient. A "good" employee is one who wants more pay, and the chance to make even more through accepting more responsibility. The good employee will likely also be seeking more opportunity and challenge. As a manager, you can meet these needs, for yourself and others, through carefully prepared HRD programs which have been coordinated with the HRU and HRE functions. You must be cautious not to allow the HRD program to raise expectations that your organization is not prepared to meet.

The question of HRD and internal mobility is a management decision. It pervades the entire organization, revolving around a very important managerial decision: Do you take a good employee who is producing well in the present job, and risk moving that employee to a new job where he may not perform as well? It is a risk decision, which is what managers are paid for. The risk can be minimized through a sound HRD program that will enable the employee to learn what is to be done on the future job before being placed there.

In large organizations, there is, of course, more room for internal mobility. But just moving employees around is not sufficient. There should be carefully evolved career plans for each employee at almost every level of the organization. The articulation between HRD and HRU is essential, with the complete support of management through significant management decisions.

Employee Satisfaction

One of the elusive elements in the work situation is the search for job satisfaction. Numerous studies have focused on this area (see the work of the

Survey Research Institute, University of Michigan) in attempts to understand what is meant by job satisfaction. It became of great concern during the early part of the 1970's, when, for one segment of the work population, it was referred to as "blue collar blues." This was dramatic, and gained much publicity in popular as well as professional journals. It also brought complaints from other parts of the workforce for increased attention to "white collar washouts" (and similar attempts at playing with the language to make a point).

Much of the research has shown that there is no direct relationship between job satisfaction and performance. Despite this, organizations spend significant sums of money, in a variety of activities, to promote job satisfaction. There are even organizations that use HRD programs to try to achieve job satisfaction! They design the HRD program to increase the happiness factor. Employees are sent to programs, not because they have specific learning objectives, but because it makes them feel good. Some managers use the off-the-ranch (outside the organization) programs as an unrecorded bonus. If the program includes golf, then it becomes a reward for a golfer in the organization. For others, it provides a chance to get away at company expense.

When HRD is used in this fashion, it may have some effect on job satisfaction. Going to one of the outside HRD programs can be considered a perk (perquisite) of the job to which one is entitled by virtue of reaching that position. Perks are fine, and are an essential part of the job (like the executive dining room in some companies), but when HRD is used by management to achieve job satisfaction, there can be disappointments for all concerned.

This should not be confused with the real need for certain kinds of programs to be conducted in plush facilities, with many amenities. This is a function of climate-setting, as part of the HRD experience. It is doubtful if this can be expected to really provide any job satisfaction, though, once the learner returns to the job.

There *are* aspects of HRD which can make a direct contribution to job satisfaction. One has been discussed earlier, showing how HRD can contribute to effective internal mobility. That can produce organization satisfaction, which is hard to distinguish from job satisfaction.

HRD experiences can also be provided to help the employee learn more about how his particular job contributes to organizational goals, product efficiency, and benefits to society. A manager should not expect HRD to take the place of job satisfaction, but HRD can certainly contribute to *increasing* satisfaction with the job.

Organizational Goals

One aim of management is to have a high level of congruence between individual and organizational goals. HRD can be one management tool for producing this congruency, but it must be used very carefully. For example, in organizations that have unions, there is the possibility of violating federal laws if the organization offers HRD programs which appear to propagandize for the organization and against the union. Such programs need not be eliminated, but should be designed to meet the goals of the organization and the legal restrictions that might be involved.

HRD can be extremely useful to managers in reaching organizational goals. For most organizations, given technology and materials, there are constant changes in the way the work gets done. Old positions become obsolete and new positions open up. During the early 1970's, with the public clamor for environmental concerns, some organizations responded by creating new positions related to ecology. Unfortunately, too often they went outside the organization to fill such positions. With adequate HRD programs, these new positions could have been filled internally, by employees who had the interest but lacked the qualifications. The goal for meeting ecology needs had not been articulated with the goal for providing opportunities for those currently employed.

More dramatic is the experience of many organizations in endeavoring to comply with equal opportunity laws and regulations. Too many managers view this program as conflicting or competing with other organizational goals. Frequently, the problem is that the managerial decision regarding equal opportunity has not been related to other management decisions regarding HRD.

Let us follow through on a management decision to offer opportunities to minority group members in the organization—whether this was done to comply with the law or because of the value system of the manager. Playing "catch-up," HRD experiences were provided for some of these minority group members who lacked some of the necessary basic skills of communication and computation. The manager made a positive decision that one of the goals of the organization was to provide compensatory learning for those who had been deprived at an earlier stage of their lives.

Unfortunately, this HRD program was not coordinated with total organizational goals. The manager identified a group of employees who had benefited from the program and who were clamoring for the chance to use their new learnings in higher level jobs. But the jobs weren't there.

What were the goals of the organization? Was the goal to provide compensatory learning situations, to encourage internal mobility in the organization, or to comply with equal opportunity laws? The activity was conducted, but the goals were not clear.

Quality of Work Life

A rapidly emerging concern is how to improve the quality of work life. In the present thinking, most of the activity in this area rests in HRU and HRE.

The quality of work life is concerned with the environment in which the employees have to work. This includes not only the physical environment, but also the psychological environment. It is involved with management providing opportunities for employees to have more control over how the work gets done, as long as standards are met.

One of the major evidences of this, at this time, is in the various kinds of flexitime work arrangements which have emerged. An employee, under this arrangement, can have more options. Picture a dreary morning, and the employee (he could even be a manager) is turning over in bed, thinking, "Oh, if I could only sink back into the comfort of the covers and sleep for about another hour—then I would be ready to face the world." Under traditional arrangements, the employee has some limited options. One is to go back to sleep, wake up at some later time, and then call in sick. (Because it is usually so complicated to figure out the arrangement for docking those who come in late, many employees opt for taking the whole day off.) Another alternative is to struggle out of bed, go through the normal morning motions, and finally get to work (of course, the mental attitude is such that the employee has diminished efficiency, and may even influence others).

Under flexitime, the employee could have another option, that of coming in two hours late, and then working two hours later that day. Sound simple? Of course it isn't, but it could be. HRD may be used to prepare back-ups all around so that flexitime does not affect production.

Quality of work life is an increasing concern, and the above is only one example. It is still a bit early to clearly identify the range of managerial decisions which will have to be made, particularly those in the area of HRD. It is included here as an indication of one of the areas where a manager should be exploring new work patterns and keeping in mind that the whole HRD program should be relating to the quality of work life at some point, somehow.

Human Resources to Match Other Resources

HRD can benefit the organization, if it is coordinated with how managers use other resources. Many examples can be given where the mismatch of human and other resources has proven costly to organizations. One of the most obvious is the experience of "out the back door and in the front door."

In a large organization, where resources are not being matched, employees can be fired or laid off because of changes in production, product lines, or shortage of materials. At the same time, another part of this large organization can be expanding and hiring new workers. This sounds ridiculous, and no competent manager would stand for such a costly arrangement. Yet, during the lay-offs of the 1973–1975 depression, this is exactly what was happening in quite a few companies.

In such a situation, it may not be possible to just take the workers who are due to be laid off and reassign them to other jobs. They probably lack the necessary skills. But this is where the manager can make a decision. It may be more costly, in direct expenditures, to provide HRD experiences for these workers, as contrasted with the cost of recruiting and selecting others. When measured only against direct costs, the "out the back door, in the front door" may look good. But what does this communicate to the workforce? How does this practice relate to the organizational image which managers are constantly striving to enhance?

On the positive side, this is an experience of one organization during the dark economic days of the early 1970's. Corning Glass recognized that they would have to lay off workers and that this could be traumatic for both the employees and the organization. They used their HRD activities to provide a two day workshop on company time. It was geared to helping the employees who were going to be laid off to make the necessary psychological and economic adjustments. The company reported that the workshop contributed to reducing tension in the whole organization. Corning did not promise any jobs, but conducting the workshop on company time and using company resources indicated that management had a concern for their employees. The limitation of resources that required the lay-offs was compensated for by providing increased resources to the HRD unit. This is a good example of how a management decision (lay-offs) could be coupled with a management decision to provide appropriate HRD (the workshop).

CONCLUSION

This introductory chapter has briefly explored some of the relationships between managers and HRD. For some managers, it has probably been a reinforcement of what they are already doing, but for many others, it may have opened up new areas where they should be functioning.

In the next chapter, we will move closer into looking at HRD and what it has to offer the organization and managers.

2 Activity Areas of HRD

In this chapter, we shall first examine the concept of HRD. Then we will take a more in-depth look at why organizations have to provide the different kinds of HRD experiences.

OVERALL CONCEPT

HRD is concerned with focusing on learning experiences provided by organizations to achieve the goals of the organization. We are able to clearly identify three different types of learning experiences, and for convenience, we shall label these as training, education, and development. We might have used the typology of others by calling them *X, Y,* and *Z,* or I, II, and III, but using words already in our vocabulary defines them more precisely. Managers are urged not to be trapped by the prior and often confusing use of these terms. Instead, let us be specific and recognize that we are dealing with concepts, not semantics.

The concepts are compared in Figure 2-1. To contrast them, and therefore to delineate more clearly among the three, we can look at them through four dimensions: focus, time utilization, financial resources, and risk. *Focus* is the major reason that managers decide to provide the learning experience.

Activity	Focus	Time Utilization	Financial Resource	Risk Level
Training	Present job	Now	Expense	Low
Education	Future job	Soon	Investment short-term	Medium
Development	Organization	Sometime	Investment, long-term	High

Figure 2-1.

The focus can be on the present job (training) or on providing learning experiences to individuals to prepare them for a future or different job (education). There is also the focus on the future of the organization, which we may not be able to specify fully, though we know that organizations will change, and that learning experiences can be helpful in preparing for the future (development).

Another dimension is that of *time utilization*. That is, when is it expected that the learning will be utilized? The provision of learning experiences requires the availability of *financial resources*. A manager deals with two kinds of expenditures—expense and investment. An expense is incurred with the expectation that it will return a direct benefit to the organization. That is, if the manager authorizes payment for rent, he expects to have a certain amount of floor space available. Then there are investments, in which a certain element of *risk* is involved. Nobody can expect that every investment will return something to the organization. However, there is hardly an organization which does not become involved in some form of investment. Some investments are low-risk, as when an organization takes its excess cash and puts it into quality bonds. High-risk investments include an organization's marketing a new line of merchandise or engaging in operations which have not been part of the organization's previous experience.

Now let us explore how these dimensions relate to the different kinds of HRD activities an organization can provide.

TRAINING

The focus of training is on the job the employee now has. Such learning experiences are concerned with actual job performance. For positions which are highly measurable and clearly identifiable, it is fairly easy to specify the job and the performance outputs. For other positions, such as from supervisor up, it becomes more difficult to measure the exact job performance, though efforts are proceeding in this direction.

It is expected that the learners will use the training immediately, on the job. The time for utilization is immediate, or almost immediate. There may be a lag if the training covers a wide range of behaviors, some of which are only occasionally performed. Still, the time emphasis is on immediate use.

Training is classified as an expense. An organization has the right to expect that if training was the reason for the program, then there should be some return on the job now being done by the trainee.

Training is a low-level risk. This is not meant to deprecate it, for low is not meant as a value judgment but as a comparison. Rather, as the organization expected a direct return, the risk of this expenditure is minimal. Of course, not every training program does produce a direct return. An organization may provide training for some employees, but then find that the training cannot be used because of unforeseen changes in the processes, the materials, or the market. So even here there is some risk, but when the organization provides training, it is expected that it will be used; hence the low risk classification.

EDUCATION

The focus of education is on preparing the employee to perform on a specific job or group of jobs in the organization, in the future. It is still job-related, but in order to differentiate it from training, the manager should recognize that the emphasis of education is on the individual preparing for a different job.

The most common use of education is to prepare an individual for a promotion. The future job already exists, or at least the description of it exists so that both the manager and the individual have some agreement as to the performance to be required on the new job. In some cases, the new job is being vacated by the incumbent; then it is much easier to identify the job behaviors expected.

The time utilization is the future, but a fairly near future. However, as will be seen later in this chapter, it is also possible to have long-range programs continuing over several years as employees are being educated for new positions. The more common practice is a fairly short period of time between education and placement in the new position.

There are two possibilities for education:

1. A definite job to be filled at a *definite time*.
2. A definite job to be filled at an *indefinite time*.

Obviously, the education for a job to be filled at a definite time can be more specific, and the risk level lower.

Education is an investment, though generally a short-term investment. If it falls into the second category indicated above, it becomes a long-range investment. Usually, managers tend to provide education to an employee for a definite job to be filled at a definite time.

Despite all the good planning of managers, it is possible that an investment will not provide a return to the organization. An employee may be educated for a job which does not become available. This can occur in large organizations where there is extensive workforce planning based on mobility within the organization and within a geographical area. However, the incumbent employee may not move at the planned time; the newly educated employee cannot be placed in a position which has not been vacated. The investment may also be lost to the organization in cases where an educated employee leaves to work for another organization. Sometimes, as a result of the education program, it becomes apparent that the employee does not meet the performance standards for the new job and probably never will. These factors all contribute to decreasing the tendency to provide education. Other alternatives are to place unprepared employees on the job and then provide training, or to recruit from outside the organization.

Education is a medium-risk activity. It is expected to pay off, and a manager provides education with a high expectation of a return. Still, it is an investment, with all the risks attendant to an investment.

DEVELOPMENT

The focus of development is on the organization. It is based on the experience which has shown us that organizations must grow and change in order to stay viable. They must be able to move with the times. Amitai Etzioni has proposed a concept of entropy, which states than an organization (like a machine) will run down unless something is done to keep it stimulated. John Gardner has said the same thing about individuals and their continuing need for self-renewal. Gordon Lippitt has extended this concept to organizations and indicated ways in which organizations can be self-renewing. Many of the writers on the subject stress the need for continual learning.

Development is concerned with providing learning experiences to employees so they may be ready to move in new directions that organizational change *may* require. Once a direction has been identified, and the organization plans to bring about specific change, training and education are more appropriate. At this stage, the need for development may be vague or unknown. What is clear is that the organization will be changing.

In some rare cases, the possible new jobs may be identified. However, they may be so far in the future, and with the specifics unclear, that the learning experience is directed more toward the purpose of development than toward training. Development should be undertaken without any thought of a specific job.

The time utilization for development is some time in the future. Indeed, the manager must be perpared for the eventuality that the learning may never be used. The purpose is highly future-oriented. Even so, there are times when what is learned may become useful on the present job, or on a job in the near future. That is fine, and should not be ignored, but the primary purpose of development is lost if there is an intent that what is learned will be used in the near future on a job.

Organizations are employing futurists, individuals whose major function is to help the organization see its way into the possible future. When managers endeavor to prepare employees to cope with the future, the learning experience is in the realm of development. For each organization, the future is different, and change is erratic and at times very rapid. Managers are probably best able to deal with development if they think in terms of the time utilization being at least one year in the future.

Given this time dimension, it becomes apparent that development is classified as an investment. As differentiated from education, development is a long-term investment. When the learning is finally utilized, it may be so long after the time it was obtained that any direct evaluation is impossible. Therefore, like some other long-term investments, the organization may have difficulty in establishing a cost-benefit ratio for this type of investment.

Recognizing the changes that occur in society, production, etc., the manager who provides development must deal with the possibility that this activity may never pay off. Learning may take place, but then the manager may decide to move in other directions for a variety of sound reasons. The rapidity with which we have been confronted with the energy crisis gives us an indication of what can happen. If the development program was concerned with courses of action requiring high-energy inputs, the turn-around in 1973 would make such a course of action less likely. Therefore, the development provided for employees earlier may now be of little or no consequence. Yet, without development, an organization is dooming itself to being only reactive—and maybe not even that.

Development is a high-risk level activity. The low-risk manager is less likely to provide for such learning activities even though such a manager recognizes the need for long-range planning for physical and financial resources. He may be less likely to see the need for long-range planning for human resources.

NOT FOR EMPLOYEES ONLY

HRD programs need not be limited to employees of organizations. There is a segment of HRD which is concerned with providing learning experiences for those who are not employees. Such programs are conducted for a variety of reasons and in each case there should be a management decision to specifically offer the program.

There are many HRD programs for non-employees and the following will given some indication of their variety and scope.

Customers

Most of the learning programs for customers involve training. The objective is to enable the customer (or customer's employees) to more effectively use the service or product of the sponsoring organization. An obvious example is that of the telephone companies throughout the U.S. They will provide, free of charge, training programs for employees of other companies on how to use the telephone, switchboard, and other telephone equipment.

For more complicated products, such as computers and some military hardware, it is almost automatic for the sales contract to include the provision that the contractor will provide training for the employees of the customer. In some situations, the supplying organization will provide this as a continuing service. The titles applied to such HRD people do not always identify their involvement in HRD-type programs. For example, IBM has a Customers Representative whose major function is to train the employees of the customer in the use of the newly purchased equipment. These representatives visit the customer regularly to train new employees assigned to the equipment, as well as to provide training for refresher purposes to the regular personnel using the equipment.

Related, but not exactly the same, is the training an organization provides so that the customer may become more effective. The U.S. government is well known for its tax collecting function through the Internal Revenue Service. Not too many people know that the IRS provides extensive training programs (directly and through learning packages) so that the taxpayer can complete his return more accurately. The purpose is not to increase "sales" (i.e., to receive more taxes) but to have fewer errors, which will enable the IRS to reach its goals with less difficulty. Similar activities can be identified in other types of organizations, usually those which are in the human services area.

Labor unions provide training for similar purposes. The training, they hope, will make the members stronger union activists. This is one of the goals of a labor union. Training programs (sometimes called worker education or labor education) are offered by some of the strongest unions as a way of reaching their goals.

Many membership organizations provide some kind of training for members, chapter officers, and other non-employees of the organization. This is necessary if the organization is to meet its objectives, usually more through the efforts of the members and volunteers than through paid staff. The American Society of Association Executives offers a wide range of training programs for association members, who are non-employees of the ASAE. The American Red Cross continually conducts training for the numerous volunteers who are essential to the operation of that important organization.

These are also learning programs designed to reach those who are not yet customers or users. The purpose is to prepare the potential customer for the use of the product. Organizations support such programs in a variety of ways. For example, auto companies make their product available, at special rates, to driver education programs. The intent of the program is to prepare young people to become drivers. The auto companies, obviously, are interested not only in having good drivers but also in introducing their product to potential customers.

More direct education programs are those in which an organization reaches out to new markets and new potential customers. Education programs are provided to familiarize the customers with the product and its advantages.

The U.S. government uses this approach, though possibly not often enough. The introduction of a new program sometimes is accompanied by an educational program. Attempts of this kind were coupled, to a degree, with the introduction of revenue sharing, or other programs involving citizens (e.g., customers).

Related Companies

Another kind of non-employee HRD program is that offered to employees of other companies who are in some way related to the sponsoring company. For example, the Whirlpool company manufactures a line of products which is sold under other brand names—a common practice. One of the major arrangements of this kind is with the international merchandising company, Sears. Whirlpool provides training for Sears personnel at the Whirlpool facilities in Michigan so they can sell and service the appliances.

There are many similar examples of one company providing HRD for the employees of another related company. The range of programs and activities in this area is quite large and often difficult to identify. In some instances, the HRD unit is not involved at all and the activity is conducted by the marketing unit or even the production unit.

Franchise Operations

Franchising has become a major entry point for small entrepreneurs. The supermarket and similar forms of mass merchandising signalled the virtual disappearance of the "mom and pop" store so prevalent in earlier years. Although the stores disappeared, there were still Americans who wanted to be their own bosses in small businesses. The franchise became a new route. Major companies, with products ranging from food to mufflers, provided the opportunity for individuals with limited capital to provide services or products. The obligation was that the franchisee meet requirements such as standardization of products, services, advertising, etc. The franchisee traded on the name of the franchiser and bought most, if not all, of the raw materials from the franchiser. The franchisee was self-employed and therefore actually a different company from the large franchiser.

Franchisers found that an essential element for a successful franchise operation was adequately prepared employees. For managers, as an example, there is a McDonald Hamburger College. Other franchisers usually provide similar learning experiences coupled with the franchise agreement.

Families of Employees

HRD experiences are provided for families of employees through scholarships and similar financial aid. For example, RCA offers 25 scholarships each year to employees' children for trade, technical, and vocational careers. There are many other companies with similar scholarships, as well as reimbursement for short-term learning experiences.

The U.S. government offers education for wives, and sometimes children, of government employees going to overseas assignments. A similar practice is found in private companies that send families to assignments abroad. It is a limited practice, despite the great need, and it varies with the economic climate and the pressure for immediate departure.

It has not been possible to identify regular HRD programs which are open to families of employees, but it is highly probable that there is considerable activity of this kind. It frequently goes unrecorded or is considered part of the public relations activity rather than part of HRD.

Cooperative Programs

It is necessary to qualify the term "cooperative" since it is used in a variety of ways. Essentially, it is concerned with the HRD programs operated between a school system and a private employer. The school system could be a secondary school, a community college, or a university. Sometimes, more than one private employer is used for a particular student.

It is unlikely that one will find training in such cooperative agreements. Usually, these programs are designed to help individuals prepare to enter the world of work in the future. Many managers have decided to become involved in cooperative programs for a variety of reasons, including community relations and helping to reduce the number of young people unprepared to enter the workforce. Generally, though, the objective of the program is to prepare the individual to qualify for a job, at a later date, and usually with a different employer than the one who provided placement through the cooperative program.

The major focus of cooperative programs is for education—the preparation of the individual for a future job. Sometimes, these are also called work-study programs, as the student works and studies at the same time. The learner essentially belongs to another organization as a student and is not an employee.

Some apprentice programs can be classified under cooperative programs. Here again, the apprentice is being educated to become a journeyman. In the process, the apprentice may work for a variety of companies under a company/union/government agreement. Such educational programs have proven valuable in providing us with a skilled workforce in a variety of crafts.

Absence of Development

It will be noticed that in the previous discussion of non-employee HRD there is no mention of development programs. There may be some, but development programs are not easy to identify for this group. The focus of development is vague, as discussed earlier, and would be especially so for the non-employee who is outside of the organization.

Time utilization is often too indefinite to be able to relate the non-employee to the sponsoring organization. Financial resources are not likely to be provided for non-employees who have little or no relation to the organization, and are not expected to have any kind of continuing relationship. All this produces an extremely high risk level, and therefore makes it unlikely that we will find much in the way of non-employee development.

REASONS FOR TRAINING

It should by now be apparent that there are some specific reasons for training. However, as managers are called upon to make decisions regarding training, it is important to re-emphasize the reasons why management should support training.

Deficiency in Performance

Possibly the most obvious reason is an identified deficiency in performance. The Kepner-Tregoe approach to problem-solving gives us one way to look at the problem: When a deficit in performance occurs, and we can identify that it can be rectified by training, management should make the necessary decisions so that training can take place.

When an employee is deemed to be deficient in performance, there are several possibilities. It may be that the HRU unit did not recruit and select as effectively as it should have. But even if the HRU unit has done the best possible job, there could still be a need for training. For the future the manager might want to re-examine the standards and methods used by the HRU unit. For the present, the decisions may range from firing the employee, transferring him to another part of the organization, or providing training to enable him to perform effectively on the job.

Job performance includes not only output, but also interpersonal relations. This is a program area usually reserved for supervisors and managers, but HRD programs in interpersonal relations can be helpful at many levels of the organization, and can aid in improving job performance. Where the output is measurable, it is possible to identify training needs by changes in output. When production goes down, the alert manager looks for the reasons and considers that training may be one response to the problem. It is sometimes difficult for a manager to accept the fact that employees who have been productive may now need training in order to regain a previous level of performance. There are so many examples of this that it should no longer need to be emphasized.

One reason for this difficulty is the difference in the nature of measurable jobs and the job of the manager. As the manager moves up the organizational hierarchy, he is moving away from the measurable into the area where performance is less directly measurable. Of course, the manager is frequently measured against the "bottom line," but the manager knows that not every action will be directly reflected in that magic number.

Newer employees may also require training. They may have been hired because they met the requirements for the job, but they may not be able to perform to the standard required by the organization. A common practice is to provide the new employee with the opportunity to observe a more experienced employee. In the U.S., we refer to this practice as "on-the-job training." Too frequently, the new employee may observe the wrong behavior unless there is a well-designed training program available.

New Products and Processes

When managers make decisions to change some element of production, they should recognize that this can produce the need for training. The new product, particularly if it requires alteration in existing processes, may require a new kind of performance from employees. Before the change, the employees would presumably have been functioning at acceptable levels of performance. The new changes may not seem significant to a manager even though they require changes in performance. If employees are not provided with training, the manager should not be surprised that performance falters and production rates slip. Of course, the manager can gamble on the possibility that the employees will "get the hang of it" and will somehow increase their performance back up to the old standards. But what if that does not happen? How often has a manager charged the supervisor with being incompetent when production on a new item has slipped? Would it not be more profitable to provide training to assure that this would not be the cause of reduced levels of production on a new item?

Production slippage becomes even more probable when the employees are expected to operate new or different equipment or use different materials. An example of the above occurred when a plastics plant, using machinery to draw the plastic into appropriate shapes, found that a change was desirable. The purchasing department discovered a new plastic which would be less expensive, and could still be used with the same equipment. As it was only a change in material, the manager involved notified the supervisor of that department that training would not be necessary. The supervisor reviewed the situation and reluctantly agreed that the material change would not make any difference in the way the machine operators had to function. Therefore, there was no training. Within the first few days of production, the new material appeared to make no difference except in a minor instance. Previously, there had been times when a machine had to be shut down because some of the plastic material did not separate from the dies. This was a fairly simple matter. The operator would call the mechanic, who was on the floor all the time, and the mechanic would shut down the machine and clear the die. This would usually take no more than about ten minutes, which included stopping the machine, clearing the die, washing it with solvent, restarting the machine, and checking the first production to verify quality. With the new plastic material, the mechanic was having a great deal of difficulty and the supervisor found that several machines were down at the same time, as the mechanic could not get to all of them. The new plastic made significant time demands on the mechanic and required different repair processes. The machine operators did not need training, but the mechanic did!

In being swept along by the enthusiasm of the purchasing department, the manager had not encouraged the supervisor to explore all possible training needs. Subsequently, a half-hour training program for the mechanic by the manufacturer of the plastic reduced down time on the machines to the old level. In the interim, the cost to the department far exceeded the cost of the half-hour training program for the mechanic.

It is not only in manufacturing, but also in sales, that we find the need for training when there is a new product. The salesperson is charged with having adequate product knowledge to be able to communicate effectively with customers or prospective customers. With the rapidity of change in new products, and even the changes in established products, continuous training of salespersons should be uppermost in the thoughts of management.

One drug manufacturing firm coped with this in an innovative fashion. Management recognized that if their salespersons (often referred to as detailers) were not completely current on the new products, they would be at a disadvantage. As new drugs are placed on the market, there are sometimes rumors about side effects, or that the Food and Drug Administration is planning an investigation. Both of these items might be correct but might not indicate the undesirability of the new drug. But since the detailers are constantly on the road and being confronted with rumors about the new product, it would not be economical to bring them in frequently for training.

A manger then made a decision requiring the use of financial resources but which resulted in continual training at a fairly low cost. He authorized equipping each detailer's auto with a cassette tape deck. Then, cassettes were prepared and shipped out to the detailers, either to their homes or scheduled to meet them on the road as they reached a new motel in a new town. The cassettes were sent through the mail and the detailer found them waiting on arrival. They could be played either at the motel or while driving on to the next stop. This provided individualized training for the detailers and gave them the material needed to cope with the rumors that were affecting sales.

New Policies

Managers continually make decisions related to policy. These decisions, in the area of human resources, relate to employees, to non-employees, and to the community. Many of these decisions, regarding new policies in the organization, require some HRD action for implementation.

Many policy decisions occur on a day-to-day basis and have only peripheral relationship to HRD. Others, however, occur less frequently but have much more impact on the organization and much more significant implications for HRD. This was particularly evident during the 1960's, when there were three major movements in American political and social life that required management decisions.

The first was the attention to the disadvantaged within our population. These could be minority group members, but also included the underemployed or the unemployed, no matter what their ethnic origin. Even before the federal government passed legislation, and provided funds, some managers made the decision to become involved, and to deeply involve their companies. The program was called Plans for Progress, and private profit-making organizations decided to help the disadvantaged. At the core of the program was jobs, but it rapidly became evident that when managers made the decision to employ, extensive training and education programs were also required. Through the 1960's and well into the 1970's, the programs persisted, with some name changes and a change in focus. The basic requirement still remains: To be part of the activity, a management decision requires a supportive HRD program.

The second movement in the 1960's was concerned with equal opportunity. Though this started with blacks, it spread and ultimately encompassed other ethnic groups as well as groups based on age and sex. There was no choosing whether or not to participate—it was the law. But *how* to participate was a different matter. Some managers chose to do so as little as possible. Where the organization chose to comply fully with the law, it became evident that the inequalities of the past could not be remedied only by back pay or rapid promotions. Compliance required active HRD programs to support the management decisions on the extent to which compliance would take place within the organization.

The third event was the proliferation of conglomerates and massive mergers. Some organizations that merged ignored the human aspect of that decision. Employees at all levels would suddenly find themselves working for a company other than the one they thought they were working for. New policies were thrust upon them, with little in the way of preparation.

In each of these events, management decision-making required an appropriate HRD program. Too often, the program was too late, or never took place. The loss in human resources staggers the imagination.

Most management decisions are not so dramatic. Still, when a decision is made that changes a company policy, issuing memos and publishing newsletters will not suffice. New learning is required, and appropriate training programs are a necessity.

REASONS FOR EDUCATION

Managers, particularly in the private sector, tend to shy away from the word "education." It apparently connotes something which is not related to business, profit-making, and the other values which are important to managers in the private sector.

As we are defining it here, education consists of those learning experiences provided to prepare an individual for a different job. Given that definition, education is certainly something with which every manager needs to be concerned.

For managers in the government, non-profit organizations, etc., education is also a necessity. In the government, it is obvious and is a common practice, and despite the limitations in the Government Employees Training Act of 1958 and subsequent legislation and regulations, education does take place.

In non-profit organizations (e.g., labor unions, voluntary associations) it is more difficult to find managers who support education. There are many reasons for this, but essentially it may be in the nature of the job of managers in those organizations. They must be much more "now"-oriented than "soon"- or "sometime"-oriented.

Let us look at some of the factors that should encourage all managers to support education in their organizations.

Workforce Planning

Workforce planning is a future-oriented activity. It seeks to identify how the needs of the organization for human resources will change in the future. The process assesses the needs against the availability of resources both within and outside the organization. Too frequently, the human resources needed are sought outside the organization. A sound education program can meet the needs by encouraging internal mobility and providing the people who could move.

Managers are accustomed to making plans for growth and expansion. It may be the construction of a new plant, the acquisition of other companies, or moving into new areas of operation. In each of these cases, the need for managerial decisions is apparent. Some managers tend to leave the human resource part of these decisions to others or to chance. The various human resource units in the organization can be helpful, each in their own way, but the managers at other levels are those who should be making the ultimate decisions.

Peter Drucker continually reminds us that we are moving toward a knowledge society. More people will be involved in knowledge activities than in just physical activities in the course of business and industry. Managers who agree with this should be aware that this movement requires more education activities within organizations.

Preparing Replacements

Education programs are designed to prepare replacements, in accordance with workforce planning. From the organizational point of view, it is important to have employees who have been educated so that they can easily fit into the new jobs. This takes time as well as careful planning. Yet, without this activity, the organization will not be able to move employees into positions in any orderly fashion. Rather, there will be a constant flurry of last minute identification of somebody who might know how to do the job, or at least will be willing to try.

At times, the organization cannot prepare replacements. Jobs are vacated for a variety of reasons and not all of them are reflective of an orderly procedure. This suggests that organizations should provide education for a larger pool of employees than will actually be moved into jobs at a future time. Each organization must decide for itself, through an appropriate management decision, the extent to which it will provide education programs for its employees. It should be a positive decision related to total organizational planning, and not a haphazard occurrence as conditions permit.

Career Planning

Just as the organization has needs, so do individuals. Given a concept of an economic society which allows for mobility in the workforce, we must recognize the needs and aspirations of individual employees.

Career planning is the method by which the organization assists an employee to identify his personal goals as related to the possibility of growth within the organization. It is workforce planning from the viewpoint of the individual employee rather than the organization, but it is hoped that both goals will be congruent.

To have effective career planning, there must be a management decision that it is desirable. Then, this decision must permeate the entire organization. Without the active cooperation and participation of each level of management, career planning deteriorates into a paper exercise which raises expectations and produces frustration and mistrust.

As we learn more about individuals and careers, new concepts emerge. In prior years, the general approach was that of the ladder. That is, an employee started at the bottom rung of a particular specialty and slowly worked up to a higher rung of that same specialty. We now recognize that goals change, some employees have latent abilities which show up in later years, and, above all, jobs change and new "ladders" emerge. Management must make policy regarding the possibility of individuals moving from one ladder to another—a concept called "branching." Where there is a union involved, this may not be as easy to accomplish, although by no means is it totally out of the question. In most organizations, branching is possible but requires different kinds of education programs than those which are based on the ladder concept. Management should be aware of this and make positive decision, rather than just letting things happen. When management has a laissez-faire approach to this issue, it is likely that potential employee talent may leave the organization to find jobs elsewhere.

Education programs are also related to an employee's stage of life. An employee who has recently entered the workforce is less likely to know what possibilities for growth exist. The general tendency should be to provide some general education experiences for such individuals as they begin to uncover their potential. An employee who is in "mid-career" is more likely to be concerned with education opportunities geared toward more specific goals which have been identified through years of involvement in work situations. An older employee will still want education, but may be more reluctant to prepare to enter completely new fields. Management must recognize that "older employee" is a vague term. The age range for this category has changed dramatically over the last decade. Neugarten now refers to the new "old-young."

Some education programs are short, but others may take place over a period of years. The American Oil Company, for example, has worked with the University of Chicago on a program to prepare a regional marketing manager to become an HRD manager. It is a long-range program taking place over several years.

Education programs are not without their limitations and problems. A major concern is that of the "crown prince effect." This is the situation in which the organization provides education for an employee in preparation for taking over a higher-level position. Everybody now acknowledges that this individual will get the promotion when it becomes available, but this may block others who have potential. In turn, such a policy can produce negative side effects. Others with capability may see little future for themselves when the replacement has been identified a year or two before the vacancy will become available. They see the person being prepared, and are aware of the education program which is preparing that person to replace the incumbent when the job is vacated. They may opt to leave the organization rather than wait years for another opportunity.

To counteract this, it is possible to educate several employees for the potential opening. This can have value, but also carries with it the possibility that some good employees will be lost in the process. Assume that three employees are educated and therefore prepared for the vacancy, but when the vacancy does occur, only one can be appointed; the others will have to wait for an indefinite period. However, these employees now have new skills and knowledge as a result of the education program. Will they be content to merely sit by and hope for another opportunity in the future? It is possible, but it is more likely that one or both of them will choose to become available to another organization for work at the higher level for which they have prepared.

There is no easy answer to these problems. Management should be aware of the implications of any policy it makes on providing education, particularly for jobs at the various levels of management.

REASONS FOR DEVELOPMENT

Development consists of those learning experiences designed to prepare an individual for the future. It is not related to the present job of the individual, and it is not designed to prepare the individual for a future, definitely defined job. It is a type of sensitizing process. It is keeping individuals in a learning state so they are ready to learn when new opportunities arise for training and education.

There are two directions for development. One is related to the organization. It is axiomatic that organizations must change if they are to survive. It has often been said they must grow, though Schumacher (*Small is Beautiful*) does not agree. There *is* general agreement on change. Organizations, no matter what they produce or the kind of service they provide, must be reflective of the society around them, and that is always changing. The sensitive organization looks for the change, and even tries to anticipate it. Marketing studies are commissioned, and there is constant research and development looking toward the future. The same future-oriented effort should be applied to the human resources. People should be provided with learning experiences so they are looking to the future and prepared to change.

The second direction is in terms of the individual. As indicated earlier, in our discussion of career planning, *people change*. At different stages of their life, they have different needs. Even the same information gets processed differently at different times. This becomes evident when one watches a movie made 20 or 30 years ago, which one first saw at that time. The first time, the viewer probably identified with the children in the movie. Today, that same viewer may find a more comfortable identification with the parent. The same movie (since, of course, it has not changed) delivers a very different message.

Another aspect of individual learning is the desirability of keeping all employees in a state of readiness to change. The organization can establish the learning community concept which encourages all employees to be constantly learning, no matter what the subject matter.

Development is high-risk, and will appeal more to high-risk managers. This indicates that we are more likely to find development in larger well-established organizations. Even though many smaller organizations need to be high-risk to survive, they usually cannot afford to be high-risk in their HRD operation, for economic reasons.

Unforeseen Organizational Change

Toffler (*Future Shock*) has warned us of the rapidity of change, although there are some who still refuse to acknowlege this situation. It is a reality. Even Toffler's book, which was such a jolt when it was first published, is partially out of date now, just a few years later, as change has caught up with it.

Organizations have to prepare their workforce, particularly at the managerial level, to cope with unforeseen change. People need to be aware and ready to move, even though the direction of movement may not be clear at a particular time.

One American organization, a textile firm, has done this by a very simple method of development. It is an international firm, and has used its overseas components to provide development for some higher-level employees. As they described it, they select executives and a few middle-managers for the development program. These employees are given the opportunity of going overseas, but not to work. It is usually a development assignment of several months duration. During this time, the employee (and family) are attached to an overseas office or plant for logistical support only. The employee is actually forbidden to do more than visit the facility. He is not allowed to accept any work assignments. Instead, the employee travels around this foreign country and endeavors to cope with new surroundings, strange language and customs, and all the elements of cross-cultural existence. The employee is *not* being prepared for a foreign assignment or for a position back home which will be in the area of international operations. It is purely for developmental purposes. The organization reports that employees who have been given this opportunity for development returned with new insights into change and differences. The organization acknowledges that the returning employee might have gained some new skills and knowledge which would be helpful on the present job, but that was not the objective of the development experience. The organization has been doing this for years and is pleased with the results of the program.

Organizations have, from time to time, sent executives to a variety of liberal arts experiences (Aspen) for the purpose of development. In recent years there has been a bit less of this, partly because in the middle 1960's many organizations increased hiring of liberal arts graduates, recognizing their potential for dealing with change and the unforeseen future.

Sensitive to New Movements

Development experiences help keep employees sensitive to trends and movements which are future-oriented. There is much in the way of hard data which can be analyzed, but this is not the purpose of the development experience. It is to help employees recognize that the possibilities of population shifts, unpredicted technological developments, and national crises exist. Indeed, it is possible that part of our difficulty in 1973, when the oil crisis struck the U.S., was the lack of managers who had been exposed to development opportunities, and therefore were not prepared to deal with the unplanned.

Some organizations have tried to cope with this problem in a different manner. They have hired "futurists" whose function is to take the data and the possible trends and to help the organization "create scenarios for the future." These futurists are probably helpful in many in-company development programs. However, true development should not deal only with even the predictable or possible futures. It should be much broader.

Considering that development is so vague, the reader may well ask whether managers want to have development for themselves. I cannot cite a study, but I can relate an experience. In July of 1973, I spoke before two groups at the famed Sydney (Australia) Opera House. (My ego urges me to point out that I was the first person to make a public presentation from the stage of the Drama Hall.) Each group numbered 544 persons, which was the maximum the Hall could hold. It was an invitational affair, with invitees coming mainly from the government of New South Wales, but there were also some private sector managers. My talk was essentially based on the material in this chapter, and its purpose was to help managers understand the concepts of human resource development. After a 20 minute presentation, I encouraged them to talk with their neighbors and write questions so I could respond to them. The first day, 52 questions were asked, and 35 of them were essentially the same: "I understand what you are saying, but how come my HRD staff has not provided any *development* for *me*?" The response was almost exactly the same on the following day with the second and similar group. Managers want development and see the need for it, although I would not want to generalize from Australia to every country in the world. Some of our colleagues in the lesser developed countries are more concerned with survival; hence, training and education are prime for them.

CONCLUSION

The distinctions among the terms "training," "education," and "development" are more than semantics. Managers should become familiar with the meaning and practice associated with each term. Then, they should be prepared to ask their HRD people about each program: Which is it, and why?

This brings us to the HRD people. What should a manager be looking for when staffing an HRD unit? Chapter 3 answers this question.

3 Staffing for HRD

Does your organization have an HRD unit? It is surprising to find managers who are unable to answer that question. Sometimes this is the result of a manager being unconcerned, but it may also be that the unit is so deeply buried within another activity that it is difficult to find.

The assumption of most of this chapter is that every organization, no matter what the size, should have an HRD unit. It can range from one person, who is expected to give only a limited percentage of his time to the HRD function, to a unit of several hundred people. At present, there are no yardsticks (or the metric equivalent) which can enable us to suggest the proper ratio of HRD people to total organization. There are too many variables to be considered. In this chapter, we will provide some guidelines which will enable a manager to consider the size of the unit and the kinds of people who should be in it.

There are managers who, for a variety of reasons, prefer to contract out their HRD effort or to send employees to outside learning activities. A manager can decide to do this, but should be aware of the trade-offs. There are some losses entailed by having the entire HRD function external, but if this is the decision, it should be arrived at after careful consideration of the alternatives discussed herein. For the most part, we will be focusing on those organizations that have some in-house HRD activity.

ROLES AND THE HUMAN RESOURCE DEVELOPER

Research over the past 20 years has given us a way of looking at the Human Resource Developer through the concept of roles. As a manager, you are probably aware that the role theory has many aspects and that there is not even complete agreement on what is meant by "role." As used in this book, a role is the expected behavior of an individual as preceived by that individual and by others in the organization. As such, any discussion of roles is like the concept of average. You have probably heard the story of the individual who had one foot on a hot stove and the other on a block of ice. He was comfortable, on the average!

Expected behavior relates to what the individual should be doing. This is composed of what the individual can do, and what the individual likes to do. If these two are the same, it is likely that job satisfaction will be high. Frequently, there are areas of mismatch between these two expectations. There are HRD people who can do much more than they are doing, but often get trapped into doing what they like to do. The HRD person might like to be a stand-up instructor and receives excellent feedback from such a performance. It is likely that, without any intervening factors, this HRD person will continue to function in this role, for it can be done, and the individual likes to do it.

The alternative is also possible. The HRD person may be a stand-up instructor, but a poor one. However, he continues in this role even though he cannot do it, for he has few alternatives. More likely, he is not aware of the alternatives and this may be due to the perceptions of others in the organization.

Too often we hear that "HRD is teaching." This is a tremendous oversimplification and represents only one of the possible roles an HRD person should be able to perform. If the organization (and that means the people in the organization) has been accustomed to seeing HRD people as instructors, then the trap is set. An HRD person who wants to do more than just instruct must fight out of the cage. This has been one of the contributing factors to the use of the OD title. (More on OD later in this book.) As OD emerged, some HRD people found that if they changed their titles, it was also possible to change the restrictive roles which had been forced upon them, even though there were situations where they had brought this upon themselves. The new title was given to the individual (or the function) and we then had a Director of OD. That did not mean the individual was actually doing OD, but it did provide an opportunity for new behaviors which had been restricted when the individual was the Director of Training. Even changing that title to Director of HRD allowed for some role changes.

Roles of the Human Resource Developer

Learning Specialist

Facilitator of learning
Curriculum builder
Instructional Strategist

Administrator

Developer of HRD personnel
Supervisor of HRD programs
Maintainer of relations
Arranger of facilities and finance

Consultant

Advocate
Expert
Stimulation
Change agent

Figure 3-1.

The concept of role is two-sided. It consists of the individual exhibiting the behavior, and those individuals to whom the behavior is being exhibited. You, as a manager, may be losing the real worth of a good employee by having only a narrow view of the possible role behaviors of your HRD people. Therefore, in this chapter, we will explore the broader role possibilities available to HRD people. Figure 3-1 presents an overview of the three major roles and eleven sub-roles of the Human Resource Developer.

The model discussed here is one that was developed through research I started in 1958. Since that time, additional research has been conducted, and even as this book is being written, the American Society of Training and Development (ASTD) has initiated a broad study of the roles.

Learning Specialist

A common role, for many HRD people, is that of the Learning Specialist. This is the term used to encompass three sub-roles, all of which are directly concerned with delivering the learning program to the learner.

Facilitator of Learning. Facilitator of learning is the general term used for a teacher, group leader, presenter, etc. It is the person who directly interfaces with the learner in the learning situation. Recent advances in learning practices have greatly altered the behavior of the facilitator from the traditional pattern.

In some cases, we still find the stand-up instructor. This is the individual who directs the learning situation through a variety of techniques, methods, and devices (i.e., strategies). The most common, still, is the lecture, despite all the research which says it is one of the poorest ways to learn. Therefore, we still look for platform skills in the individual who wants to be an instructor.

Among the recent advances is the use of "educational technology." This means using some kind of machine-mediated instruction rather than a stand-up instructor. The practice can range all the way from machine-mediated instruction that merely supplements the human instructor (e.g., audio-visual materials) to having absolutely no person involved (e.g., self-instruction). In those rare cases where there is self-instruction, without a human mediator, there may still be a function for the HRD person—probably as a coach. Self-instruction can be very appealing to you as a manager, for it allows learning to take place with a minimum of time off the job. This can apply to you or to your subordinates.

Another and newer trend is self-learning, which is not the same as self-instruction. In the later, there is a previously well-defined package or route which the learner must follow. In self-learning, there is a much more fluid and evolving situation. An important element can be the use of a contract, which specifies in written form the learning objectives, the resources to be utilized to accomplish the learning, and the ways in which the learning will be evaluated. You, as a manager, may do this for your own learning, with the Human Resource Developer serving as a resource. For your subordinates, you would probably work in conjunction with the HRD people to identify the various elements of the learning contract.

Despite the new trends, there is still a great emphasis on the instructor, for this is the most obvious part of the learning program. It is what people see, and, unfortunately, when one discusses HRD, it is too frequently put into terms of class hours and instructor performance.

The remaining roles and sub-roles are less evident in many organizations, yet are as crucial to success in HRD as in a good instructor. And there are situations where one or more of the other sub-roles are even more crucial to success.

Curriculum Builder. In its most direct terms, the curriculum is the sum total of the learning to be accomplished. It is the content and the sequence of the material to be learned.

The main activity of the curriculum builder is to design the learning activities. There are many ways to do this and the competent curriculum builder must be familiar with the various models available and the theories of adult learning.

The curriculum builder need not be a subject matter specialist (SMS), and is perhaps more valuable to the organization when he is not trapped into providing the subject matter. The range of behaviors expected is from building a program from scratch to being able to recommend which already available learning programs will best suit the identified need. This latter requirement should not make the curriculum builder a booking agent, which, unfortunately, some tend to be. It is not a matter of merely knowing what is available and posting it on the bulletin board. This can be helpful, but this is not the role we are discussing here. Rather, it is the curriculum builder who starts with an identified need and then designs the content and sequence of learning.

The curriculum builder keeps in mind who will do the instruction. The content and sequence will have to be modified, depending upon who will actually be the instructor.

To a manager, the curriculum builder is a much different kind of employee than is normally found in private industry, or in much of the public sector. The curriculum builder works behind the scenes to provide a product which is consumed within the organization. The work he produces is essential to the performance of another member of the organization, the instructor.

Instructional Strategies Developer. When the curriculum has been built, there is the need for some specialized instructional strategies to enable it to function. This includes a variety of activities, such as writing cases, developing role-plays, and making videotapes. Some curriculum builders prefer to make their own tapes, and when they do, they are actually combining the sub-roles of curriculum builder and instructional strategies developer. More sophisticated materials may require special people who have the skills and ability to produce materials of professional quality.

During the 1960's, many people made extensive use of the overhead projector, and today that particular piece of equipment is still used more than ever, with many materials available to produce the necessary overhead transparencies. But in the 1960's, materials were not as readily available. Those of use who used the equipment produced their own overhead transparencies using a form of letters which could easily (the manufacturer said) be transferred onto the clear overhead transparency to produce a "professional quality item ready for projection." For some time, I had deluded myself into believing the manufacturer's claim, until one day, at one of my sessions, a participant was heard to remark that the transparency, when projected, "reminded one of a ransom note, with letters pasted on in an attempt to avoid detection of the person who made it." Since then, I have relied on professionals and have benefited from their advice and skill.

Utilizing specialists for methods or materials can produce another result. At Standard Oil of Indiana, based in Chicago, they have an extensive and elaborate set-up for producing slides. They used to have this done externally, but then found it would be less costly to actually set up their own unit. Once they did, the use of slides increased greatly. This helped unit cost, but did require additional equipment and personnel to service the additional requests.

The continuing development of new forms of audio-visual materials, and other forms of non-book and non-written devices, makes this sub-role even more important. There are many specialties within this sub-role, and some large organizations have production capabilities which could compete with those organizations producing movies for TV. Indeed, some of the facilities actually do this, but they are called videotape-recordings (VTR) and could compete with any of those produced for commercial consumption.

Administrator

Administrator is the general term applied to those behaviors which are done by any administrator, but in this case the word will be sharpened to focus on the HRD function. Given our terminology, this role could just as easily be called manager and does include those behaviors related to the management of the HRD function. As with the Learning Specialist, these sub-roles could all be done by one individual, or there could be separate units for each. The listing of sub-roles does not present any particular hierarchy and none is intended. They are all possible, depending on the needs of your organization.

Developer of HRD Personnel. The emphasis here is on *HRD* personnel—those persons who are involved in the HRD function. It relates to the folk saying that "the baker's child goes hungry and the shoemaker's child goes barefoot." HRD people are so busy taking care of the learning needs of others, their own are sometimes overlooked.

Many kinds of HRD personnel are included in the category. The most obvious are those who are full-time HRD people, serving in one or more of the sub-roles discussed in this chapter.

Another category consists of the temporary people. They are employed by the organization, and for a limited period of time are assigned to the HRD function. In this sense, temporary means for a few weeks, or at most a month or two on a full-time basis. Longer than that might better be handled by considering the individual as an HRD person. Temporary people might be instructors, where the subject matter is highly specialized and the particular people are needed during the conduct of the program. This can happen with engineers, sales, and some of the technical HRD programs.

Part-time is another category. In this case, the individual does not leave the regular job, but spends several hours a day in the HRD function. This is the case where a supervisory training or education program is conducted by a person who is already a supervisor, and where the instruction is given either a few hours a day or concentrated into four or five days. In such a situation, the supervisor/instructor has a part-time assignment to the HRD function.

You, as a manager, have probably been called upon to either conduct sessions or to sit on a task force to build curriculum. You did not leave your regular job, but there were hours, and perhaps even a day or so, given to this duty. You were part-time in the HRD function. Then, you may question, "What kind of HRD experience did I need?" Perhaps none. Or, perhaps, if you were going to instruct, you asked one of the HRD people to help you prepare, to listen to you, and to give you feedback on your performance. This is one example of the kind of activity we list under this heading.

Generally, it is unlikely that a person would be assigned to this sub-role on a full-time basis, athough where there is a large instructional staff, this is more likely to happen. Where the major function of the organization is instruction (i.e., a school system or a community college), this is a very important function. Only lately, with less emphasis on hiring and more on improving existing staff, have such organizations begun to explore this activity more closely.

If your organization utilizes outside resources for any of the Learning Specialist functions, this sub-role of developer of HRD personnel is still important. You can hire very good people, but they need to be linked into your organization. They may need to know about past programs, and something of the culture of your organization. This time spent doing this is chargeable to the sub-role of the developer of HRD personnel.

As noted earlier, it is unlikely that a person would be assigned to this sub-role full-time. For that very reason, it tends to be overlooked. The person in charge of the HRD unit will likely do these functions in relation to performance appraisal, and this is good. If your organization has a weak performance appraisal system, then this sub-role will also tend to be very weak.

There are many good and valid reasons to emphasize this sub-role. They are the same reasons that require HRD opportunities to be provided to every member of the organization. For HRD people, there is an additional reason. It is helpful, from time to time, for an HRD person to "be on the other side of the desk." Just being a leaner for a time is in itself an important experience.

Supervisor of HRD Programs. This is the sub-role concerned with the day-to-day management of the HRD programs. It includes the record keeping, selection of learners (in cooperation, it is hoped, with managers and supervisors), obtaining feedback on performance where appropriate, identification and utilization of instructors, liaison with the curriculum builders, etc. It is the linking pin among the various HRD sub-roles. Usually, the manager of the HRD unit will be found in this capacity, but this is not necessarily so. Where the program is small, the manager is probably doing this supervisory task but where the program and activities are broader, the manager would delegate this sub-role to another person or persons.

This supervisor is concerned not only with the programs actually being conducted, but also with those being planned. As such, this supervisor cannot do the job sitting behind a desk and filling out forms, even though this is an essential element of the job. It is equally important to be out where the action is. If it is a manufacturing concern, the supervisor of HRD programs should be making trips to the shop floor to become familiar with the operations and climate of that part of the organization. Organized follow-up activities would include conversations with supervisors, foremen, and any others who have been involved in HRD activities.

As a manager, you want to know what is going on in the HRD function. The supervisor of HRD programs should be gathering data for you, showing how the HRD function relates to company operations and management decisions. Too often, the supervisor of HRD programs reports what is important to him, or is limited by the kinds of records he can keep. This produces what is sometimes the "head count": the function is reported in terms of how many heads rolled through the program. Often, it will be in terms of program hours or number of courses. This could be helpful, but what do *you* really want to know?

Essentially, from your HRD people, you want to know what problems were solved. In what ways did the HRD function contribute to the implementation of management decisions? Your HRD supervisor should be able to give you this information. He *is* able to do it, in fact. Perhaps he doesn't feel that you really want to know. Our recent concern with "the bottom line" (of the P & L statement) and the use of computers have over-emphasized the quantitative aspects of reporting. Of course you want to see measurable results, and you should be asking for them. But if you insist on only this kind of data, then do not be surprised if the programs your HRD unit runs are only those which can be reported in those terms.

If your management is humanistically-oriented, then you realize that not all performance is amenable to quantification. If it is not possible to quantify performance, then is it really possible to expect your supervisor of HRD programs to report to you in quantifiable terms? (Later in this book, evaluation is discussed, and some of the ways you can find out what your HRD program is doing for you are explored, as well as the kinds of reports you should expect from your supervisor of HRD programs.)

Maintainer of Relations. How many times are you, as a manager, called upon to give speeches? Some of these can be to various groups within the organization. These are not reporting sessions or staff meetings. Rather, you are just being asked to describe what your part of the organization does.

How about external relations? Do you get called upon to speak to the local

Rotary, Chamber of Commerce, or high school on career day? You are not "selling" anything in the sense that you want your listener to immediately go out and buy your company's product. Instead, you are sharing information and, you hope, building the image of your organization.

These are the kinds of behaviors expected by an HRD person when he is a maintainer of relations.

There are two distinct communities. The internal community includes those groups within the organization with whom contact should be maintained. For the HRD unit, these are supervisors, managers, salespeople, office personnel, etc. They are the various groups within the organization, and the variety is extensive. Of course, if there is a union, then those who are part of the bargaining unit are one community, while those outside the unit are another.

Externally, a variety of communities exist. For the HRD person, they seem to be almost endless, as mirrored by the numerous requests for talks, papers, press releases, and participation on panels.

As a manager, when was the last time you invited your HRD people into your staff meeting (presuming you do have these) just to talk about the HRD function? You don't want this HRD person to sell any program, nor do you expect that as a result of his appearance, any programs will result. Actually, you just want your people to know how the HRD program relates to organization operations and policies. Or, you might call your HRD person in as the most likely individual to help unscramble TA, TM, EST, and the other alphabet soup of behavioral science. If your HRD person does not know these terms, and is unable to discuss them with you and your staff, you may have uncovered a need!

Arranger of Facilities and Finance. Earlier, we discussed the need to support the HRD function with adequate facilities and finance (more will be said about this in Chapter 4). Usually, this sub-role is left to others outside the HRD function, and this is unfortunate.

An example of what can happen occurred in a course I was teaching about instructional strategies. One of the students came to me and the following dialogue ensued.

Student: In this course, will we be covering videotape-recording (VTR)?

Instructor: That depends. You know, we keep saying that there are so many strategies available, and with a limited time, the selection will depend upon the choices made by the students.

Student: But I have to cover VTR.

Instructor: Why?

Student: I report to a manager who has HRD as one of his many areas of responsibility. Last year, he got excited about

	VTR and purchased 15 outfits at $2000 each. He spread them around in various HRD units we have in different parts of the country. I happen to be in headquarters, and I got mine.
Instructor:	Fine, you have what would appear to be a good portable VTR outfit, given that price.
Student:	I don't know. I never unpacked it! I didn't see any need for it so I just kept it stored. Now, he wants a report on how I have been using it all year! If I'd had the $2000 in my budget, there are many, better ways I could have used the money. Now, I have to report on something I didn't request, didn't want, and haven't used.
Instructor:	Don't you use VTR at all?
Student:	As a matter of fact, we do. I have a monitor and we rent selected video tapes when we need them. But I don't have the capability for producing our own.

The story could go on. Of course, I assisted the individual in developing the minimal skill to make his report and protect his job. As he and I explored the situation, this was only one example of how his budget was spent by his boss. He should have had more control over his own budget.

By no means should the manager be seen as the "heavy" in this situation. All too often, HRD people have preferred to concern themselves only with learning programs, and have encouraged the organization to have somebody else handle the finances.

As with any manager, the manager of an HRD operation needs to know budgeting, finance, and the financial operations of this organization. Cash flow is important. There are certain times to make requests, and times when a manager should not make any request which dips into the limited cash available.

Perhaps your HRD people should be more closely involved in your budget cycle and your deliberations on expenditures. You may find that they are capable in the learning area but don't know anything about depreciation or liabilities. They may not even know the difference between your company's stocks and bonds. While you are not trying to make them financial experts, you should prepare them to handle the financial aspects of HRD effectively.

Where your HRD person does have an accounting background—and some do—he may be trying to hide this. Once again, we are involved in roles and expectations of the specific roles. If you box your HRD people in so they are only expected to know learning, that is what you will get. If you broaden your expectations, and let them know about it, you might find that they know more about management and finances than they have exhibited in the past. You could have some fine managerial material sitting in your HRD unit!

Consultant

The label of "consultant" has been put on so many behaviors that it becomes difficult to use it to describe anybody or any role. Unfortunately, we have no alternative. This is the term applied generally to the behaviors we will be describing in this section. It is also the term used by many managers when they seek the kind of help we will be describing.

There *is* a limitation to the term. It is often used to describe an external resource as if there was some general agreement that the old descriptive phrase had been altered to read, "One is a consultant when away from home," or "One is never a consultant in one's own country." (Obviously, we have replaced *prophet* by *consultant*, along with the implication that there is a difference!)

Consultants can be *either* internal or external. For our purposes, we will not make the distinction here, but will do so later in the chapter. The focus at this time is to describe what a manager can expect from a consultant.

There are many kinds of consultants. The question a manager should ask a person offering consultant help is, "What do you consult about?" Consulting is a form of behavior, but the subject of the consultation can make a significant difference in the expected outcomes and the respective responsibilities.

During a consulting relationship, you, the manager, will be referred to as a "client." You may not like the term, but it is preferable to "patient"! The designation of client is not meant to put you into a dependency situation, but rather to signify that any consulting relationship involves two parties—and practice has labeled them as client and consultant.

One way of seeing this relationship is through the four sub-roles. These roles should indicate to you the various ways your HRD people can serve you when they function as consultants. It is hoped that they will realize that consultant" tells too little about mutual expectations. By exploring the possible sub-roles together, both of you can more readily come to a decision about the kind of help being sought and the expected outcomes.

The consulting relationship should begin with the client indicating a need for help. In the culture of the U.S., this is sometimes difficult. A manager is being paid to manage and may think, "If I have to ask for help, maybe I am not a good manager. If people see me asking for help, my job may be in jeopardy—at the very least, my judgment will be questioned." Where the manager is a male, there is the complication of the male ego in our society. Where the manager is a female, she may be even more hesitant. Her reflection might be something like, "If I ask for help they will all say I-told-you-so. They'll point out that they knew a woman couldn't do the job." Of course, such soliloquies could be written for minority groups, young people, old people—anybody. If a manager wants to reject help, it is too easy to rationalize why it should not be sought.

The mature manager recognizes that, at some time, all of us need help. (I had a lot of help in writing this book.) Even consultants need help. It is not uncommon for consultants to call in other consultants to help them. There are many forms of informal arrangments to do this, and even some formal ones.

Once an individual recognizes he can use help, the question becomes: "What kind?" As with other sub-roles, the order of presentation is not meant to signify any hierarchy or level of importance.

Advocate. In this sub-role, the consultant is offering advice, and at the same time giving a specific answer. There are times when what is needed by a manager is a specific answer. Too often, as a result of the influence of leaders in the field who stressed the non-directive approach, consultants rely on questioning behavior as their main technique. Or, they rely on seeking motivations or other behavioral components. These are helpful, but only in response to the right need.

As an advocate, the consultant is responding to the need of a manager who says, "I have a problem and I know what it is. The answer lies in HRD and I want your advice as to specifically what I should do." Of course, the consultant/advocate should explore to be sure the problem is as stated, and that there is agreement on the problem. Then, if possible, he should give a specific and direct response.

Suppose the manager says, "I intend to hire minority group members. What should be the first training program for our current employees?" It should not be too difficult for the consultant/advocate, if he is experienced, to realize that the first program should be for the first-line supervisors. We have a great deal of evidence that this is one of the most crucial activities, one that must take place before the event.

If the consultant, instead, responds by asking, "Is a training program necessary?", he is not being responsive to this particular need of the manager. It is always a good question to ask—is this program necessary?—but given the facts stated above, the question has already been answered.

As a consultant/advocate, management has a right to expect a specific answer to a specific question. Management has made a decision, and now wants advice from the consultant on how to implement the decision.

Expert. There are situations in which the consultant cannot respond so readily, because even though the need is clear and the management decision has been made, there are alternatives to be considered. Here, the manager wants a consultant who can offer advice with alternatives. There are based upon the expertise of the consultant, who can say, "Based on research, evidence, and experience, here are some of the alternative ways in which you can satisfy the learning need you have stated."

Let us take the case of a manager who has decided he wants to implement a career development program for his employees. (Career development is one of the emerging areas, and for inexplicable reasons is appearing within the HRD function.) The consultant/expert should ascertain what management means by career development. They might agree that it is a carefully designed program to assist employees in identifying their career goals and developing individual development plans. Now, the consultant/expert can react and offer several different ways in which this could be done. There could be a strengthening of the personnel group, who really should be handling this area—perhaps they need training in counseling. Or the emphasis might be put on individual supervisors, in which case the supervisory training program should be revised to include components on counseling. Another approach is to use outside firms that specialize in this kind of counseling.

You might ask: If some see this as an HRD program, why give it away? My own belief is that counseling of this kind is not an HRD function, but probably indicates a need in another part of the organization. The HRD function is the implementation of the individual development plans where learning is a component.

In this instance, if the consultant were to respond by saying, "Let HRD do it," he has moved into the consultant/advocate role. As a consultant/expert, he should be offering alternatives to management and having them make the decision as to the one they think is most appropriate for their needs.

Stimulator. In this sub-role, the consultant serves in the capacity of one who does not have the answers, but knows how to ask questions. The outcomes are much more vague than in the previously discussed consultant sub-roles. In this situation, the manager has a problem, or, in any case, something is not going right in the area of HRD. He wants somebody to talk to, and somebody who can ask him questions to get him thinking. The example given below explores the task of the stimulator (and the confusion that may result when the stimulator does not know he has been consulted as a stimulator!).

When a very large U.S. company was faced with the problem of getting minority group members into supervisory and management positions, there was no pipeline for such employees. Traditionally, in that company, everybody rose from within the organization. The first four levels of the organization were pre-supervisory. At level five, one became a supervisor, and then there were three levels of management above that. To avoid massive fines, they had to put people in at level five who had never been through the first four levels. Historically, this had never happened. They could not see any way to put somebody into the higher level until the internal HRD person, serving as a consultant/advocate, suggested that a well-designed education program could bridge the missing levels. The company bought into that, and the manager had to deliver.

The consultant called in a consultant! Although the internal consultant was a manager and had a large staff, he felt he could benefit from outside help. The external consultant spent a great deal of time with the internal consultant, and finally reached the stage where he was ready to present a report. Time passed, but the internal consultant did not ask for either a report or for another meeting. The external consultant, a professional colleague, shared his frustration with me. (I was a consultant to a consultant to a consultant in this case!) I listened, serving merely as a consultant/stimulator, but not a very helpful one in this case.

Some days later I met the internal consultant, who remarked, "Do you know Mr. X? He has been doing some consulting work for me—and he is great. I don't know what I would have done without him. I would strongly recommend him for this kind of work again." Puzzled, I contacted Mr. X and conveyed what I had heard. We had another meeting. This time, I questioned him regarding the sub-roles. Mr. X knew of them but had not used them in this case. He called the internal consultant and suggested they should have one more meeting to close out the consulting relationship. The internal consultant readily agreed.

As reported to me, Mr. X discovered at this meeting that the internal consultant had wanted a consultant/stimulator while Mr. X had seen his sub-role as a consultant/expert. Mr. X had answers ready, but the internal consultant's needs had been met by the questions Mr. X had been asking!

Change Agent. Change is the name of the game. Managers are constantly confronted with change and make decisions regarding change. The HRD consultant/change agent can be helpful in assisting management plan the kinds of change that relate to human resources.

Many managers, during the early 1970's, made some management decisions related to human resources as a result of the deteriorating economic condition. One of these was to develop systems to encourage people to retire early. This included giving extra points for early retirees, or just reorganizing and diminishing the job of the "retiree." Some older employees were offered the choice of reductions in pay or early retirement.

Some managers used a more positive approach. They recognized, or their consultant/stimulator helped them recognize, that retirement was an emotional and social concern as well as a financial one. It has been said by a housewife that when her husband retired she had twice as much husband and half as much income!

The managers in one company called on their consultant/change agents and posed the question: "How do we bring about the changes which will encourage early retirement among those who want it?" This approach generated many kinds of programs that proved beneficial to both the retirees and the organization. It included a wide array of approaches, including learning programs, alternative work scheduling, voluntary realignment of duties, and even some reassignments at the request of the proposed retirees.

For those HRD people who are doing OD, here is the sub-role that describes them: if they are engaged in OD involving financial or engineering changes, then they are probably doing something else and functioning in non-HRD areas.

For a consultant to function as a change agent, within organizations, he must know more than learning theory. Here is where the field involves multi-disciplinary work. The consultant/change agent should also have studied or had significant experience with organizational behavior. More and more consultants concerned with OD are building their professional skills by focusing their own growth in the areas of learning and organizational behavior. It is a necessary mix if one is to be helpful as a consultant/change agent.

Applying the Role Concepts to the Organization

Once there is an understanding of the roles, it is possible for a manager to utilize the HRD unit more effectively. Mutual expectations can be surfaced and service to the organization enhanced.

The Air Force Systems Command (AFSC) used this approach when looking at the HRD people (called Employee Development Specialists in the federal service) employed at its various installations around the U.S. They collected data from various levels of managers on what they saw the HRD people doing, and what they expected them to do in relation to the roles. It had been expected that in AFSC, supervisors would see the HRD people as Learning Specialists, the middle managers would see them as Administrators, and the executive level would see them as Consultants. The actual result was that all three levels saw the HRD people almost exactly the same way in relation to each role! Level in the organization was not a significant factor in perception of the roles of HRD people.

As a manager, if you are interested in what the study showed, look at Figure 3-2. You might even ask your HRD people to do a similar study in your organization. Given the above descriptions of functions in the sub-roles, how do *you* see *your* HRD people? If you do this, then ask them how they *think* you see them. The comparison could be a valuable learning experience for all concerned!

The AFSC study did not stop at just looking at what the various levels of managers perceived the HRD people as doing. The researcher went on to explore expectations. He found that all levels wanted the HRD people to do less administration (i.e., paper work) and more consulting. This kind of study effectively paves the way for an organization to bring expectations into agreement.

The roles can also serve to bring the expectations into line through mutual discussion. As a manager, you can list the sub-roles, indicating those areas where you expect service from your HRD people. Then, taking this list, you

56 CORPORATE HUMAN RESOURCES DEVELOPMENT

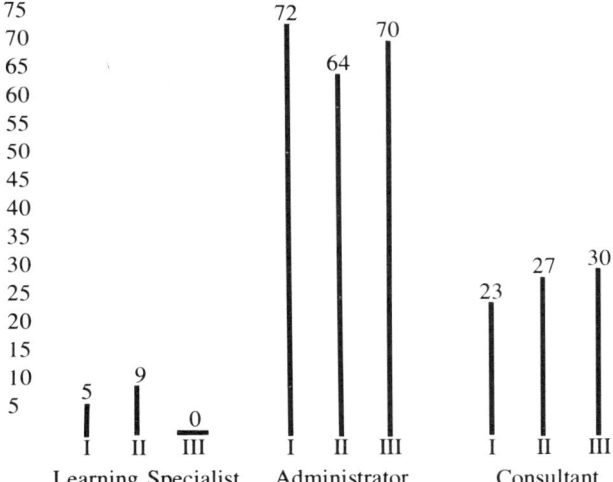

Key
  I. Supervisors
  II. Managers
  III. Executive

Figure 3-2.

can discuss this with them—or at least with the manager of the HRD unit. After there is agreement on which sub-roles would be of help to you, it is possible to get down to specifics. Now, you and the HRD people can identify the specific kinds of activities in each sub-role which has been mutually agreed upon, and what you expect in the way of service. This provides a fairly specific agenda and can clarify expectations on both sides.

An organization, through the roles, can examine how it is organized and who is doing what, and determine if what is being done is necessary. One major automobile company decided to utilize this approach in looking at its corporate level HRD staff. After gathering the data on who was doing which roles, and the actual behaviors in each role, they made some drastic cuts—at the corporate level. At the time of study began, there were 32 people working as professionals in the HRD unit. There were 10 Learning Specialists, 20 Administrators, and 2 Consultants.

After reviewing the work of the Learning Specialists, there was a good management decision to reassign these personnel. They were doing a good job, but it was determined that they were conducting courses through the corporate level which should really be offered through the division level. Not only did they reduce the staff, but by doing so they also freed up some space which had been used for classrooms. They kept one person as a curriculum builder for specialized management programs where they wanted to make inputs from the corporate level.

The Administrator group was reduced to three people, one of whom was the individual who headed up the HRD unit. Without programs, they did not need any supervisors of program. They also found that they had two people who, as arrangers of facilities and finance, kept extensive records on the company's tuition refund program. It was a good program, and the company had a right to be proud of it. A close examination, however, disclosed that the information they were compiling was readily available through the Comptroller's office and the computer system they had. Obviously, all expenditures went through the Comptroller's office and they kept complete records of all tuition reimbursement. As the company was unionized, these figures were important for negotiations, but could be supplied from another source. The two arrangers of facilities and finance were reassigned and the head of the unit retained the responsibility for the budget of the unit, as had been the practice in the past.

The Consultant group of two persons were involved in some OD work. On closer examination, it appeared that what they were doing was fine, but they were spread too thin. Actually, the company had six operating divisions on the domestic side and two additional units which were concerned with international operations. Accordingly, they added six more HRD people as Consultants, and each one serviced a division. The division managers were enthusiastic about this resource, particularly when the manager of the HRD unit emphasized that the performance of the consultants would be based on feedback from the manager/clients they would be expected to serve.

Four additional people were retained, for a while, in a Research Section. When I asked about this, I was given an honest answer by the HRD manager: "We really aren't doing any research. I was just afraid to cut back too soon. Perhaps the roles weren't a good way to go, so I built in a bumper by holding onto four additional positions." Within a year, these four HRD people were also reassigned.

A frequent question asked by managers is: "Does this mean there should be eleven people, or three people? What combination makes the most sense?" This is one of those questions best answered by: "It depends." In this book, we are giving some indications of the variables that must be considered.

If the organization has a large HRD operation, the mix should reflect some management decisions. For example, some companies (of which Exxon is one) have made the policy that all supervisory training will take place out in the field at the respective installations. Therefore, for Exxon, the central HRD unit in Houston does not have any instructors on its staff for supervisory training. They do have curriculum builders, who continually look at the course content and make the necessary revisions. The courses are specifically designed to be conducted in the field.

The staffing of the HRD unit should follow management decision, not the presssure of some individuals to build up their departments. If the organization is becoming involved in change and increasing the use of consultants, the HRD unit should be staffed to reflect this movement.

Where an organization uses a great deal of self-learning materials, it is likely that there will be a section within the HRD unit which prepares and produces these materials. Note: a *section,* not a single individual.

Small organizations tend to have one person as the Administrator, and then supplement this individual with part-time and temporary assistants. The variations in staffing almost defy description. The important point is that the staffing should reflect carefully thought-out management decisions, relative to the contribution the HRD unit and staff can make to company goals.

The role concepts can assist in many other ways, but each organization must search for its own way of applying the roles. It takes understanding by managers of the role possibilities and the cooperation of the HRD people. If it is expected that the application of the roles will be used as a weapon for beating down the unit, do not be surprised if it is greeted with less than enthusiasm. All concerned have to "buy into" the role concept, at least on a preliminary basis. So far, every organization that I have worked with or known of where the roles have been applied have benefited. In most cases, the HRD unit ended up doing much more of the work they wanted to do and could do, but had thought the organization would not let them do.

STAFFING PRACTICES

Before reading further, you might want to take a look at the policies your organization has for staffing the HRD function. If you cannot find anything in writing, don't be surprised. Too few organizations have put their policies into writing; they suffer from the "everybody knows" syndrome. Obviously, the result is that "nobody knows" and the HRD unit is staffed on an ad hoc basis or as a result of personal pressures.

You can use the roles we have discussed to look at the HRD function, the people, and what you as a manager can expect from this function. It will probably take time to identify the questions you want to ask and to process the responses you get. You will have to become involved in dialogues with your HRD people, and all of this is important if the HRD function is to contribute to the success of your organization in the meaningful ways it can.

Immediately, you will be surfacing the implied policies. These will be items such as the following.

- If they don't have any other job for you, you are assigned to the HRD unit.
- Anybody who stays more than (fill in the time) years in the HRD unit is automatically passed over for promotion.
- Being assigned to the HRD unit puts a stop to your career.
- People being groomed for managers are usually assigned to work in the HRD unit for a period of time.

Some of these statements appear to be in conflict, but remember that we are dealing with *implied* policy, not stated. When staffing is left to implications and perceptions, we should not be surprised to find contradictory statements from people within the same organization.

Any or all of these statements may be correct for your particular organization. But how do you know? Finding the implied policies related to HRD can be difficult, but the end result can be a much improved HRD contribution to organizational success.

The written statements are easier to find, and may be included in policy manuals or organizational manuals, or whatever your company calls the compendium of written policy statements. Once again, do not be surprised if you find few or no statements related to HRD. In too many organizations, the staffing of this function is not done on a planned basis. Instead, there are reactions to pressures and trends. One major New York City bank built a large HRD unit composed almost entirely of curriculum builders and instructional strategies developers. This was a reaction to the head of the unit, who was an exponent of programmed instruction and swung the entire HRD operation in that direction. When the effort collapsed, as any single approach effort must, the HRD unit was almost totally wiped out. Within the following two years, they began to slowly rebuild, recognizing the need for a well-balanced HRD unit. Most current employees voiced disinterest in such an assignment and did all they could to stay away from it. The recent history of this organization showed that the HRD unit was built on the charisma and push of the manager of HRD. When he failed (and there was always that possibility), the whole unit suffered. This piece of organizational memory and its implications forced the company to staff by recruiting almost all new personnel hired from the outside. There was no written statement to this effect, but as the Personnel Office recruited and staffed, the message was clear that nobody inside the organization was willing to take the risks they had in the past.

Many major companies have implied policies which might look like this, if they were written:

- At corporate level, the HRD person stays from three to five years.
- At division level, the HRD person stays from one to three years.
- At plant level, the HRD person stays from six months to one year.

How does your organization staff, in terms of time within the HRD, function? During that time, what sub-roles are staff members expected to perform?

I was called into one major company to conduct a "training of trainers" program. This was for the plant level HRD people. I worked with them using one model for designing training programs, the Critical Events Model. By the end of the four days, it was apparent that they were essentially a bright group and had mastered the Model and its use. The subsequent evaluation confirmed this.

About three years later, I was once again invited to conduct the same experience for the same company. I asked, "If it was so great three years ago, why do you need it again now?" The response was: "None of those trainees is still in the HRD function. They have all moved out to other jobs. We now have a new group." This made sense in terms of their company policy, which had never been stated. It also suggested that we should do a role examination this time, and we found that the plant level trainers did nothing as Learning Specialists. Essentially, they were responsible for identifying plant HRD needs and communicating these to the division level. They were functioning more as Consultants, with some Administrator behavior, since they were responsible for "policing" (their word) the programs being conducted. With this information, we were able to design a program which more closely met the needs of the plant level HRD people. We also worked with the plant managers to clarify the sub-role behaviors they could expect.

Categories of HRD People

If you have talked to any group of HRD people, whether to those in your own organization or to others, it is obvious that they represent a wide range of human beings. Among themselves, they have difficulty communicating and this has given rise to many rude jokes, which will not be repeated here. Rather, let us explore some of the reasons and implications.

At present, there is just about no undergraduate program in HRD. If you look at most of the other functions in your organization that are classified as professional or specialties, there will have been some undergraduate work which turned out people who had a common terminology and had read many of the same books.

Generally, organizations do not seek HRD people with a particular degree. Over the past decade, this has started to change, and the want-ads and similar sources indicate that employers are asking for graduate degrees in education, the behavioral sciences, psychology, or some combination of these. Graduate programs in HRD are now being developed, though it is likely that George Washington University holds the distinction of having offered the first courses in the field (1948) and of maintaining one of the largest programs giving graduate degrees specifically in Human Resources Development through the School of Education and Human Development.

With little or no undergraduate supporting programs, and few graduate programs, it is painfully obvious that we will have people with various backgrounds. What is most unfortunate about this is that it usually results in the process of "rediscovering the wheel." The decade of 1965–1975 saw a significant amount of research in HRD. This does not mean that there was none before, but the amount and quality increased remarkably during this period. And although this increase has proliferated since then, we still find people new to HRD who are unfamiliar with the research and who continue experimenting when the data are already there for them to see and use.

Even more important is the confusion that results from having various kinds of people, with different backgrounds and goals, doing the same kinds of work. This is not unique to HRD, but occurs even in established professional groups like medical doctors and nurses. The model presented in Figure 3-3 is based upon research in hospitals that was done in 1960. The model has been revised to reflect the HRD field.

Those in the field who are *professionally identified* (Category I) represent a minority and probably will for a long time to come. This is not necessarily bad, unless the organization and the individual clash. An HRD person who is in Category I will tend to get a graduate degree in the HRD field, and will seek to remain in that field for a significant part of his professional life. Given the changes in individuals and society, we should not force anybody to commit his entire life to any one field of endeavor. Upon approaching retirement, looking back, people may find they have lived in essentially one professional area. But this is no longer a requirement in today's mobile society.

The Category I person, as any professional employee, is faced with the dilemma that arises when the profession suggests one direction and the employer suggests another. I know of a Category I person who took the HRD concepts discussed in the previous chapter and conducted the organizational diagnosis of HRD suggested there. He found that the organization was great on training, was doing a bit of education, and was involved in no development. On the other hand, this HRD person had a professional bias which said that an organization that does not have identifiable development activities is not going anywhere. He wanted to be with an organization that was evolving. Being in Category I, he moved to another organization. If he had been Category II, he would have waited until he was reassigned.

Most HRD people are in Category II, and this is not meant to be a derogatory remark. Internal mobility in an organization is important, for a variety of reasons, and if HRD is one of those functions that people move through, then we must expect many Category II people.

The unfortunate part of it is that Category II people usually come in with little or no preparation for the job. They are there for a limited period of time and are expected to make an impression while they are there. For a Category II person, the biggest fear is being trapped into any one function beyond the time in the stated or implied policy of the organization.

Categories of HRD Personnel

Category I. Professionally identified
Category II. Organizationally identified
    A. Time definite
    B. Time indefinite
Category III. Collateral duties

Figure 3-3.

To some, it would seem that doing a good job would mean the individual would be retained in the position. Yet, where the company policy is to move people, doing a good job means the individual is now ready for new and higher challenges. This puts great pressure on Category II to produce at a high level in a short period of time.

The Category IIA person may be under the greatest time pressure, for the termination of his assignment is known at the time he is transferred to the HRD unit. Usually, this is about a two year assignment. It takes time to get the operation moving, and the new Category IIA person will try to seek out the "name" people in the field, the current "hot" programs, and the other very visible factors which will indicate to higher levels that here is a person who knows how to move into a situation and get the job done.

The Category IIB person will also be under pressure to show some immediate results, but the vagueness of the length of the assignment produces another pressure: to produce HRD activities that can be completed and evaluated in short periods of time; that is, while the Category IIB person is still there. Long-range planning is left to others.

Complicating the situation even farther is the level at which the Category II people are brought in. It might seem logical that the HRD function would be headed by a Category I person, though staffed with many (if not all) Category II people. It doesn't always work that way.

People who are being rotated through the organization, in managerial positions, are obviously being groomed for high-level spots in the organization. Therefore, when a Category II person is moved into a unit, such as the HRD unit, the possibility is that he will be put at the top. This is based on the folk-saying that "a good manager can manage anything." The Category II people are trying to prove they are good managers, and the organization does not hesitate to put the Category II person in charge of the function—in this case, the HRD function!

(As an aside, Category I HRD people sometimes tend to be paranoid—though not clinically so. They think that this imposition of a manager who knows nothing of the function is done only in HRD. They talk of HRD being used as a unit that one just passes through. Reality indicates that this is done with many units in an organization.)

One major company, using this staffing policy, took a leading marketing person and put him in charge of the HRD function at corporate level as a Category IIA manager (although they obviously did not label him as such). This new HRD manager took a look at the situation and decided that what made sense for the organization and for him was to initiate an "Executive Development" program (actually, an executive HRD program which would contain training, education, and development). He held a meeting of his HRD staff, and laid out their goals. He then applied Management by Objectives (which he had learned in an earlier assignment) and, with the stated goal, had each HRD unit member specify how his efforts would contribute to reaching that goal. All other activities were to be suspended, or cancelled! An Executive Development Program was the goal, with a time limit of three months to get it initiated. He had the budget, and outside resources could be made readily available (I was one of them and that is how I got to know this situation). It is not possible to end the story with a perfect conclusion, since this happened during the depression of 1973–1975, and the program was scrapped due to financial difficulties. It took several years before that HRD unit was once again able to function and to recover from the drain of focusing all of its efforts on one program decided by the Category IIA HRD manager.

Some Category II people, assigned as HRD managers, do a magnificent job. As good managers do, they start by finding out what the unit has been doing and how this relates to the organization. They endeavor to discover the strengths and weaknesses of the staff in relation to the functions to be performed. Unfortunately, too many Category II people see Category I people as lower-level people who have been caught in a trap and are not going anywhere. There is also the projection, on the part of Category II people, that everybody wants to get to be a general manager (and movement is essential for the career of a general manager).

Where the Category II manager and the Category I staff work together in a positive fashion, there are benefits for both. The Category II person discovers how the HRD function can contribute to the organization. The Category I person gets to work with a Category II person as a superior, rather than as a learner. This can be mutually helpful.

The other situation is where the Category II person is brought in on the staff with a Category I manager. This is where the sub-roles become even more important. The Category II person will only be there for a short period of time, as compared to Category I. The Category II person brings strengths and weaknesses, as well as his own professional and personal goals. He is an important resource to the Category I manager, if used effectively. This depends on the particular sub-roles which are more appropriate for the individual and the organization. Some sub-roles require years of preparation (e.g., the consultant/expert sub-role) and it is unlikely that the Category II person has this background. The Category I manager can make this assignment a rewarding one for the Category II person. Conversely, the Category II person may leave the assignment with negative feelings toward the staff and work of the HRD unit.

Whatever the category, it should be clear to all what is expected of each individual. "Moving through the HRD unit" should not be seen as demeaning to the individual or the unit. The staffing of the unit with various categories can be helpful, if the expectations have been clearly identified.

So far, little has been said about Category III, and perhaps little need be said. This is usually found in small organizations that do not have an HRD unit. There will be a person, frequently a personnel director, who is also asked to do something about HRD. Many of these personnel (utilization) people attend conferences and institutes of the ASTD and similar organizations in order to find out more about what they should be doing in this function. Some of the more traditional groups, such as the American Society for Personnel Administration, still see "training" as one of the functions of personnel directors. As such, they try to find out what they can about the HRD function, and this is admirable. However, they are still Category III people, with the HRD function as only a small part of their responsibilities, and they cannot be expected to be familiar with learning theory, trends in the field, the current research, and the other elements that contribute to an effective HRD operation.

Some organizations have their HRD unit within the Personnel/Utilization section. As such, the Category I person is there but has great difficulty functioning effectively. The emphasis is always on promotion, and promotion is into a personnel position. This forces the Category I person to become Category II or leave the organization. The other implication is that the HRD person has been "passed over" and, after a while, nobody in Category I really wants the job. Where HRD is under personnel, the long-term staffing is usually with either Category II or Category III, and the organization loses the benefit of what the Category I person can bring to it.

RESOURCES FOR STAFFING HRD ACTIVITIES

There are many ways to staff for HRD. As indicated earlier, the use of the sub-roles is a very helpful way for an organization to look at its HRD unit and come to some agreements on staffing. In addition, there are other dimensions of staffing which need to be explored.

Internal and External Staffing

One issue of continuous discussion is the relative merits of internal and external staffing; that is, from within (internal) the organization or from outside (external) the organization. There is sometimes confusion over the use of these terms. For our purposes here, if the salary is being paid by the organization, the HRD people are internal, no matter where they are physically located on the organizational or geographical map.

Related to this is the poor use of the word "consultant." It is too often used to signify anybody brought in from the outside. In light of our earlier discussion on roles, it is hoped that we can now use the term consultant in a more specific manner to describe behavior rather than location. Usually, by saying "consultant," a manager means an "external resource." This external resource can be brought in to conduct a course (i.e., an instructor), which certainly does not make this resource a consultant.

Generally speaking, the Learning Specialist and Consultant roles can be filled by external resources. The Administrator roles must be accomplished through internal staffing.

Some organizations find that it is to their financial advantage to bring in external resources for instruction. One reason is that if a staff member is to do instruction, this requires time for preparation, and the cost of instruction is higher than it might seem if one just counts the actual class/contact hours. In addition, if the staff member is to function only as an instructor, then there must be sufficient instructional need to justify a full-time person in this position. On consideration, the cost of an external instructor may not be as high as it first seemed. Some activities, such as secretarial, orientation, supervision, and—more recently—affirmative action, may best be served by a full-time instructional personnel. Of course, if these personnel also have the capacity to fill the other two sub-roles of the Learning Specialist (curriculum builder and instructional strategies developer), that would be more beneficial to the organization. It is easier to find external resources for instruction than for the other sub-roles.

Where the subject matter is highly specialized (e.g., quality control), the organization may benefit from having the curriculum sub-roles serviced by external resources.

The Consultant sub-roles can be handled either internally or externally. There has been a continual discussion as to which is better, but this is probably not the crux of the question. To date, there is little evidence to suggest that an external consultant is more effective than an internal consultant. There is a tendency to use external consultants because of reputation and easy access—also easy termination. At the present time, internal HRD staffs are improving their consulting skills and may possibly be utilized to a greater extent in the future than they were in the past.

The Administrator sub-roles can only be done effectively by somebody within the organization. When these are done by external resources, the organization loses effective control and responsiveness to daily shifts and demands. In my own experience, I have hardly ever found an organization that utilized external resources for this role. When it did occur, it usually signified either a disinterested management or a high-pressure external resource who was able to sell the service. In either case, the external resource benefited at the expense of the organization.

There are no absolute criteria for selecting an external resource. The general admonition is to look for that person or organization with a track record; that is, an organization or person who has done this work before, and has satisfied previous clients. This organization should be able to give you a list of past clients and you should be free to explore prior performance. Of course, there are some ethical limitations on what can be shared, but there is certainly no harm in trying to get information before buying—and you are doing the buying.

As the field grows and changes, there will be new people and products constantly emerging. This precludes the possibility of checking by previous performance. In that case, some kind of demonstration of capability would be within reason. This should not be used to exploit the external resource, but the organization under consideration should be able to demonstrate what it can do for you.

Your HRD unit is probably familiar with the vast array of organizations that can supplement the internal resource. These external organizations range from those having large multi-national staffs to the single entrepreneur whose essential value is in the service he personally performs. Being large does not necessarily mean being better. Some of the individual and smaller organizations may be spin-offs from larger organizations. It is also possible that the individual wishes to specialize in a particular aspect and therefore cannot meet the needs of a large organization that requires a flexible staff.

The HRD staff can easily be supplemented by these external resources, and many of them can be found in the numerous buying guides and postcard services which sprang up during the mid-1970's.

There are major publishing houses which have varieties of HRD packages and have vast "off-the-shelf" resources. When the term is used, it denotes something which has been previously prepared and tested and is generally available on the open market to anybody who wishes to purchase it. Some of these materials are excellent, but there are also those which do not live up to their advertising. If you, as a manager, are interested in these resources, you should discuss them with your HRD people.

These various resources are ways of supplementing an internal HRD staff; they *cannot* be used to replace such a staff. If an organization relies entirely on external resources, it is unlikely that the organizational climate which encourages a concern for human resources will be built.

Another way of looking at staffing is to take each sub-role and indicate some of the possibilities. The sub-role of *facilitator of learning,* for example, can be filled *internally* and usually quite easily. There are probably many people in the organization who know the content or can readily master it. They may need help in presentation, and here the developer of HRD personnel could be helpful.

When an organization has many sites and large number of employees needing a particular program, the instructors can be identified locally. Each manager may be asked to recommend those who could serve as either part-time or temporary instructors, depending upon the nature of the instruction and the design of the program.

There are advantages to a manager having his people do some instruction. It has been said, "You learn best by teaching." Almost anybody who has instructed knows the truth of this axiom. Therefore, by making personnel available to instruct, a manager gets the added benefit when that instructor returns.

As discussed earlier, it is generally less desirable to expect the HRD staff to function too frequently in this sub-role, though there are times when it is desirable and essential. Historically, it has been expected that HRD staff will include people who can conduct management programs—whatever they are. Some organizations will not allow an external instructor when the program is conducted in-house. Of course, they will still send some of their managers to out-of-house programs.

The *facilitator of learning* sub-role can also be filled *externally*. There are many excellent resources available outside the organization for many of the HRD needs that have been identified within the organization. There are HRD service organizations that specialize in offering various programs that can be utilized in-house. There is an unlimited number of these, and they emerge and disappear—in some cases rather rapidly. Once one gets on mailing lists, each day's mail will bring new notices of offerings (called public seminars), some of which may well meet the needs of the organization. A prudent manager would not merely enroll, or send people, without first discussing the offering with the HRD staff. They too have been receiving these mailings, and are probably in a better position to offer some insight, if not a full evaluation.

When new equipment is purchased, particularly when it is electronic or computer, it is likely that the supplier will be in a position to offer a training or education program as needed. In fact, when writing a purchase contract for equipment which will need some HRD, the manager is advised to consult with the HRD unit. Before the contract is signed, there should be a decision as to whether the instruction will be provided by the supplier or whether this service will be provided by the organization's own HRD unit.

Other external resources are the colleges and universities which are plentiful in our country. In addition to the regular on-campus offerings, they also are a resource for off-campus, non-credit, and non-degree programs. There are some varying definitions of these terms, but the following reflect the general usage.

"Off-campus" usually signifies that the learning experience is being offered at some site other than the regular college campus. This could be at the site of the organization requesting such a service. Despite the language, an off-campus program can also be on-campus! This arises from the distinction some colleges make between their *regular* offerings (i.e., on-campus) and their *special* offerings (i.e., off-campus), even though they may be conducted in the same place. This may be confusing, but if you are to utilize a college's system as a resource, it is well to become familiar with its terminology.

A "non-credit" course is one which does not offer any college credit—usually. There is a variation of this called the Continuing Education Unit (CEU), which is an attempt to give some kind of validity to the various external (off-campus) programs offered by colleges and universities. It can have value for some organizations and individuals and should be explored carefully before being advertised as an additional benefit. Non-credit courses are usually not bound by the same restrictions of time, length, etc., which are imposed on credit courses. The manager has every right to expect that the quality of the course will meet the needs of the learners. Once again, this is a point where direct consultation with the HRD unit can avoid disappointment and needless expense.

The "non-degree" offering is one for which credit is available, but for which that credit cannot be used toward a degree. This kind of offering is useful when a regular credit course can meet an HRD need, but the learner does not have the prerequisites. Frequently, the college or univeristy will allow the student to take the course, but will not count it toward a degree. More often, the learner needs a particular course, but does not wish to go on for a full degree in the subject. The learner may already have a degree, and the course may merely be meeting a training need in a specified area. This option of non-degree should be used very cautiously. It may be that the learner *should* go for a degree or that the learner should have the option of taking the course at a later date, if he should decide to go for a degree. Some organizations have a policy that they will not pay for a degree, though they will pay for individual credit courses. The manager should explore all these possibilities with the HRD people, in order to identify the company policy and the most appropriate choices for a particular learner at a particular time. This is always subject to change, so constant communication with the HRD unit is essential when a manager utilizes colleges and universities as instructional resources.

Community organizations, such as the Red Cross, can also be an instructional resource. When the subject matter is concerned with minorities, community organizations might be the best source for instructional services. Sometimes they already have previously designed programs, and it would be the responsibility of the HRD unit to review these offerings to see how they could relate to the learners from your organization, as well as to company policies. Professional societies, which often conduct extensive learning programs, are also a resource of this kind. Accounting societies offer periodic courses related to changes in tax laws, and ASTD offers programs to improve the skills of HRD people. It is probable that most professional societies offer some learning opportunities, even if only at their annual conferences.

The *curriculum builder* sub-role can be done *internally*, and requires people in the HRD unit who are skilled in program design. The common practice is to link them with other in-house people, the subject matter specialists (SMS). These latter will be regular employees who know the subject matter that needs to be learned. A good curriculum builder will seek out those who can function in the SMS role, and there are usually many people who can, in any organization. They may be supervisors, but even lower-level employees can function in the SMS area. To facilitate this process, you, as a manager, must decide to make such people available. If not, the HRD unit may have to go outside the organization for this resource, presenting the possibility that they may then design a program which does not meet your needs. This is a waste of resources, and you should be prepared to make employees, including yourself, available to serve in the SMS function.

When needed, *external curriculum builders* can be found in many of the same places as the instructors. One source is the faculty of colleges and universities who can provide the most up-to-date information on research and practice, from their vantage point. The instruction can still be done internally, even though the curriculum builder has come from an external source.

Using an external curriculum builder is desirable, if the HRD unit does not have personnel with design skills. A caution is that the external curriculum builder may incline toward producing a program which can only be taught by an external instructor—who is the same person or organization as the external curriculum builder! This is most likely to occur when material included in the design is the property of the external resource. This combination may be good and may save the organization time and money in developmental costs. Even with an external resource to do the design, you—the manager—can still be called upon to provide some internal SMS assistance.

The *instructional strategy developer* sub-role can be filled *internally*, but requires special staff in the HRD unit. There are few companies who have the need, in their regular operations, for the kinds of skills required by the instructional strategy developer. Therefore, either the sub-role must be specially staffed, or reliance placed on external resources.

There are many kinds of strategies and materials. If the need is for graphics or specialized audio-visual materials, it might be best to contract externally. For example, if it is necessary to produce videotapes, this requires special skill and equipment. (It is unlikely that the organization will have such people in the HRD unit, unless this is done extensively, such as at the American Airlines Flight Academy in Dallas. There, they have a whole unit that specializes in producing not only videotape but many other forms of audio-visual materials of a high level of sophistication and made with great skill. They also package these materials for use in the HRD programs in the widespread American Airlines installations.)

Writing case material is another skill, which at first appears easy. It is difficult and time-consuming to write good cases, but well worth the investment. Some curriculum builders prefer to write their own cases, while others are more interested in having the cases written by specialists. It is possible to have internal people with this skill, if the case method is used extensively.

A limitation of staffing this sub-role internally is that the resultant products are limited by the skills of the staff and the equipment they have. If the operation is large enough to warrant sufficient and varied staff and equipment, it is probably best to do it in-house. We are still finding significant bursts of technology in this field, so an organization that chooses this method of staffing should make the budget available for the purchase of new equipment as it comes on the market.

There is insufficient data, but it is unlikely that most organizations rely on *external* resources for filling this sub-role. Either they contract out, or they bring specialized people in-house for limited periods of time. Such external people may come from colleges and universities, but most likely they will be freelancers. They may work within the organization, as in the situation of case writers, or they may utilize their own facilities where specialized equipment is required.

The sub-roles of the *Administrator* will almost always be staffed *internally*. It is difficult to find a situation in which this role can adequately be handled by external people. Selected positions might be staffed by external people, but in very limited circumstances. *External* resources might be brought in to help assess the learning needs of the HRD staff and to suggest appropriate learning experiences. In this case, the external resource is functioning as a consultant to the HRD unit, not as a developer of HRD personnel. The actual learning experiences can be done internally or externally. Here too, that function being performed is that of instructor or curriculum builder.

Looking at all the functions of the Administrator, it becomes apparent that these are best performed internally.

The *Consultant* can be either *internal* or *external*. Most important is that the sub-role be clearly identified. If this is done, it is possible for the manager to decide if there are sufficient internal resources to accomplish the task.

Where there is a great deal of consulting work, it is possible to staff internally. Indeed, many HRD people would like to function as Consultants to their own organizations. They may have the skill, but does their organization have the need? Consulting work is much more variable than that of the Learning Specialist. In the latter case, it is possible to forecast the need and schedule the learning experiences or the times for designing programs. For the consultant, such scheduling is impossible. Consulting arises from a need for help, and it is usually not possible to anticipate when this need will arise. A large organization can keep one or more people in the HRD unit with the responsibility for consulting, assuming that the kinds of consulting needs match the skills of those available.

Most frequently, and for many reasons, the Consultant is staffed externally. Before calling in an external Consultant, the manager should work with the HRD unit to clarify the kind of consulting help needed; then, if the HRD personnel cannot provide it, they can assist the manager in thinking through the kind of Consultant who would be most helpful. It is also likely that the HRD people have the contacts (particularly if they have been maintaining community relations) and can readily identify the kind and quality of people needed for the particular consulting assignment.

A new trend is emerging which almost defies classification. It has become most apparent in the Consultant roles. Good consultants are in demand. An organization can have a good consultant in its HRD unit (or even more than one) and can even utilize this person full-time. However, many people with consulting skills and experience find it challenging to work for a variety of organizations in different settings. They are Category I people and are willing to stay—and interested in staying—with an organization, but they yearn for the external consulting assignments which present variety and the opportunity of working with other consultants.

This has resulted in various arrangements, to the mutual satisfaction of the Consultant and the organization. Though details vary, the arrangement usually allows the Consultant to accept work outside the organization as long as it is not with a competing organization. The Consultant usually charges this time to vacation, though this is not entirely desirable. Even Consultants need vacations. Therefore, some arrangements are based on a fixed salary, but with the Consultant being permitted to work a certain number of days outside the organization, not chargeable to either vacation or "leave without pay." Of course, this type of arrangement is more prevalent in large organizations and among Consultants with excellent reputations.

CONCLUSION

Staffing for HRD should not be done haphazardly or on the basis of who is temporarily available. The HRD function can be staffed by both permanent and temporary personnel, but this should be the result of careful planning by managers and the HRD people.

Three major roles have been identified: Learning Specialist, Administrator, and Consultant. Within these, there are 11 sub-roles. Managers should be aware of these possibilities and encourage the kind of staffing for the HRD unit which will provide the best service for the organization.

The Learning Specialist and the Consultant can be either internal or external. The Administrator role is best serviced by internal personnel. As a manager, you should be working with the HRD unit to identify the mix of internal and external resources most appropriate for your particular programs and activities.

These decision must be congruent with the kinds of financial and physical resources that exist and with the expectations there are of the HRD function.

4 Providing Physical and Financial Resources

No activity in any organization can function without the necessary physical and financial resources. One of the major functions of any manager is to make effective use of these resources. If the Human Resource Development activity is to contribute to the goals of the organization, resources must be provided.

HOW MUCH SHOULD WE SPEND ON HRD?

An essential resource is the financial, for with that the HRD unit can obtain the necessary physical elements it needs. This requires that we look at the financial picture.

As of now, there is a woeful lack of data on what kinds of financial resources are provided by management to the HRD function. There have been some attempts to gather such data, but so far they are to no avail. A major reason is the lack of agreement as to what costs should be included in this financial data. It is becoming so important that we are likely to see some generally agreed upon classifications in the future. As of now, comparative data are not possible.

A manager cannot ask, "How much should we be spending?" or "How much do other companies in our field spend?" It is not that the data are secret—they just do not exist! If any comparisons are to be made, they must arise from within the organization, and that is the place to start. Your organization can establish classifications for expenditures related to HRD and track them from quarter to quarter and from year to year. At least you will know how expenditures for HRD are managed in your organization and how they relate to the rest of your operations.

One way to approach this problem is to decide how to organize the HRD unit as a financial unit. At present, there are three prevalent ways of organizing: budget item, cost center, and profit center. Each has advantages and limitations. Each represents some aspect of the philosophy of the organization as well as the mission of the HRD unit.

Budget Item

The budget item approach is the most traditional way the HRD function is organized. The expenditures for the HRD operation appear as an item in the budget, and as an identified unit. It can be at many levels of the organization or only at the corporate level. The budget is stated as a specified amount and represents the total that is available for HRD, unless there are later budget adjustments.

The process of arriving at the budget figure is probably as vague as the process for many other units of the organization. It is based on some kind of assessment of past performance and a guess as to the future, particularly during the fiscal year for that budget. If the corporate policy is to increase budgets by 10 percent (perhaps for inflation) then the HRD figure benefits from this decision. If the corporate policy is to cut back, and every department will take a 15 percent cut, then HRD is usually cut in a similar fashion.

This approach makes for easy bookkeeping but does an injustice to the contribution that HRD should make to the organization. An increased budget allocation to compensate for inflation can readily be justified, but the HRD function should also be reflecting other elements of corporate policy. The budget item approach allows for that, if the manager recognizes the relationship between policy decisions and needed HRD activities.

There is an underlying concept related to the budget item approach which should not be missed. It is based on the idea that the HRD unit is not being asked to make any financial recovery for the expenditure. This does not mean that the HRD people are not accountable for the use of the budgeted funds. There should still be a positive attempt to show that the HRD activity has used the budgeted resources to reach objectives. This can be done by showing increases in productivity, improvement in quality, reduction in rejects, improved customer relations, increased sales, etc. Where the organization does not have any such measures for job performance, as it frequently does not have for managers, it becomes impossible for the HRD unit to show any measurable changes.

The advantage of the budget item approach is that the amount to be spent can be specified and agreed upon. Given an exact budget, the HRD unit can plan specifically and make the necessary commitments for the year. Planning is facilitated and the whole procedure can be accomplished in an orderly fashion.

A limitation is that there can be reduced accountability. The HRD unit must still show what it accomplishes for the money, but it recognizes that it is unlikely that there would be a severe budget cut as long as the staff continues to provide the services recognized by the managers in the organization. This tends to encourage the HRD unit to focus more on the managers than on any other group. It is possible that managers need more learning experiences, or it may be that budget-wise HRD people recognize that it is easier to get the budget if they are more visible to managers.

Another element has been introduced which could have an impact on the budget item approach, and this is Zero Based Budgeting (ZBB). It has been around for several years but received a significant impetus when the Carter administration introduced it at the federal level. There are many variations, but essentially, the ZBB approach is based on the idea that each activity starts each budget cycle at zero. The traditional approach is to start the budget cycle by looking at last year's budget and performance. Under ZBB, the previous year is important but is not the basis for the current year's budget. Rather, the question that must be answered is: "What difference would it make if we gave you no budget this year?" This requires that the unit under question, in this case the HRD unit, clearly indicate specifically what it will do during the coming budget year to enable the corporation to meet its goals. When the activities are agreed upon, then the HRD unit must justify the amount of financial resources it will need to provide that service. The lump sum approach cannot be used. Each activity becomes a separate item and all HRD people must respond to those questions of "What difference . . . ?" and "How much . . . ?"

Theoretically, the approach has much to offer. Practically, the major criticism is that it makes the budget process too laborious and time-consuming for the benefits which might be derived. It is likely that alternative approaches will evolve, if the ZBB concept proves to be useful. We have already seen one approach, at the federal level in Congress, which goes by the descriptive title of the "sunset clause." This means that some legislation contains a clause which puts a limited life on the activity and funds authorized in that legislation. At a given point, the program ceases unless new legislation has been passed.

Applying this to the budget item approach, which some organizations are considering, means that there are some HRD activities which are budgeted each year, though the amount may vary. There are other activities which are budgeted for a limited life and will not be rebudgeted without new justification. For example, a manager might agree to fund a program for hiring new employees because a new plant is being activated. The budget item for this will automatically terminate at the end of a specified period, probably when the new plant is in operation. To get additional funds for this activity, the HRD unit would have to present a new justification.

Although the budget item approach is probably the most prevalent system for HRD, managers should be aware of other possible alternatives.

Cost Center

Organizing the HRD unit as a cost center has been a popular approach with many large manufacturing organizations, and it is also used by the U.S. Civil Service Commission.

The essence of the cost center approach is that the HRD unit charges out for all the services it performs. It is given only a very small administrative budget. To survive, it must sell its services internally to the various parts of the organization. By the end of the year, it should have a net balance of zero; it should have covered all its costs by billings; it should have spent all that it received from its "customers."

Accounting for the HRD operation is much simpler and cleaner under the cost center approach. It also has significant implications for the HRD programs. If they do not sell, they do not survive.

The cost center approach transfers a good deal of control of the HRD function from a central unit to the line manager. It requires that the line manager make provision in his budget for HRD, or it will not happen. Many line managers have discretionary funds, but HRD should not be paid for on this basis. The line manager should have funds in the operating department budget specifically for HRD activities, but released only when paying for specific services from the HRD unit. (There is one exception to this, and it will be discussed later under *limitations*.)

If the cost center approach is utilized, management sometimes includes another element. The HRD unit must be able to provide the service at the same or lower price than an outside competitor, or the line manager can use the funds to purchase out-of-company HRD programs. This makes the HRD unit highly competitive. The in-house HRD unit has many advantages over the external resource, but the decision lies with the manager. Each manager should make the decision on a case-by-case basis. There are times when, even though more costly, the in-house HRD unit should be used.

The difficulty for a manager lies in assessing the relative cost and cost benefits. When dealing with machinery or raw materials, the manager can obtain some absolute, comparable data on which to base a decision. With HRD, it is not always possible to quantify in absolute terms. The manager recognizes that most decisions dealing with people cannot be compared as easily as those decisions related to physical objects. This is one reason it is so much more difficult to manage people than it is to manage the physical resources of an organization.

The cost center approach has the advantage of focusing very highly on cost effectiveness. The HRD is under constant pressure to provide cost data to managers: what it will cost, and what it will save.

Another advantage of the cost center approach is that it is likely that cost data related to the HRD activity will be more readily discernible. The HRD unit will will have to institute significant financial controls in order to determine how to cost a program, and its related activities, so they end the year with a break-even figure.

One limitation, briefly indicated earlier, is that a cost center deprives the HRD unit of research and development (R & D) money. This can be budgeted, but it would reduce the impact of the cost center approach. What does the HRD unit do when it needs money to develop a new program? One way is for the HRD unit to approach one or more managers and ask them to contribute some risk capital. Of course, these will have to be managers who would benefit from the new HRD activity. There must be agreement that if the program cannot be sold to others, the line manager bears the risk, as there can be no recovery of the initial cost. If the program succeeds (i.e., can be sold to others), the line manager will recover the initial risk capital.

Such an approach assures that the HRD unit will be as responsive as possible to the needs and wishes of line managers. It prevents the HRD unit from exploring and experimenting with new approaches unless there is some indication of need and the possibility of financial success. The company (the market) must be large enough so that the HRD unit can sell its new program to other parts of the company and recover its original R & D expenditure. A small company would have difficulty implementing a straightforward cost center approach, but might couple it with a budget approach.

The cost center approach encourages a low-risk attitude on the part of the HRD unit. The HRD staff will tend to focus its activities on just what the manager is willing to buy. There will be a tendency to continually offer those programs that are sure-fire sellers. The evaluation is almost strictly in terms of what managers are willing to pay for. This is based on the assumption that if it does not benefit the manager, he will not pay for it. The emphasis will be on strictly observable skills, and particularly those which can be measured. It should be recognized that this is the underlying premise of the HRD function in a cost center approach.

Profit Center

Another form of financial arrangement for the HRD function is that of the profit center. Under that system, the HRD unit is expected to make a profit from selling its services both internally and externally.

Internally, the HRD unit will function more like a cost center—that is, it is expected to break even on its sales to other parts of the company. If the internal fiscal policy is that goods and services sold from one part of the company to another are priced with a mark-up which produces a profit, this would also apply to HRD. There may also be the policy that if the purchasing unit can obtain the same service at the same quality standard from outside the company, it is free to do so. As with the cost center approach, this encourages the profit center to compete with outside suppliers.

A major difference is that the HRD unit is now expected to market its services externally to other companies. The marketing unit may use the name of the parent company, so we find names such as Westinghouse Learning Corporation and Litton Learning Corporation. The name of the parent company is retained, with "learning" or some similar word introduced into the title.

It is not necessary for the company to spin off new companies for its HRD products; instead, it can handle them the same way it does its other products. DuPont found a demand for the excellent program it had developed over the years in factory maintenance, and it uses some of the regular company marketing resources to sell the program.

When organized as a profit center, the HRD unit is expected to operate on the open market and return an agreed-upon profit to the company, just as any other unit does. Obviously, this produces a change in the nature of the HRD services. The emphasis is on packages or on HRD programs that can readily be marketed through the numerous channels available. Only infrequently does the HRD product include direct personal service. More often, the product is one which had been developed for some specific unit in the company, but which was deemed to have broader applications and, therefore, could be marketed outside the company. The pressure is to develop those products which would be generally marketable and could meet the profit goal assigned to the HRD unit.

If you choose this form of organization for your HRD unit, do not be surprised if the HRD people are not as responsive as you would wish. You have trapped them into looking for salable products rather than to giving direct service to managers. It is an ambivalent position and has caused a great deal of discontent and frequent turnover among the HRD people in such situations.

One of the advantages to management of the profit center is that there is a high concentration on cost data. It is necessary to know the cost if there is to be a profit margin. There is a direct return, financially, to the organization, and this can put the HRD operation in a new light. Instead of being considered part of the overhead, managers can look to the HRD unit to produce a profit.

The limitations are obvious, but they must be considered by managers who plan to organize their HRD units as profit centers. There must be an increased concentration on marketable items. Almost the sole criterion for any HRD activity becomes whether it can be marketed. It also means that HRD programs have to be packaged. If they cannot be packaged, it is doubtful whether profit center personnel should be devoting time to them. Yet there are HRD activities, particularly consulting, which cannot and should not be packaged. The profit center limits such behavior on the part of the HRD staff.

Organizations that have their HRD operations functioning as profit centers will most likely have the units headed up by managers from other parts of the company. The executives in the organization will look for a marketing manager, or one who knows how to turn products into profits.

Variations

It is apparent that there is no one best way to organize the HRD function from the viewpoint of financial resources. Managers should be cautious and not make decisions which cannot be reversed as needed.

The manager who is aware of the various possibilities will also recognize that all three can exist within the same HRD unit. It is possible to identify those programs that are best serviced by a managerial decision to provide a budget item. There are other programs which should prove themselves by being handled as cost center activities. There are still other HRD programs which can be marketed and provide a source of revenue for the organization.

A management decision is necessary to determine which programs fall into which categories. Even after the decision has been made, it may be necessary to move programs from one category to another. With this kind of flexibility, it is possible for management to have the advantage of three different approaches and to lessen the impact of the limitations. This can be done by having three different approaches in operation at the same time, but this can also cause an imbalance within the HRD unit.

FACILITIES

Managers must provide their HRD units with adequate facilities if they are to get the job done. There is no absolute list or criteria, but there are some areas where managers can ask questions so they can make effective decisions.

Later in this chapter we will explore the issues of internal and external facilities. First, let us look at some of the kinds of facilities which must be provided by management.

Space

When an HRD program is squeezed into poor facilities, this communicates a lack of managerial interest and, perhaps, the intent of management. In most companies, space communicates the position of management toward a given activity. Thus, there must be adequate space. No matter how small the HRD activity is, at the very least there will be the need for some kind of administrative space. The space should be equivalent to administrative space for other similar units. Usually, the HRD activity will also require some classroom or instructional space. This tends to be more difficult. As a manager, you know the need for administrative space, but you may not be as aware of the need for a good climate for instruction.

Since classrooms may not be in continuous use, there is the tendency to give the HRD unit some space which they can share with others. One of the most frequent pairings is conference room and classroom. On the surface, this may seem adequate, but it depends on the use of the conference room. If there are regular meetings which have priority, then HRD will be seen as less important and may have to be scheduled around the regular meetings.

Classrooms should contain storage space for equipment and materials. If managers do not provide the space, then the HRD unit will probably have to increase its costs in order to obtain materials and equipment on rental—and not be sure exactly what they will have each time.

Having the space is important, but where the space is located is equally important. A beautifully prepared room that is in the basement, near the utility services, may communicate that management does not consider the HRD activity of any importance. As a manager, you know you want your office to be in a particular part of the building because of what that communicates to the rest of the organization. The same holds true for the HRD function. Location communicates a great deal about the status of a function in the organization.

Equipment

The field of learning has come a long way from the Mark Hopkins picture of "a log with a student on one end and a teacher on the other." This sounds like good individual instruction, but in the world today something more sophisticated is frequently required. It is unlikely that this model would provide good learning today, no matter how many logs you purchased for your HRD unit.

Managers should not purchase equipment! The type of equipment purchased will determine the nature of the HRD program. The people in the HRD unit should be asked to make recommendations and be given the budget for equipment purchases. What they purchase will reflect the learning philosophy of those in the HRD unit. This also suggests that managers should not be surprised, when they hire new HRD people, to find that they are flooded with requests for different equipment.

It is not possible, and probably not necessary, to provide managers with a list of the various types of learning equipment on the market. One reason is that the hardware (machines) and software (what goes in or on them) changes so frequently that the list rapidly becomes out of date. What managers need to know is that every time they are asked to provide the funds for a purchase, that purchase should be questioned—not by asking, "Is it needed?" (we can assume that it would not be requested if it was not needed), but by asking what the equipment will bring to the program that was not there before. Purchasing a videotape recorder (VTR) may be an indication of a whole new thrust for the HRD unit. This could be desirable, but the manager who is providing the funds should know that. Any good HRD person would be happy to be called in by the manager to explain how a piece of equipment will contribute to a specific kind of learning need in the organization.

HRD also requires special furniture and appointments. Earlier, we discussed the possibility that the conference room could be used as a classroom. One problem usually is that of furniture. The type of conference table and chairs that are usually purchased for a conference room are very different from those needed for an appropriate classroom. In a few cases, they might be used for both, but the instances are rare.

The increased use of various learning technologies has brought with it specialists in various kinds of equipment. Management should be talking to these specialists in the HRD unit to avoid the kind of problem observed in one organization (which shall remain nameless here). This organization had built a magnificent hall, with a wide variety of possibilities programmed into the environment. These could all be worked from the podium, which was similar to the controls of a large airplane and would make a computer operator very happy. There were myriads of colored buttons, lights, toggle switches, etc. All were utilitarian, and from the podium the speaker could handle a wide variety of learning possibilities for large groups.

The room was equipped with rear view capability. The special screen was of one piece of specially produced glass which provided excellent viewing from any part of this vast auditorium. The screen could be hidden from view by various drapes and other hangings. In an awed voice, my guide for this visit to the facility (an HRD person) described how they had brought the glass screen into the auditorium and installed it before the building was completed. This was the only way they could bring in this seamless piece of glass.

The next question is almost obvious, and painful. "What if the glass was scratched or broken during use? How could it be replaced?" The reluctant response was that they would have to use a seamed glass, which would not be at all in keeping with the requirement! This was a question that managers should have asked while the facility was being planned. Other alternatives were possible then, but later was too late!

Supplies

There are few learning experiences today which can function without supplies. These are classified as expendable factors related to the learning situation. The most obvious are the pencils and paper which are available in any organization.

There are some supplies which are only found in the HRD unit. These would usually be workbooks, exercises, and other materials provided to learners that are not expected to be returned. There is the need for control and accountability for such items and provision for availability when they are needed for a learning situation.

As in the case of equipment, the manager can learn a great deal about the HRD operation by the types of supplies they purchase. It is not expected that a manager will read every purchase order or review each request for supplies. It might be helpful for all concerned, however, if managers occasionally visited their HRD units and took a quick look at what was there. Ask questions of the HRD people. They will be only too happy to explain, and this can provide a significant learning experience for the managers about the kinds of resources available for HRD within the organization.

If a manager can purchase HRD supplies from his budget, and plans to purchase outside, it would be a good idea for him to first ask if the material is available internally. I observed one company where a manager had decided to use an outside resource to conduct a training program. The external trainer said he needed a significant quantity of newsprint (the name for the paper which goes on the easel, also called tear sheets or flip chart paper). The manager rushed out to purchase the newsprint, even paying extra for the quick delivery of this bulky item. It was delivered to the HRD unit by mistake! They asked the manager why he had made the purchase and he explained. The people in the HRD unit then invited the manager to visit them and showed him the large supply of newsprint they had in stock, for they also used it extensively. They purchased in significant quantities, without paying for a special delivery, and therefore could have provided it for him at a lower cost than he had paid.

Internal

There is constant discussion over the relative values of building and maintaining internal facilities for HRD, as contrasted with renting external facilities. Let us start with a look at some of the factors a manager must consider in arriving at this decision.

If you decide to have internal facilities, you are not alone. You would be joining the ranks of companies such as Pepsi-Cola, Motorola, General Electric, Xerox, and Holiday Inn—all of which have extensive and expensive internal facilities. Note that when the term "internal" is used, it does not mean that the HRD *facility* is within a plant. The companies cited above have extensive sites located at areas outside of the manufacturing or corporate office facility. The "internal" signifies *control,* not location.

There are some companies that build the facility as part of a plant or office complex, but with some space—and usually an entire building—specifically designated as the HRD facility. Standard Oil of Indiana has such a complex in its headquarters buildings in Chicago.

If you are considering an internal facility, you should recognize that this design requires a different kind of architect and planner than you would consult for a facility that will be used for multi-purpose operations. To get the most out of your facility, you must commit the space—and budget—and then have the requisite experts advise on the various aspects. The list of possibilities is almost endless, but must represent the philosophy of HRD in your organization: the nature of the programs, the type of learners, the company philosophy, etc. If you have no specific and stated policy on HRD, it is probably unwise to build an internal facility. Though it may look magnificent, it may not be adequately used.

Of course, philosophies and policies change, and practices change even more frequently. When you have an internal facility, the question of change must be considered. A new HRD director, new advances in the field, and the constant impact of new learning technology all require that the internal facility be capable of constant updating and revision. It is the same kind of decision you have to make about any part of your organization that has equipment which can become obsolete.

With an internal facility, you must also have staff; the larger the facility, the more staff you will need. Having an internal facility may also confront you with a decision about centralization or decentralization. Organizations that have built internal facilities have moved toward concentrating most of their HRD staffs and operations in those facilities.

Making a decision about internal facilities involves more than just the physical aspect. Many internal facilities also provide for live-in situations. This is particularly important if your organization has many sites and many employees who will be coming from long distances. But this need not put you in the hotel business. A convenient way to handle the sleeping and food arrangements is to contract out this responsibility to some of the large corporations that specilize in this kind of housing and mass feeding. If appropriately negotiated, the service will be more like a deluxe hotel than a hostel. The decision rests on the amount of money to be made available and the kind of non-verbal communication which is expected to emanate from the facility.

Up to this point, the discussion has focused on what may seem to be very elaborate facilities. There are other alternatives, however, and a frequent practice is to have smaller internal facilities.

If it is more desirable to have the learning take place near the job site, then the internal facility should be used to meet this purpose. This is often the case when the learning is expected to be of short duration, since it would be too costly to send people long distances for short-term learning. Often, people cannot be spared, and the expense of the learning should not outweight the benefits which might be derived from it. Also, as the early experiences of the National Training Laboratory showed, you can face a problem of "transfer of training." That is, people can learn new behavior in a controlled environment but then have difficulty using it back on the job.

An organization with an elaborate internal facility may also have additional but lesser facilities at their various plant sites or office locations. These may be tied into the larger facility, organizationally or technologically. Through the use of closed circuit television, which now has direct feedback capability, the instruction can be offered at the major facility, with the in-plant facilities tying into the program on a prearranged basis. In addition, the major facility may generate programs and materials which can then be sent out to the various sites around the country or around the world.

External

In contrast to the previous alternative, your company can use external facilities. (At this point we will make it either/or, but later on we will discuss combinations.) As used here, an "external" facility is one which is not controlled or operated by your organization. It is a facility available to the public and one for which you have to negotiate and contract to secure time and space.

During the 1970's, there was a tremendous expansion of facilities built expressly for the purpose of servicing the external HRD needs of organizations. Usually, the words "conference center" appear in their titles. Do not be misled—not every facility which uses these words was built for that purpose. I recall going to a "conference center" to conduct a program for a client. On arriving, I found that it was a golf club. The management had found out that during winter the facility could prove equally lucrative if made available for meetings and conferences. Just as I was unpacking my bags, I received a call from the front desk. Would I please not disturb the clothes which were in the room! The employee then went on to explain that the room I had was actually Judge Smith's room during the golf season and his clothing and other personal effects were in there. They would appreciate it if I would use the one drawer which had been cleared out for visitors, and the one-half of the closet which had been likewise prepared. Also, would I refrain from using any of the toilet articles which remained in the bathroom. Of course I complied, but wondered if during the night I might not be asked to share my bed with Judge Smith!

The newer conference sites tend to have special equipment, facilities, and highly qualified staff. The National Conference Center in New Jersey, built and managed by Coleman Finkel, is an outstanding example of this and has won accolades in the professional literature. The chain known as Harrison Houses also has a good reputation, and there are many others in the same caliber. It remains to be seen if the various external facilities can continue to warrant their favorable reputations.

Before contracting with an external facility, you should conduct an in-depth, on-site visit, as well as engage in discussions with others who have actually used the facility. But you cannot merely rely on the opinions or the experiences of others. The HRD program you are planning may be different. You should be working with your HRD people as you look for an external site, and they should be able to provide sound guidance based on their own experiences in selecting external sites.

If your HRD people are going to use an external site, they should discuss this with you prior to making any commitments. The external facility they choose should be a reflection of the kind of HRD experience you want your people to have.

Other sources of external sites are hotels and motels. These can be a problem, for most such facilities do not have HRD programs as their prime objective, as is the case with conference sites. Rather, hotels and motels focus on transients. They usually have also provided facilities for banquets or monthly meetings of civic and business organizations. Such a facility *might* be adequate for your HRD program, but usually it is not. Lighting, seating, and availability of equipment are quite different for HRD activities than for monthly meetings or socials.

Recognizing the increased revenue which can be derived from HRD activities, many hotels and motels have improved their facilities and services to cater to this market. Unfortunately, it is not always possible to tell from their brochures just what capabilities they have.

Our country has the largest university system in the world, and this includes two-year colleges as well as major universities. Beginning in the 1960's, some of them built "continuing education centers," usually with money provided by the Kellog Foundation. Today, some of them are still referred to as Kellog Centers, but the labels used by the continuing education centers are variable. If you are considering using such a facility at a local college or university, it is best to find out what the college is calling this facility and what it really is, in order to avoid wasting time with the wrong people.

Many of the newer community colleges have built buildings specifically planned for use as external centers by others. Some of them have facilities and equipment which are comparable to those found in the best conference centers, discussed earlier.

In some situations, the university or college will also provide qualified staff to assist in designing and even conducting the HRD experience. If you have an internal staff, be sure to avoid any conflict between the two. They are competing for the same market—you.

If you graduated from high school many years ago, you may not realize that our public schools today are another resource. The adult education programs in some schools consist of much more than basket weaving and folk dancing. (There is nothing wrong with these activities, but you are unlikely to need them as part of your HRD program.) You may not be aware that the public schools also have facilities and staff for other kinds of learning programs which fall more closely into the field of HRD.

As a taxpayer—and your organization may be the most important taxpayer in the community—the public schools are available to you. Generally, they dislike conducting a learning program for a single employer, although in most cases, this is not a matter of law. Usually it is a matter of trying to meet extensive needs with limited resources. Despite this, there are times and places where the use of the public schools for HRD programs can be of benefit to all.

Take the case of a community which is trying to bring in new industry—and it could be yours! Do not be surprised to find that the public schools will provide the necessary learning programs so that when you open your plant you will have a supply of qualified labor. This requires planning, but it can be done—and has been done many times, in many places.

The public schools have certain obvious capabilities that should not be overlooked. You may be looking for a learning program in "Better Letter Writing" for yourself or for some of your subordinates. There may not be enough potential learners to require a full class. Check with your public school adult education program. They may be offering such a course, and by looking at their course outline (curriculum) you can determine if such a course would meet your needs. If so, the action to take is simple and obvious. If a course is not available, you could work with the adult education people to develop the appropriate course. They have many good professionals staffing the adult education programs who might be quite willing to work with you. Most likely, they have not contacted you directly because that is not the way such adult programs usually operate. Why not contact them when you have a need?

The public school cannot be considered a significant source for an external facility, although that is not outside the realm of possibility. Particularly for programs concerned with the "disadvantaged," you will find that the public schools are very ready and capable to assist.

Internal and External

Up to now, we have concentrated on either external *or* internal facilities. Obviously, it is possible to use both. This requires careful and well-planned decision-making, involving many people.

The HRD unit may have been given the mandate and resources to establish an extensive internal facility. If you, as a manager, then choose to utilize external facilities, it could be a waste of resources. If the capability already exists in-house, why go outside? There are times and reasons, but the decision should be carefully made, considering the long-range implications as well as the immediate need.

As HRD programs expand and contract, so will the need for facilities. Larger organizations find there is a constant mix of internal and external facilities. The decisions concerning which facilities to use should be constantly re-examined. If you, the manager, have your own budget for HRD, recognize that your choice of internal and external facilities is a decision that goes to the very core of HRD in your organization. Having such a budget, you can expect to be wooed by those with external facilities to sell. You owe it to your organization and your HRD people to discuss such decisions with them.

FINANCIAL POLICIES

Your organization has financial policies regarding its operations. For high cash flow operations, such as purchasing and payroll, the policies are specific, for the very existence of the organization is at stake. For other areas, there may be fewer clearly stated policies, yet policies do exist. They may be the result of practices which have been in use by non-policy makers and not scrutinized by managers.

What Are the Policies Related to HRD?

At this moment, could you put your hands on some kind of manual or set of statements specifically delineating the policies for HRD? If so, your organization is unique. The closest most managers can come to this is to say that "the same policies which apply to all of the organization apply to HRD." This ignores the fact that HRD has some activities which are so unique it is unlikely that financial policies which apply to the entire organization can be directly applied to HRD.

If you do have financial policies directly related to HRD, how were they arrived at? Were they the result of careful consideration of how such policies relate to the effective use of HRD? The field of HRD is constantly altering as it reflects changes in internal policies as well as external pressures. Are you sure that your current financial policies are consistent with the changes that have taken place in your HRD operation?

Everybody in the organization should know the financial policies which are related to HRD. This can lessen the possibility that HRD may become a perk (perquisite or added benefit) or a fringe benefit item, rather than a direct cost to the organization for which there are some specific expectations. How do you, as a manager, know that the financial policies related to HRD have been adequately conveyed to your people?

Record Keeping

If you are to make financial management decisions related to HRD, you need data which are derived from records. Do you know what records are kept by your HRD unit?

PROVIDING PHYSICAL AND FINANCIAL RESOURCES 87

If your HRD unit does not have adequate records, do not start out by blaming them or looking for a "cover up." The HRD field suffers from a lack of agreement on terminology, and this must be reflected in the record keeping function. The major records you will find in your HRD unit (because this is what it is possible to get agreement about) will probably reflect the number of hours employees have been in HRD programs, or the total number of employees who have been in HRD programs. Through simple mathematical manipulations, these gross figures can be related to the total expenditures to produce an "average cost per employee" or "average cost of learning hour." If your HRD unit makes the important distinctions among training, education, and development (see the discussion in Chapter 2) the resulting calculations can fine-tune the data to produce better results.

Beyond those general figures, the record keeping becomes confused. The situation can be improved if managers will agree about what kinds of information they want from records and on simple definitions of terms, so that data can be compared. HRD people sometimes try, unilaterally, to establish classifications to clear up the terminology, and endeavor to present some meaningful report to management to reflect the application of the financial policies. Too often, managers have difficulty with such reports and resort to accusing the HRD people of using jargon to obfuscate. Of course, there are some HRD people who do this—and they are not alone in this practice. You can reduce this possibility by informing your HRD people that you would like to reach agreements on terminology so you can communicate more effectively.

It is possible to get good records of the financial aspects of HRD—but what then? Why should you, as a manager, want financial records of a different unit in the organization?

To begin with, the HRD unit, as a staff unit, serves the entire organization. Therefore, what they are doing with and about financial resources is of concern to all managers. Even more significant is that managers are responsible for financial planning. The more good data you have, the better chance of making informed and correct decisions. Good financial records for the HRD function can facilitate sound financial planning within the organization.

The records have another and more far reaching implication. HRD rarely serves only one part of the organization. It should, in fact, be serving *many* parts of the organization. Managers are responsible for bringing about organizational change, and the HRD activities should be reflecting these changes. If management is planning to open new facilities requiring additional employees, and the HRD budget does not reflect this increased need, managers should know about this early enough to take appropriate action. The financial policies of almost any part of the organization have a ripple effect, and some of those ripples must rock the HRD boat.

There is one major difference in the HRD records which should be kept in mind by managers. Most financial records in a company are the property of that company and privileged unless the company is required to show them by law. The usual laws with which management is familiar are those related to taxation or possible civil and criminal actions. There are also laws, enacted in recent years, concerned with privacy of the personal information which appears in school records. At the time of this writing, this has not yet been extended to employers, though it is not unlikely that the interpretation of the legislation could move in that direction. If so, managers need to be aware of their liability and responsibility for information in the corporate files in the HRD field. It is not possible to give specifics here, as the laws are constantly changing. Managers should be asking their HRD people how these laws apply to them.

A related legal area is in Equal Employment Opportunity (EEO), where there is no one set of rules but a veritable maze. Experts are required to sort out the various reporting requirements. Here too, at this writing, there are pieces of legislation in the congressional hopper which could have a profound effect on the kinds of HRD records which must be maintained. If you want to avoid surprises, be sure your HRD people know what is expected of them in this area of record keeping.

In earlier days, record keeping for HRD activities was a fairly simple matter. Today, with the many reporting requirements, and the expanding use of the computer, the situation has become much more complex. If you want financial records from your HRD unit, be sure that both you and the unit have made appropriate provisions for the human and financial resources required to establish and/or maintain such a system. As with any other system, it must be reviewed periodically to be sure it is providing the needed financial data and is not becoming only an end unto itself.

Tuition refund is probably one of the clearest examples which can sum up this whole section. There are various names used to describe this practice, such as tuition reimbursement, educational entitlement, and tuition expense. There is no agreement, but each of these does indicate some possible difference in policies. What is the policy in your organization for tuition refund? It can range from reimbursement for all expenses related to that learning, which takes place outside the organization, to reimbursing nothing. Is the program available only to employees, or are the benefits extended to their families? First, there should be clear financial policies related to this practice, and they should be open for all to see. Good record keeping is essential if managers are to assess the operation of the program and make recommendations or decisions regarding its continuance or termination, its expansion or contraction.

HUMAN RESOURCE ACCOUNTING

There are many cutting edge areas in HRD—growing edges where the people in the field are reaching out to explore ways to make HRD more relevant to individual and organizational needs. Human resource accounting (HRA) is one of these areas.

Essentially, this is an approach that brings together the field of human resources with the practice of accounting. It is an attempt to quantify the expense and investment which goes into human resources.

At first, managers who are humanistically-oriented may find it difficult to think of people in terms of accounting. The thrust in the field is not to deprecate the role of humans or to consider them extensions of machines. The purpose of HRA is to find a way of taking the financial resources related to the human resource and producing some forms of quantified data.

There are many avenues of exploration under consideration. One of these seeks to keep a continuing financial record of what the organization spends on individual employees. So far, the intent is not to see how much of this is returned to the organization in terms of revenue. This is, perhaps, a risk inherent in the HRA approach, that some interpreters of data will try to establish direct connections. Some managers are already trying to make such connections, but without sufficient data, and based strictly on hunches and rumors.

A more useful purpose of HRA is to provide terminology to the HRD field. There have been, and will continue to be, attempts by managers to understand HRD in terms of financial data rather than attendance data. It is possible to utilize some of the HRA thinking and general accounting thinking, even now, to sort out some of the financial aspects of HRD. To do this, we must return to the classifications of HRD—training, education, and development.

Training

As you will recall from Chapter 2, training consists of those learning experiences provided by the organization to improve performance on the present job of the employee.

Training is an expense. This is defined as an expenditure of financial resources with the intent of getting something directly in return. When you, as a manager, authorize an expenditure for supplies, you expect to see those supplies. When you authorize the payroll, you expect that there has been some performance at this time which will show a direct return to your department and your organization.

This is the case with training. As the results of training are expected to be seen immediately, on the job the individual now has, it is an expense. As with any other expense, the manager should expect to identify the return at this time.

Education

Education consists of those learning experiences provided by the organization to prepare employees for future positions.

Education is an investment. This is defined as an expenditure of financial resources with the intent of getting a future return. As with most investments, there is a certain element of risk, since there are many events that may cause the investment risk to become a loss, or to give less than a full return.

In the case of education—preparation for a future job—in the time between when the employee completes the education program and is actually assigned to a new job, that job may change, making the learning comparatively useless. Another possibility is that the new job may be cancelled before the employee is transferred to it. There is the ever-present possibility that between the end of the education program and the availability of the new job, the employee may leave the organization.

Given all these possibilities, why should a manager take the risk of making financial expenditures for education? The most direct response is that managers are expected to take risks. Part of the job of any manager is to take risks in the hope of increasing return to the organization. Education is just such a risk. The manager who does not wish to risk is not doing the job for which the organization is compensating him.

Education is a low-risk investment. It is conducted because there will be an opening and the manager should be preparing an employee to fill the anticipated opening. Sometimes it may be a promotion, but even if it is a lateral transfer (or a demotion), it is still the responsibility of managers to take appropriate steps and provide the needed education. It is a low-risk investment because there is a direct intent to prepare an employee for a defined but different job.

Development

Development is an investment, but it differs from the risk of education. In development, the manager is providing a learning experience which is not directed toward a specific job, but in the general direction the organization may be going (or at least wishes to consider). Long-range management plans can change.

Also, as discussed earlier, there is no direct relation to a specific job; therefore, the direct and even indirect return may be difficult to identify.

As a result, development is a high-risk and long-range investment. As with any such investment, there must be policies and controls. Too much of this kind of investment can wreck an organization. But having none of this kind of investment can also contribute to the demise of an organization. Without development and its attendant risks, an organization may be relevant for yesterday, perhaps struggling through today, but completely unprepared for tomorrow.

COST SYSTEMS

There is no one way to obtain good cost data, as has been discussed earlier. There are attempts in progress and a good manager should support these endeavors even though they may not yet be able to produce the kind of data required for hard decisions. Until certain agreements are reached, it will not be possible to provide the kind of cost data that managers need to make decisions regarding HRD. If your HRD people are not providing the kind of cost data you would like to have, it is not because they do not want to or because they are hiding anything. The problems are in the area of lack of clarification as to what is a cost, and how to economically measure the benefits of learning programs.

There are ways of looking at cost systems, and they will be discussed here. Both require the cooperation of managers if the cost information is to be meaningful and helpful.

Cost-Benefit Comparison

This is a cost accounting approach which endeavors to couple the expense or investment with a direct return to the organization. It starts with identifying exactly what the HRD activity costs, on a program-by-program basis. Every element of cost is identified and listed. This sounds easy, but it requires agreement on what the cost items are, and then making data available to the HRD people.

Some of the direct costs are readily discernible, such as the operating cost of the HRD unit, transportation expenses, materials and equipment, and other items directly chargeable to HRD. The use of the physical facility should be allocated on the same basis as that charge for any part of the organization, if that is the practice. Given the difficulty in allocating some of these costs, some organizations calculate a general overhead figure to be borne by each unit of the organization. The same should be applied to the HRD unit.

More controversial are some of the other cost elements. For example, while an employee is in training, should his salary or wage be chargeable to the HRD function? What of loss of production or service during that period—who should bear the cost? It is not possible to provide answers to these questions in this book, but it is hoped that the questions will give managers the basis for examining these practices in their own organizations.

Once agreement can be reached on what is included in cost, it is possible to make some comparisons. One way of looking at this is the "bottom line" approach. This refers to the bottom line of the P & L (Profit and Loss) statement. If the cost is known, it might be possible to determine whether a program adds to the profit or contributes to lessening any loss. Applying this approach is based on the availability of other data, as well as on the philosophy of the organization.

In order to utilize this approach, the job must be measurable. It is not possible to quantify change unless there is some benchmark or prior data. If the job is not being measured, then there is nothing against which the cost can be compared. If your organization does not have base line measurable data, it is not possible to use a cost-benefit approach. If the data are available, then at least you can explore using a cost-benefit method in your cost system. The entire situation needs to be examined closely to be sure it is being correctly analyzed.

Once again, we have to return to the concept of HRD. For training, the cost data can be extremely helpful. Increased or improved job performance, if measurable, can be contrasted with the cost of the training. Education and development are much more difficult to deal with in a cost system and no generally acceptable methods have been recognized, as yet.

Front-End Approach

The cost systems discussed above are all based on comparison after the program has been conducted. Is it possible to use cost system before a program starts to determine if it might be cost effective? There are those who urge that this approach is not only possible but essential. Theoretically, none would differ. Who would argue for a program which will not return anything to the organization for its use of financial and physical resources? Regretably, the situation is much more complex than the simple questions which have been posed.

To use the front-end approach, it is once again necessary to have cost data. As the program has not yet been conducted, these will be estimates rather than actual costs. If there are the agreements discussed earlier on what cost elements are to be included, then the HRD people can at least provide managers with a cost estimate. This must be compared with the estimate of the manager as to what savings would be gained by conducting the program. If the manager cannot provide this figure, then any comparison for front-end purposes is not possible. In such a situation, the front-end approach would not be feasible.

Let us assume that the cost data are available from both HRD and management. What then? Going further, if the cost exceeds the benefits, should there be an automatic decision not to provide the learning experience? Obviously, the answer should be a a resounding *No!* Decisions regarding HRD should not be made on the basis of cost alone. There are other factors to be considered, but with the comparative cost data, a manager is in a good position to be able to make a sound decision. Whatever the decision, the basis for it should be shared by the manager and the HRD people. If they do not know why you are making the decision, they are reduced in their effectiveness to be of continuing assistance to you. The decision is still yours, as a manager, but your thinking on the decision should be shared.

CONCLUSION

Without adequate physical and financial resources, HRD cannot function. Managers need to make decisions regarding how HRD is to be funded, and the kinds of physical resources which will be made available.

There is no suggestion that HRD be excluded from the normal constraints on other organizational units, but to date we have had a great deal of difficulty in measuring the results of HRD in financial terms. With managers and HRD people working together, at least the basic elements of a responsible cost system can be developed and be helpful to all.

5 Instructional Strategies for HRD

When you send your subordinates to a learning experience, you should know something of what will be happening to them during this experience. You are not expected to make any hard decisions in this difficult area, but there are some aspects you should at least know about.

If you come from one of the hard science areas, you are in for a disappointment. The field of learning is mainly theories—that is, assumptions under which we operate but which, in most cases, cannot be absolutely proven. We continue to use some of these learning strategies because they appear to work—i.e., to reach the objectives of the learning situation. We introduce new learning strategies because they have promise, and at least a minimal basis in some research or studies. If they do the job, they are retained. If not, they disappear into the textbooks or are coupled with existing strategies in some other form.

The terminology in the field is likewise confusing. Do not let yourself be put off and fall into the trap of muttering "jargon." The area is complex and includes many professionals who have come into this field from disciplines other than learning. They brought some of their terminology with them. The impact of manufacturers of hardware has also introduced terms and names which slowly are becoming common to the field.

This has led to the term "instructional strategies." For years, there were discussions as to whether a particular approach was a method, a technique, or a device. There are some who still try to make the distinction. As there is no agreement on those terms, others have slowly begun to accept instructional strategies as the overall term describing how learning can be organized and supplemented.

In this chapter, there will be a discussion of some of the concepts of learning and the terms associated with them. There will be an exploration of some of the strategies in common use which you can expect to encounter either as a learner or as a manager. This familiarization should facilitate communication with your HRD people and enable you to ask some intelligent questions and understand most of the replies.

There are many ways in which your HRD people make selections of the appropriate strategy. One of these is based on what we do know about learning theory and which strategies are most likely to bring results, given the objectives, the material, and the learner. Another factor in this decision-making rests with the history and culture of the organization. In some organizations, it is almost mandatory that case studies be used for management learning programs, and that all learning programs for executives are conducted off-site.

A third element is administrative decision-making. If a manager indicates that he will not release employees for a whole day, but only part of it, this will influence the range of strategies available to the HRD people. Therefore, it is important for managers to know enough about instructional strategies to enable them to make appropriate decisions or be prepared to alter previous decisions.

In this chapter we will also indicate some trends. The field is constantly changing and some of the directions will be of interest to managers.

SOME CONCEPTS

There are vaious ways of looking at learning, and herein we will discuss the use of models, the curriculum, and learning theories.

Models

Most HRD people, in designing learning experiences, are using one or more of the many models of learning prevalent in the field. For the manager, the use of a model is important, for it provides a form of road map so that the HRD people and the manager can at least be looking at the same road. Models are usually drawn in diagram form rather than narrative. Some are fairly simple, with a few boxes, words, and arrows. Others appear to be line wiring diagrams for TV sets and are best understood by those with an engineering background. A manager who comes from an engineering or technical field will find those diagrams reassuring and easily read. For those from sales or similar fields, the model can appear to be one more example of how people in the HRD field tend toward obfuscation.

Models are helpful to all concerned. If your HRD people cannot show you the models they are using, you have a right to question whether they know where they are going and how they will get there.

There are many existing models, though your HRD people can certainly create their own. You need to explore carefully, for underlying every model are assumptions about the learner and how people learn. It is presumed that you agree with those assumptions. We will look at this a bit later in this section when we discuss some learning theories.

Curriculum

The term curriculum is most commonly used in the school system, but as more academically prepared people enter the HRD field, the practice is growing to use the terminology of the learning profession. A manager should not be made to feel inadequate if he is not aware of some of the terminology.

In essence, the curriculum is the content to be learned and the sequence in which the learning is to take place. Some HRD people will also include the actual instructional strategies as part of the curriculum, while others consider this a separate area.

As a manager, it is your responsibility to review the curriculum being offered to your subordinates. The content should include what you think is necessary for their jobs as reflected in the objectives of the learning. The HRD people should invite you to examine the curriculum and discuss it with them. Of course you are busy—you have much to do, and looking at the curriculum may not seem an important way to use your time. If you choose not to look at the curriculum, you are running the risk that the learning program may contain items which are either not important for operations or are contrary to policy. The HRD people are not doing this purposefully. If managers do not communicate with the HRD people, how are the HRD people to know if they are in conflict with policy or practice?

When reviewing the curriculum, avoid commenting, "But that is not what *I* learned." The curriculum should not be limited only to what you learned, or even to what you now know. This is particularly true where the curriculum is for a position below yours. Since you last did that job, there may have been many changes in process and technology. As a manager, you may not have kept up with those changes, and are not expected to have maintained your competencies in those jobs which you left.

Reviewing the curriculum can be a learning experience for a manager. You can discover what has changed and what is happening in the field. If the curriculum is well-designed, a close examination by you can be an informal self-directed learning experience!

If you have questions about any aspect of the curriculum, arrange for a discussion with your HRD people. They may have utilized subject matter specialists with an approach different from yours. The HRD people should have consulted you about the selection of the subject matter specialist, and you may have even recommended the person they used. When the material is finally reduced to writing, in the curriculum, it may be somewhat different from what you had anticipated. Further exploration with your HRD people can be extremely helpful to all concerned.

Learning Theories

There are so many learning theories that they can easily prove confusing. It is not necessary for the manager to know such theories, though the general headings may be of interest. The manager will hear references to humanistic, mechanistic, organismic, etc. These terms could be defined in this book, but all that would do is produce the possibility of a "one upmanship" situation. The manager might then begin dropping these terms into the conversation, to the chagrin and embarrassment of the HRD staff. It would block communications rather than facilitate them.

More important is that the manager should be able to ask the HRD staff some questions about learning theories and how they apply to the instructional strategies.

Does the HRD staff:

- Accept the concept of andragogy (adult learning) as different from pedagogy (child learning)? There is no complete agreement on this distinction even in the field of adult learning, but exploring the differences is important.
- Follow the behaviorist approach to learning (usually identified with Skinner)?
- Subscribe to individual learning, rather than group learning, and under what conditions?
- Use self-directed learning, and when?

These are only a few of the questions that a manager should be prepared to ask. The specific answers may not be as important as the dialogue which could result between the HRD staff and the manager.

SOME COMMONLY USED STRATEGIES

There is no one best strategy for all kinds of learning and all kinds of learners. Rather, this is a mix and a range of possibilities. This is what makes HRD so difficult, yet so challenging.

Most of the strategies will automatically call for certain kinds of support in the way of facilities, equipment, and materials. As discussed earlier, if the manager does not make the necessary physical and financial resources available, it is unlikely that effective learning can take place.

Most learning is considered either formal or non-formal. (Some prefer the term informal, but there is no agreement on the distinction between those two words.) The need for planned instructional strategies and appropriate support is fairly obvious when one speaks of formal learning. This requires the classroom (conference room, conference site) and the paraphenalia which is usually part of such a facility.

Less understood is that even non-formal learning utilizes strategies and requires appropriate support. Non-formal is commonly found in the area called "on-the-job" training (though it could be education) and is most often provided by a supervisor or somebody delegated by the supervisor to perform this function. It can be used when the new employee (singular) is assigned to a unit, or when an existing employee is not performing up to standard. Too often the OJT (on-the-job-training) is considered to be nothing more than giving simple instructions. If there is the need for learning, then whoever is conducting the experience should know how to instruct, and know what strategies are most appropriate for that situation. The HRD staff is an excellent resource for this—not to do the instruction, but to assist the line personnel in doing it.

Group Learning

The most prevalent form of group learning is the classroom situation. The actual "classroom" can be on the shop floor, a conference room, or a specially prepared area. They are all considered classrooms. The one thing they should have in common is that they should look as little as possible like the classrooms one is apt to find in traditional school buildings. The furniture should be movable and the chairs of sufficient size for an adult body rather than for that of a child. The older reader will recall the traditional classroom. For the younger reader, this label can be meaningless. Since 1960, school buildings have been built in a wide variety of shapes, sizes, and dimensions. There are windowless classrooms, and unwalled areas in some classrooms.

The major impact of this variation is that there may be a wide variety of expectations among the learners, depending upon age, geographical distribution, and type of school attended. There are still some universities where the majority of rooms contain chairs bolted to the floor in theatre style or auditorium style. Few of these should be found in the classrooms in factories and offices. If the nature of the subject matter to be taught requires a more formal setting, the chairs may be arranged in theatre style, but not bolted to the floor, thus allowing for variations in seating arrangements.

Even in the classroom setting, it is possible to have a variety of large group learning situations. Lecture is still the most prevalent strategy despite all the research which tells us this is the least effective way to facilitate learning.

Small group techniques are used to make the learning more appropriate for the wide range of learners usually found in a group learning situation. I recall one manager who observed several small groups in a large room, and commented loudly, "I see they are using sensitivity groups again!" Small groups are not necessarily T-groups. Small groups are used in many situations which have nothing to do with sensitivity work. More important is why the instructor uses small groups and how.

Imagine a demonstration of some job performance element which is being conducted for the entire class. Then, the learners are divided into small groups so they can cross-check with each other on what they observed and what they learned. This is only one use of small groups. A frequent use is coupled with case studies and exercises. After the presentation of the material (case or exercise), the class is divided into small groups so they can "process" the experience. Through checklists, instruction sheets, and similar aids, the small groups engage in in-depth discussions of the experience. This allows for involvement by everybody and encourages peer learning.

The variety of group possibilities is almost endless, but there are two points to be wary of. First, groups should not be used merely as an opportunity for the instructor to take a break, do paperwork, or have some free time. Second, using small groups takes skill. It is more than just dividing up a large group. There must be objectives, a clear task, and some form of feedback. It takes skill to design and use small group learning effectively.

Individual Learning

Since the early 1960's, there has been increased emphasis on providing for individual differences; that is, providing for individual learning. That is based on the sound notions that not everybody needs to learn the same material and that not everybody learns the same way. These differences encourage us to seek new and improved ways for individual learning.

This strategy also allows for some, if not all, of the learning to take place at the job site. The mistake most often made is to think that this is a less costly way to produce learning. In fact, it usually proves more costly in the development of appropriate materials, controls, etc.

For a person to learn individually, the objectives and curriculum must relate to individual performance. If the learner is to improve performance in working with others, the learning program must have the possibility of interaction and practice with others. For learning which is not influenced by a need to interfere with other people, it is possible that individual learning can be more effective. It can allow the learner to set a personal learning pace, make his own mistakes, and profit from direct feedback on performance. Individual learning requires more mechanisms for direct feedback to the learner as to the quantity and quality of performance of the newly learned behavior.

The major breakthrough in individual learning occurred in the early 1960's with the development of programmed instruction. As with many new instructional strategies, it arrived on a crest of a wave with the implication that this was *the* answer to all learning problems. As the years passed—and with them, more experience with the strategy—it became obvious that it was helpful, but by no means the only approach nor always the best.

The two variables in programmed instruction (commonly referred to as PI) are the learner and the nature of the subject matter to be learned. Some learners need others around them—they have high social needs—and have difficulty learning alone. There are also those who are "gestalt"-oriented—they see things as a whole. Such learners have difficulty with the frame-by-frame approach of PI even if variations such as branching (which provides learning opportunities in breadth and depth) are used.

Some subject matter does not lend itself to PI, particularly where attitudes are involved. There are programs which purport to improve attitudes through PI, but as attitudes are acted out in relation to other people, doubt has been expressed about PI programs dealing with attitudes. Also, there is some question as to whether skills can really be learned through PI, though these has been some significant experience with the "skill" of listening. The most common use of PI is where knowledge must be learned, and the knowledge is stated specifically and unequivocally. In such cases, where no variations is allowed, PI can prove to be an important way to provide for individual learning.

From PI came machines, and then, toward the end of the 1960's, the coupling of PI with media: mediated learning; that is, learning which is made possible through the use of media (tape recorders, projectors, PI machines) rather than through the mediation of a live instructor. Various kinds of teaching machines (hardware) appeared on the market, but few survived more than a few years, mostly due to the lack of adequate programs (software) for the machines. The cost of producing the software is extremely high, and therefore is only warranted if there is a large market where the cost can be spread over many learners.

On a more sophisticated level, there are computer-assisted-instruction (CAI) and computer manager-instruction (CMI), both of which had brief periods of use and then were used only in rare cases. With the advent of simpler programs for computers, and computers in the home, it is possible that there will be an increase in the availability of software and rejuvenation of the CAI approach to learning.

There is an individual learning strategy which relies on an instructor-mediated approach. This is commonly called coaching. There are many variations of coaching, but it is probably one of the oldest and most commonly used individual learning strategies. In coaching, an experienced individual watches another perform and then gives advice, assistance, guidance, etc., to improve performance. It sounds easy but is actually quite difficult. It requires that the coach set a climate of mutual respect so the learner will be receptive. Being too critical can block learning, and not being critical enough can cause the learner to lose confidence in the coach.

The coach is required to be sensitive and observant. The instructions from the coach must be given at the point where they are needed, and this is sometimes when the learner is at the highest level of frustration. Good coaching is a valuable strategy for individual learning. Another label for this kind of coach is mentor.

There are situations when the coach is not a superior, older, or even more experienced individual. The buddy system, as applied to coaching, is to match up two individuals at the same level who will work together and learn together. Time must be provided so one individual can watch the other, and not be working, and then there must be time to provide the feedback essential to coaching.

TRENDS

There are some movements, outside of the regular instructional strategy area, which managers should be aware of. Over the years, some of these will develop further and make a significant impact on the field of learning and on organizations. Others will either fall into disuse and merely be recorded in the books, or will change as new pressures, research, and technology open up new vistas.

Behavioral Science

This term is still unclear and is viewed by some with suspicion. As originally used, it was intended to embrace a broad look at the field of human endeavors and not be limited to any one discipline. The exponents of behavioral science saw the learner as being composed of many elements, which suggested that learning should be approached on several levels.

The major impetus came out of the work of the National Training Laboratories and the sensitivity movement. To most people, even today, behavioral science means T-groups. It should not. Behavioral science goes far beyond any one strategy, though some areas rely very heavily on experiential (laboratory) learning rather than on passive approaches.

Some newer trends in the behavioral sciences are worthy of mention, as they relate to instructional strategies. The earlier period placed heavy emphasis on the group, and on group learning. Newer approaches recognize that there is also a place for individual learning.

More emphasis is now placed on providing the learning as close to the point of use as possible. This has brought newer strategies right into the company and has spun off other approaches, notably, organizational development (OD), which is discussed below.

The term "behavioral science" is itself falling into some disuse. This is partially due to its history, during which the term was used to describe a wide variety of activities. As a result, it lost some of its specificity and therefore does not communicate as well as it once did. Even further, over the past 20 years, the field has divided into various forms, some of which are mentioned later in this chapter. This has enabled us to consider just what kind of behavioral science is involved and determine exactly what the contributions to learning from various sources are.

Organizational Development

We are still at the stage where this term, OD, defies any generally accepted definition. We have even stopped trying to define it, in some instances, but instead use it as a working term covering a wide variety of experiences in the organization.

One part of OD has moved toward organizational behavior and the identification of how to manage behavior in organizations. Another group is moving toward improving learning situations in organizations, seeing the organization as a learning community. This latter group is still highly concerned with interpersonal relations and how to improve, through learning, the performance of individuals in organizations.

The activities in this field are changing rapidly. It is possible that the next decade will see many more variations arising, but the term itself may lose its effectiveness. There are those who are looking for a more precise label for this area of activity, although so far none has gained any kind of general acceptance. So OD continues to be used, though it now covers a much broader area of human and organizational endeavors than it did in the early 1970's.

Some researchers are starting to examine high-performing organizations. This is in contrast to previous efforts, which were designed to improve performance of less effective organizations. Not enough has been done about identifying high-performing organizations, or in clarifying the instructional strategies which are needed to have an effect on high performance.

Transactional Analysis

The transactional analysis (TA) movement received its impetus when Eric Berne categorized relationships as being "adult," "child," or "parent." His purpose was to find a way for psychiatrists and other therapists to communicate more effectively with their patients. Building on this came the concept, "I'm OK, you're OK," which made the philosophy of TA more understandable to the layman.

TA has moved from therapy into instruction. All of us, even those of us with no particular emotional difficulties, can find some help in understanding relationships if we know something of TA. It should not, however, be used as a technique to control or manipulate others, although it is all too easy to use it that way.

As an instructional strategy, some elements of TA are helpful in understanding supervisor/subordinate relationships. This is most obvious when the supervisor tries to function in place of a parent. TA can give insight to a supervisor about his own behavior, as well as helping him to understand the behavior of his peers and subordinates. It can even help a supervisor understand his boss!

There are many programs in which TA can be a valuable instructional strategy. One of these is in customer relations or for those employees who have direct contact with the public. In a simplistic fashion, TA helps an employee understand and respond with an appropriate approach to the individual and the situation.

As with other instructional strategies, TA must be used carefully, and by qualified individuals. It is easy to determine if an operator can work a projector, but it is not so easy to know if the person offering TA is indeed qualified to do so. The TA field has tried to police its own behavior by developing some forms of accreditation. This does not prevent any other person from offering TA. Many good HRD people have been able to develop competencies and build some concepts of TA into their programs without being accredited.

Managers should be wary of TA, as of any other instructional strategy. At one point, a consultant was called in by a manager of a large motel chain and asked if he wanted a contract (a very large one) to do TA with the front desk people. The consultant asked some questions, and the following dialogue ensued.

Consultant: Why do you want TA?
Manager: Because my people need it!
Consultant: Can we talk in terms of objectives? TA is a response. First let's talk need.
Manager: Easy—my front desk people don't know how to handle people coming into the motels. These people are tired, hungry, worn out, and they come into the motel after many miles on the road. Sometimes the weather has been bad, or they have been traveling with children.
Consultant: (Responds with a grunt of recognition.)
Manager: The first person the driver sees is at the front desk. The driver may be angry, frustrated, tired—whatever, and the front desk person bears the brunt of it. Front desk people will tell you horror stories of all kinds of behavior short

	of being physically beaten, and we even have examples of that. TA will help them handle the situation.
Consultant:	There you go again. We may settle on TA, but first let's look at the situation. What is the main objective for the front desk people? What does your organization reward them for?
Manager:	Getting the people into rooms as fast as possible. We pride ourselves on having some of the best rooms and facilities in the industry. We don't want people hanging around the front desk and complaining. This holds up the process and sometimes has a similar effect on others entering the motel. The rule is: get them registered and to their rooms as fast as possible.
Consultant:	Fine—and with TA they will start a dialogue with the customer and keep them at the front desk. Is that what you want?
Manager:	No! I want to get them away from the front desk as soon as possible.
Consultant:	Then why TA?

At that point, what was going on became obvious. The manager had read about TA and the fact that some companies were using it. Those were other large companies, and if it was good for them, he assumed, his company should have it, too. He oversimplified. Many of the other companies did not have his problem, or his goal.

On the other hand, American Airlines has reported that through its use of TA, customer relations have improved and the problems faced by the flight attendants have been reduced. Where the customer and employee must remain together, as in an airplane, there is much to be said for TA. It fits the need of that particular situation.

There are many other situations where TA could be helpful. It is slowly becoming one of those strategies which is used by being coupled with others, such as role-play, case study, and exercises.

Assessment Centers

The history of the assessment center, as we know it today, goes back to about the end of the 1950's. Attempts were being made to select good employees through a technique known as multiple role-playing, in which everybody in the group was involved. Then, in-basket was added to this. In-basket is an exercise in decision-making and handling the crises which are prevalent at various levels of management. What slowly emerged was the realization that it was possible to predict performance before the person was placed on the job. In other words, future performance could be assessed.

As a selection tool, there is no doubt that assessment centers have a sufficient history of success to be accepted. They have become more sophisticated and, usually, special training is required to enable internal employees to handle an assessment center. It is also possible to contract for outside organizations that specialize in this personnel selection technique.

As a learning tool, its use is highly debatable, but some people have made the jump into using the assessment center to "assess" the learning needs of the participants. There is a fundamental difference between this and the sort of assessment described above. Learning is a risk activity. If the learner is not prepared to try out new behavior in order to identify his learning needs, it is doubtful the needs can be identified—and if the needs cannot be identified, how can learning take place?

In the assessment center exercise, the participant is not taking risks but is playing it as safe as possible. The participant wants to show those in charge that he is capable of doing the job, or exhibiting those behaviors which will make him elegible for promotion. He will be a low risk, and rightly so. He will exhibit the behavior he thinks the organization (examiners) want and suppress anything else. This may be fine for selection, if the examiners are qualified, but does little to identify real learning needs.

Some assessment centers do present the possibility of identifying learning needs. When carefully controlled, and where the behaviors are measurable, it is possible to determine whether the participant can do the job, or what might be needed to have him do the job. This also means the situation has to be as close to reality as possible. This is fine, but there are less costly ways to achieve this result.

As a tool for identification of learning needs, there may be some slight justification for assessment centers. As a learning strategy, it is difficult to see how an assessment center contributes to the process.

Behavior Modeling

These words, behavior modeling, have been used in so many contexts it is difficult to use them to label only one kind of instructional strategy. Growing out of work at AT & T and General Electric, a program was put together and given that label. Let us examine it only in this context.

Behavior modeling is based on the idea that we have spent too much time giving supervisors and managers theories about human behavior, which they then had difficulty in translating into direct, on-the-job behavior. The basic assumption is that people in such positions must first be sure they know what the correct behavior is, considering the organization and its practices and policies. After that, it may be acceptable to delve into theories and concepts.

Behavior modeling is accomplished through video presentations which have been carefully prepared. Then, the participants in the group try to emulate what they have seen. When they can do this, they are given new but similar situations so they can try out the new behavior in as many situations as possible.

This strategy addresses the question, "Which do you change first, attitude or behavior?" Traditionally, it has been thought that if you provide learning related to attitudes, the learner will alter behavior to conform to the new attitude. The behavior modeling approach does not deal with attitudes, but only with behavior. It says that the learner should learn the new behavior without having to explore his attitudes and even without additional knowledge. What the organization wants is the new behavior. Then, if needed, there can be work on attitudes and knowledge to reinforce the behavior—but first comes the new behavior.

The strategy is having some success but is not without its critics. Some will just not accept it at all. They say it produces rote behavior but is only useful if the participant comes up against the exact same situation he has practiced in the learning situations. Others point out that when a person becomes a supervisor or manager, he usually wants to know the "why" and not only the "how."

Those using the instructional strategy of behavior modeling can point to some success but there has not been enough time to know if the benefits of this approach are long lasting, or if they can be transferred to other situations.

Self-Directed Learning

At first, this appears to be similar to PI, but it is not and should not be confused with that approach. Self-directed learning comes out of the work of Allen Tough, of Canada, where his research showed that many learners assumed responsibility for their own learning, though they did not come near a classroom or an instructor in the traditional sense. Such learners feel the need to learn, and they seek out the appropriate resources to assist them in their learning.

For managers, this suggests that provisions need to be made within the organization for such self-directed learners. The HRD unit should be able to provide resources and support, and the managers should provide encouragement. It is likely that subordinates will look to managers for role models in this area of learning. Accordingly, managers should be knowledgable about this area and explore its utilization for themselves as well as for their subordinates.

An element of self-directed learning is the learning contract. A form of this has been developed by Malcolm Knowles and appears in his excellent short book, *Self-Directed Learning*. The HRD unit can probably provide additional assistance in devising some form of learning contract which is applicable to the local situation.

The value of the learning contract is that it specifies what is to be learned, the resources which will be utilized, and some indication of how that learning will be evaluated. It is developed by the learner, who usually requires some assistance; it becomes the visible goal of the learning to be accomplished; and it provides for individual differences, although it is possible that a group of learners with the same needs could form a class.

CONCLUSION

This chapter has discussed some of the more common approaches to learning but by no means is it meant to be all-inclusive. There are whole books and volumes setting forth the vast range of learning strategies.

For the manager, it is important to know that a large range of learning strategies do exist. We are far beyond the simple classroom-lecture approach. The HRD unit can be a valuable resource in helping managers learn more about appropriate learning strategies.

It is not expected that the managers will have any degree of expertise in either selecting or utilizing instructional strategies. Rather, managers need to know what to look for, and what to ask for. As newer strategies appear, the manager should not hesitate to query the HRD unit about the assumptions behind the strategy and about those areas in which it can be most helpful to the learner and the organization.

6   Evaluating the HRD Effort

How many times have you heard, "Evaluation is like the weather—everybody talks about it but nobody does anything about it"? Perhaps, at one time, this was true. At present, there is little reason not to evaluate learning experiences. The difficulty is that the word evaluation covers such a large range of possibilities.

The first thing we must do is separate evaluation from research. These are two different and distinct activities, each used for a different purpose. As people tend to use some of the same techniques for both, it becomes very easy to confuse them.

Evaluation is concerned with finding out *what* happened. Let's presume that a program was activated so that certain learning would take place. Evaluation seeks to answer the question, "*Did* that learning take place?" Also, "Does the learner now have the basis for producing the desired behavior?" And then, "How do we know?"

Research is concerned with finding out *why* it happened. Research asks, "If learning took place, why was it successful?" and "If it did not take place, why was it not successful?" This requires much more expertise and more sophisticated techniques than are required for evaluation.

Some other differences are that evaluation starts with objectives and tries to determine if the objectives have been reached, while research starts with hypotheses which will be tested out; evaluation is always concerned with using the results, while research can be conducted without any intent to use the results.

There are those who talk of "evaluative-research." Perhaps it is possible to mix the two, but by no means are they identical. One can lead to the other. An evaluation may disclose that the learning goals were not reached. Sometimes, this can be easily determined. There are times when the search calls for more intensive approaches, with control groups, and then we are into the area of research.

The distinction needs to be made for some very specific reasons. Every learning experience should be evaluated—but not every learning experience needs to be researched. Every HRD staff should contain at least one person with skills in designing and conducting evaluation. For most organizations, at the present time, to keep researchers in the HRD unit is too costly. Usually, researchers are contracted for from outside the organization as the need arises.

THE MANAGER AND EVALUATION

Managers need the data from evaluation in order to make decisions. Without evaluation, the manager may be repeating prior errors and wasting resources. A lack of information about accomplishments in the HRD function may encourage the manager to make incorrect decisions—or no decisions.

What should be evaluated? Essentially: Did the learning take place? If it did, but there is no change in performance on the job, this gives the manager a clue. Additional learning will probably not make any further change in behavior, but there is something about the job which needs to be explored. The evaluation should be related to the objectives of the learning, and managers should be involved in setting the objectives.

Managers and organizations have tended to shy away from evaluation where the results might be unpleasant. Few of us purposely want to look for unpleasant situations, but managers cannot avoid entering into the process.

The behavior of the HRD unit, in the area of evaluation, is actually controlled by the manager. If the manager ignores the evaluation results, the HRD unit cannot be expected to continue forwarding these data to him. The results of evaluation should be used to improve learning programs and not as a source of punishment. If the learner, or the HRD unit, is given negative feedback, it is unlikely that either will be interested in participating in any evaluations.

The manager must first be prepared to receive the results; then he must study them and react, at least in terms of having reviewed the results, whether they are good or bad. Then, action should be taken as appropriate. The results may be the basis for a meeting with the HRD unit. At first, the manager should be sure that the results are being communicated and that they are being understood. Then, through joint exploration, the manager and the HRD unit should identify the appropriate actions for each. Even where no action appears indicated, a meeting to discuss the results is beneficial.

CONCEPTS OF EVALUATION

There are many ways to evaluate. In this section, one model will be presented. By no means is it the only model, but it will provide a basis for discussion of the process. When the manager talks with the HRD unit, a good place to start is with the model the HRD people are using. If they have no models, then the manager has helped them identify a need within their own operation. Frequently, the HRD people do have a model but they have not put it down on paper. Rather, they assume that everybody knows what is included in evaluation, and such an assumption can lead to some significant distortions as to how various people perceive the evaluative function of the HRD unit.

As a process, evaluation follows these steps:

1. Determine the objectives of the learning
2. Conduct the learning
3. Evaluate
    a. Gather data
    b. Analyze
    c. Give feedback

We will look at each of these in more detail, but first let us take a broad look at the process.

PLANNING FOR EVALUATION

Although evaluation cannot take place until the learning starts, and, in some situations, until it ends, the planning for evaluation must take place during the design of the learning experience. Evaluation should be a part of the learning design and not something which is added afterwards. In designing how the evaluation will take place, and what will be evaluated, the planners (HRD unit and manager) will be clarifying mutual responsibilities as well as design.

There are two points at which time evaluation takes place for training. One is as part of the training program, while the second is after the trainee has returned to the job. The purpose of evaluation during training is to influence the learning process while it is in process. Obviously, if we wait until the learning experience has been completed, and the learner is back on the job, there is little that can be done. The time to make the necessary corrections and modifications to reach the learning objectives is *while* the learner is in the learning situation.

Perhaps a dramatic case will illustrate. I had a contract to do a learning program for a government agency that brought people from other countries to study in the U.S. In this case, it was a 13 week program, and traditionally it had been "evaluated" through an interview conducted with each learner just prior to departure. I insisted that I would not take the contract unless a formative evaluation were built in. Surprisingly enough, this had never really been done before. There had been the requirement that the learners produce a weekly report of their learning, but this usually was a list of names, places, and what was talked about.

A mid-training evaluation was designed and discussed with the managers in the agency concerned. They made suggestions, and the evaluation was administered in the sixth week. During the seventh week, the data were shared with the agency, and as a result, there were a number of changes made in the total program for all learners and some provisions made for individual needs which had not previously surfaced. Accordingly, the balance of the program was redesigned, as needed, to utilize the results of the evaluation. When the final evaluation was conducted, prior to departure, the participants singled out the mid-evaluation as being one of the most helpful experiences, and they appreciated the changes which had been made as a result of using that data.

A mid-evaluation should not be planned unless there is willingness on the part of the HRD unit and the managers to make adjustments. This may call for a change in the objectives, as well as in the content and instructional strategies.

When using a mid-evaluation, another element can enter the picture rather strongly, and that is the learner. At the outset of the learning experience, the learner may understand and agree with the objectives. As the learning proceeds, the learner may identify new needs or may discover that some of what had been contained in the objectives can clearly be done. Here we are faced with both learning theory and managerial behavior.

If the learning theory subscribed to is that the learner goes into the program and marches through it without any interference or change, then it is unlikely that a mid-evaluation is necessary. If it won't change anything, then why do it? Where the learner cannot influence the situation, a mid-evaluation is a waste.

If changes can take place, as a result of the evaluation, what is the role of the manager? Too many managers treat the learning experience like fireworks. You light the fuse and then all you do is stand by and watch the results. If there has been mid-evaluation, the manager has a significant role. He should be ready to review the evaluation and then make decisions about changes which may be indicated.

In addition to improving the learning situation, mid-evaluation also communicates to the learner and the HRD unit that the manager is very concerned about the learning experience and is committed to helping make it successful. This overt behavior on the part of the manager can communicate a great deal and contribute to the success of the program.

As part of the training program, there should be a final evaluation. This is the more familiar kind, taking place at the end of the learning activity. It is not less significant than the mid-evaluation, but the processes and expectations are different. It is conducted at the completion of the training experience, to determine if the learner has learned even before returning to the job. It is hoped, of course, that this has happened, and it is the responsibility of the HRD people to determine this.

An ethical dilemma can arise during this procedure. Should the manager expect the HRD unit to provide the results of this evaluation to him on a learner-by-learner basis? There is no exact response to this ethical question—it all depends. If the program was conducted internally and the manager made the resources available, he wants to know what he has received for his expenditures. If there is any question about this information being made available to the manager, that should be clarified at the outset. There may even be times when a manager would prefer not to incur the expense without having access to the information on how each learner ended up in the learning experience. When the learning has been conducted externally, this may present a problem. If the contractor agrees at the outset that the results of the learning program can be made available, there will probably be no difficulty. To ask for the information at a later date will raise ethical questions.

The second point at which training is evaluated is back on the job. As defined earlier, training is the learning experience designed to improve performance on the existing job. You, as the manager, should be extremely interested in determining if performance has actually improved. If it has, then the training was worth the expense. If not, do not start by blaming the HRD people. There may be other reasons why the learner cannot produce the expected performance, and it may have more to do with you, the supervisor, the job, the materials, etc., than it has to do with the learning ability of the employee or the quality of program conducted by your HRD people. If performance does not improve, your HRD people can be a valuable resource in helping you identify what has to be changed in order to improve performance.

A limitation that has existed in the past is the concept of some managers that once the learner returns to the job, the HRD people are out of the picture. If you operate in this mode, you are preventing the HRD people from conducting an on-the-job evaluation and completing the process of learning and evaluation.

For education, there are likewise two points of evaluation, but much further apart in time. The first is much like in training, in that there can be a formative and then a summative evaluation at the end of the education experience to determine if the learner has actually learned. It is not possible to evaluate job performance until the employee actually moves to the new job. If this is still within your unit, the HRD people should be involved in this second evaluation. It will help in improving the education programs in general, as well as in identifying any additional training needs once that employee is on the new job. If the employee is in a different unit, the HRD people may have to arrange for the evaluation through some interdepartmental channels. When you are the manager who receives an "educated" employee, it is hoped that you will make the employee and the job site available to the HRD people so they can conduct the second point of evaluation.

For development, only one point of evaluation is possible, and this is as part of the learning experience. As the purpose is not to improve performance directly on a job, it is not possible to implement the second point, and at this time is not needed.

WHAT ABOUT OBJECTIVES?

During the above discussion, there has been a constant reference to objectives. This is a word which has engendered much conflict, particularly since the early 1960's. It is not that objectives were not used before then—there have always been some kind of objectives in any learning situation. With the appearance of educational technology in the early 1960's, the need for specified behavioral objectives became more significant. It impacted on the whole field, even on some of the more humanistic programs.

Objectives for learning programs are important. They provide targets which allow for agreement among all concerned. The more specific the objectives, the more likely that agreement can be reached. You should read the objectives of learning programs for your employees and compare them with what you expect the learner to do after returning to the job. If there is an intermediate supervisor involved, the objectives should be reviewed by that level also. The learner should also know the objectives before the learning program begins, if only to be able to see what the expected performance looks or sounds like. The HRD people are directly involved and frequently do the writing of the objectives, but they should not do this alone and should involve you in finalizing them.

The process of writing objectives is part of the learning experience, and you must be involved. If you do not understand any of the special words used, stop the action and ask for an explanation. The purposes of the objectives is to reach agreement on the learning situation, not to impress you with any special language.

Objectives are essential to evaluation. If there are no objectives, it is difficult to determine what needs to be evaluated. Also, you should not expect the evaluation to go beyond the objectives. It is possible that during the learning experience and the formative evaluation, some of the objectives may need to be changed. This is a real possibility if the informative evaluation is to have any meaning. If so, you should be involved in any restatement of the original objectives. Those which are agreed upon at the outset of the program should not be made so confining that it is not possible for additional learning to take place. The objectives should be the rock bottom of what must be learned, but they should not put a limitation on how much more can be learned.

Earlier, there was mention of *specified behavioral objectives*. There are many people who have been involved in this endeavor, not the least of whom is Robert Mager. Over the years, others have had much to say about this type of objective, and currently there is no complete agreement on how to write objectives. Generally, it is agreed that learning objectives should specify what learning is to take place and should avoid words such as "understand," "to know," "gain an appreciation of," etc. These should be replaced by words which require some kind of observable action, such as "identify," "list," "demonstrate," etc. These words should be capable of producing action which can be seen (observable) and, preferably, even be measured (quantifiable).

For some performance, observable and measurable actions are fairly easy to define. Where the job is quantified in terms of output, papers processed, or something else which can be counted, the measurable is a good index and a basis for a specific objective. Some jobs may only be observable, and these are usually those with some aspect of supervision or management. For example, how would you be able to evaluate a change in *your* performance after a learning program? If there is some kind of observable behavior, this should be specified in the learning objectives. If you can find some kind of measurable behavior, this too should be specified.

Care must be taken with the measurable to be sure the right things are being measured. In one instance, dealing with managers of retail stores, a program was conducted to enable the managers to improve their skills in managing part-time permanent employees, as contrasted with regular full-time employees. The initial evaluation at the end of the program showed that the managers had learned and the objectives had been reached. Several months later, the reports from most of these stores indicated that gross sales had fallen drastically. The first criticism that was heard was that the managers had spent so much time practicing what they had learned, they no longer paid sufficient attention to sales. It appeared that the training program had reached its objectives, but that performance was lower than at the outset of the program. Fortunately, the managers themselves looked at the situation and were able to convince the home office that the reduction in sales had nothing to do with the HRD program, which had ended in November. It was the winter of 1976, and the bitter cold and snow kept people in their homes and out of the retail stores! The training program could hardly be blamed for that.

People who are more humanistically inclined have some difficulty with the concept of specified behavioral objectives, particularly when advocated by the extremists in the field. The humanists contend that people cannot be so directly and overwhelmingly manipulated. Learning, they say, is still a complex situation about which we know far too little. To limit possibilities by specified behavioral objectives can deprive the learner of the spontaneous learning which so often occurs and which is frequently beneficial.

A moderating voice in this controversy is Benjamin Bloom. He is well known for *The Taxonomy of Educational Objectives,* but in a chapter in a later book on evaluation, he has encouraged us to focus on another aspect. There are many variables to be considered and he has highlighted one of them. The term "mediated" describes how the learning opportunity is presented to the learner. Bloom contends that programs which rely heavily on machine-mediated learning require specific behavioral objectives. The machine (computer, slide projector, audio-tutor) can be programmed in only one way, with all the possibilities built into the program. Usually, once the learner starts the program, he continues through until the conclusion, when the learning objectives will have been met.

When the program is instructor-mediated, there need be less specification of learning objectives. It is possible for the instructor to make changes and modifications based on the needs of the individual learner, the nature of the material, the experiences in the learning situation, etc.

Obviously, there are many different points of view. In this brief discussion, not all of them have been presented, but it is hoped that you will now have a feeling for the nature of the controversy. Most likely, you will have your own ideas of how learning takes place and how specific the objectives need to be. What you believe, and what your HRD people practice, should be congruent, if possible.

EVALUATION ELEMENTS

There are many different models for evaluating learning programs. You should ask your HRD people what models and plans they have for evaluating the HRD programs they are doing for you. The following discussion will present one way of looking at evaluation, and you can use it as a basis for discussion with your HRD people.

The evaluation model presented here assumes that there have been clear objectives and that you have been involved in formulating those objectives. This has been followed by some action: the learning program. The application of the evaluation itself will take place, as discussed earlier, either during the program (formative) or at the end (summative). The planning for the evaluation should take place before the program starts.

Data Gathering

In order to evaluate, it is necessary to have some kind of data which indicate what has taken place. There are many ways to do this, and the most common way is to use an instrument to gather the data. This can be a questionnaire, a structured interview, or a checklist. It is not easy to construct such instruments, but your HRD people should be able to do this and verify it with you. The instrument should be directly related to the objectives, so it provides you with another opportunity to determine that the objectives are directly related to your needs.

One form of instrument is the test. There is mixed feeling about this instrument for adults, particularly those who have been out of school for a while. If you are one of those people who is not bothered by a test, you may have difficulty understanding those people who find a test a torturous experience. Even highly-schooled individuals may find that the mere mention of a test evokes a physical response, including moist palms, increased heart beat, and nausea. For such people, a test is unlikely to produce positive results and can reflect incorrectly upon the whole learning experience. This does not mean that there should not be an evaluation, but that it is necessary to construct some other kind of data gathering instrument.

Where the learning experience is intended to produce a change in job performance, it may be desirable to gather data that is related to the actual job. For production workers and others who are in quantifiable situations, this may not be too difficult. Where there are service workers or managers, job performance may be more difficult for data gathering.

The data gathering should be focused on two elements: learning and performance. The learning aspect can be determined at the end of the learning experience. The performance aspect cannot really be determined until the employee has returned to the job, and then it requires your help to provide for the data gathering. There are those who try to determine performance at the end of the learning experience, before return to the job. This is done by simulations and other artificial means. If there are no alternatives, as with pilot programs or other cases where the risk is great, then it is essential to use performance tests at the end of the learning. Recognize, however, that the learner must still face the prospect of "transfer of learning," or being able to take the learning directly to where it will be used. There can be a loss during this transfer which makes it urgent that there be data gathering at two points, if at all possible—at the end of the learning and on the job.

One of the ways to gather data is to utilize a "pre" and "post" measure. The performance of the potential learner is measured before the learning begins. This is helpful in identifying learning needs and setting objectives. It also provides a basis for comparison. After the learning situation, a similar data gathering process occurs, and then it is possible to identify the change that has taken place as a result of the learning. The difficulty with this approach is the necessity for assuring that the "pre" and "post" data gathering are comparable. They must be absolutely free of any bias, or the data will reflect something other than the learning situation. Developing such data gathering mechanisms must usually be left to the professionals, probably the people in your HRD unit, but you should certainly be involved.

Analysis

After the appropriate data have been gathered, it is necessary to do some analysis. The data, by themselves, do not tell us anything. The clue is in the analysis, and this must be watched very carefully. (It is not implied that people will distort the data, but it is always possible to have a variety of interpretations, given the same data.)

The form of the analysis should be directly related to the feedback process in the organization. Before any analysis is done, the question must be answered: "Who is going to use this data, and for what purpose?" Also, "What is the usual procedure for providing feedback in our organization?"

Each organization should have a feedback process. If there is such a process in your organization, what is it? It might consist of formal reports, informal discussions, or reports at staff meetings. How do you get feedback about the learning programs provided for your unit? If you have a process, then it is important that you communicate this to the HRD people so they can provide the appropriate analysis for that process.

If you do not have a process, you could be depriving yourself of the possibility of receiving an analysis of the data. If you expect your HRD people to analyze for you, they must know what form is most appropriate for your style of management. You can force them to discover this for themselves, but it would obviously save time and anguish if you would explore this with them. If they know the feedback process you have, or would like to have, they can prepare the appropriate analysis.

How do you like your feedback? Some prefer charts, while others look for the narrative. Some managers want a brief cover page, followed by the data and analysis, whereas others do not want this massaging to take place before they have seen the data for themselves.

It saves a good deal of time, energy, and resources if you communicate your preferences to your HRD people before they put the reports into final form. Indicate to them what you want, and what form it should take.

With the advent of the computer, there has been an increased tendency to use statistical and quantifiable data to assess human behavior. It is possible that we have overemphasized that approach. Perhaps the comment of Norbert Weiner has much more relevance now than it did when it was made in the late 1940's. Discussing the use of the computer and his contribution of cybernetics, he warned that the computer could control our behavior. Of course, there was the usual scoffing at such a remark and even some muttering about sabotaging the growth of this new and important tool. Weiner went on to explain that it was highly probable that when computers became more universal, we would produce only behavior the computer could handle. His prediction has been all too accurate. The tendency to quantify human behavior has grown far beyond our capacity to deal with human behavior. For some, it is much more comfortable to deal with human behavior when it is reduced to statistical data and comes pouring from the computer.

For some human behavior, particularly that which is production related, the use of statistics and similar quantifiable data is not only appropriate, but necessary. Your HRD people may not be "showing off" when they give you reports loaded with chi-square, standard deviations, and correlations. They may be honestly trying to interpret the data so that they are more useful to you. Before they engage in such valid manipulations, you should discuss with them your specific need for statistical analysis. It may mean that you have to brush up on your understanding of statistics, or that you need a training program in statistics.

The analysis they prepare for you should also have a narrative which will highlight certain elements. Unless you given them preliminary guidance, they can spend time on components of the HRD program which are either of no interest or no help to you. They need to know what you consider important and what you intend to do with their report. It is not being suggested that they will distort the analysis in any way. On the other hand, since there are usually so many aspects which could be analyzed, they should not be wasting their time analyzing what you will not find helpful.

Feedback

This brings us to the most important element of the evaluation process: Who will use the evaluation, and for what purpose? There are many different audiences, and those doing the evaluation should have identified their probable audiences before conducting the evaluation.

Using an approach suggested by Ronald Havelock and Mary Havelock, it is possible to identify a variety of audiences that would receive the feedback on the learning program, through the evaluation report.

1. *Program developers*. Those who designed the program, so that they can improve the design of future programs. In some cases, it may be possible to actually redesign while the program is still in existence.
2. *Facilitators of learning*. Those who actually conduct the learning experience can learn a great deal from the evaluation. If they are regular full-time instructors, the feedback of the evaluation can help in the present program. It can certainly help them to improve their performance in future programs.
3. *The learners*. A properly done evaluation can assist the learner in understanding what happened during the learning experience. It can be

of benefit in aiding the learners to understand something of their own learning, their general behavior, and how it all relates to the learning objectives and the conduct of the program.
4. *The manager.* This is you—the sponsor who sent the people to the program. Perhaps you even used some of your resources to enable the program to happen. You want to know if your resources were effectively utilized, and whether the learning objectives have been met.
5. *Future learners.* Others who might be going into the same program, at a later date, might benefit from knowing the results of earlier evaluations. These should not be used to compare one group of learners with another—unless that was the specific purpose of the evaluation. Rather, it can provide the potential learner with some idea of expectations, right alongside the objectives of the learning program.

We have said that it is important that feedback be given to the right people. What is equally important is the timing. The right information given at the wrong time can be useless and even damaging. You should inform your HRD people, at the outset of the program, when you will expect to receive feedback on the evaluation. A specific date should be agreed upon as to when the feedback material will be provided to you, and in what form.

If the material arrives too long after the completion of the program, it can be historical and nothing else. There might not be anything anybody can do with the results except discuss them. When the evaluation indicates additional needs, or that goals have not been met, you will want to know this soon enough so that you won't have unrealistic expectations of those who have completed the program.

Recognize that the HRD people are not walking in your shoes. They know something of what is happening to you, but perhaps not enough. They may prepare the evaluation and provide it by the date agreed upon, but by that time you may suddenly be in some crisis they do not know about. Don't penalize them by throwing the report back to them, giving the implication that either the report was worthless or that you are no longer interested. If the date has arrived for the report, and it comes to your desk, but it is not possible for you to deal with it at that time, then tell them so. Arrange another time when you can receive the report and give it the attention it deserves.

The feedback process should be in two parts. The first is your receipt of the report (with time to study it). Then, there should be a face-to-face meeting with the HRD people and others who might be involved in the outcome of the learning. You may have questions, and some of these might be sent to the HRD unit beforehand so they can have the answers. This will save time at the meeting.

The meeting should not be an adversary proceeding with the HRD people trying to convince you the learning program was beneficial and you (and your people) trying to prove either that you didn't need the program, or that it didn't make any difference. The learning program is history and the decision to offer it was made at an earlier time. The meeting is of value now in trying to understand, on all sides, what happened as the result of the learning, and whether the experience should be repeated. One of the outcomes of such a meeting should be to provide you with the basis for decision-making about future HRD activities.

THE HRD CONCEPT

We can link together the HRD concept discussed earlier with the whole picture and process of evaluation. (Refer to Chapter 2 for the definitions of training, education, and development.)

Training

As training is job related, a training experience should be evaluated in terms of changes in job performance. Where the preformance is quantifiable, and the objective of the training experience was to increase production or productivity, then there should be a measurable change in the output from the job.

To accomplish this evaluation, there must be the bench-mark data (or what the level of performance was before the training). If these data are not available, it is not possible to measure any change attributable to the training program.

There is a preliminary evaluation possible, and that is to determine if the learner has learned. This can be accomplished during, as well as at the end of, the training. That is not sufficient, however, as the reason for the training was not the learning, but the application of the learning to the actual job situation. Thus it is essential that you provide an opportunity for the HRD people to do some evaluation after the trainee has returned to the job. If you do not make provision for this, you are preventing them from doing a complete job. Too often, managers have resented what seemed to be the intrusion of the staff or headquarters people onto the job site. This can happen when the HRD unit is located at some point away from the job site, even in another city or country.

The on-the-job evaluation may not have to be accomplished by the HRD people. It is possible that it can be done by examining production records or other data sources which relate to the objectives of the training. If the HRD people are not involved in this process, they can lose valuable feedback on the results (or lack thereof) of the training.

As a manager, you must make sure that your supervisors will cooperate in this process. The supervisors should see the training as a direct help to them in improving job performance. They should also see the evaluation as being helpful in determining whether or not the training has produced results.

This can be a problem. It is possible that the trainee has learned new behavior which the supervisor finds threatening or undesirable. This can happen even when the supervisor has been part of the process of designing the training and approving the release of selected employees. It happens all too frequently when safety training is involved and the new safety procedures which have been learned go counter to existing practice. You may question why the supervisor would approve the course content, knowing that it is contrary to practice. It may tell you something of the kinds of short-cuts supervisors may have to take in order to meet the quotas imposed from above.

There are many cases in which the training was successful, as measured by evaluation in the classroom setting, but was a failure (or at least less of a success), as measured by job performance. There are numerous factors which can contribute to this discrepancy, and a few will be discussed here. If a discrepancy does show up, don't start by blaming the training. Instead, first examine the reasons why there may have been a loss during "transfer of training."

Some learners function very well in the protected environment of the classroom, but have difficulty applying the learning outside that situation. It is not that they haven't learned; they simply need help in making the transfer. It may require some additional support and even instruction by the supervisor. Perhaps the supervisor needs training in how to help employees bridge that gap.

In the learning situation, the trainee may have been receiving some valuable support from peers which was lacking in the job situation. After a successful learning experience, the trainee may return to the job and be met by comments such as, "O.K. you had your fun—now let's get back to work and make up the lost time." Or, "Hey—did you have fun with the shrinks? What kinds of games did you play?" Such a greeting on returning from training will encourage the employee to revert to the pre-training behavior and even point out the crazy things learned during training which have nothing to do with the job! (We will discuss organizational support systems in more depth later.)

Where performance is not measurable, it is still important for evaluation to take place on the job. The data will probably be more anecdotal than statistical, but could be equally important. The evaluation should relate to the previously agreed upon objectives, and the evaluators should seek out those incidents and reports that relate to the evaluation.

Education

As education is related to preparing an individual to perform on a different job, it must be evaluated differently.

At the outset, it will be the same as for training, in that the first evaluation needed is, "Did the learner learn?" This can be measured at the conclusion of the learning experience. More difficult is the second phase of the evaluation: on the job. There are factors which make this much more difficult than the evaluation of training.

Time lag. There will most likely be some time between the completion of the learning program and placement on the new job. This can vary from one week to about a year. If education is provided with the intent that the learner will be placed immediately upon completion of the program, evaluation is easier to accomplish. Provision should be made for the employee to make some adjustment to the new environment before evaluation takes place, or you will find yourself evaluating job adjustment rather than the results of the education.

If the education is provided too far in advance of the placement, then it is reasonable to expect fade-out or the loss of learning due to lack of use. With no reinforcement, most new learning disappears after a period of time, and sometimes it is a short period of time. Try learning a new language and then not using it for a year. It will almost be as if the learning had never taken place.

Assuming there is a reasonable period of time, the second evaluation should take place on the job, and this can present problems.

New supervisor. When the learner was sent to the education experience, it was while working for a different supervisor or manager. The new supervisor must be brought into the picture by being informed about the objectives of the education the employee received. Where possible, for education, the prospective new supervisor should have been included when the objectives were being determined. Unfortunately, this is not too common a practice.

The new supervisor may also feel that the evaluation is of the supervisor and not of the learner. The whole process must be handled very delicately; it requires a good deal of support from the manager if the supervisor is to assist in the evaluation.

Changes in job requirements. As there is a time lag between the original development of the education program and the final placement of the learner on the new job, it is quite possible that unforeseen changes have taken place. The most obvious is that there may be new equipment or different processes than those utilized in the education program.

If the job is clerical, sales, administrative, etc., there may have been changes in regulations, laws, policies, and personnel. All these factors could impact on the job for which the employee was being prepared. Therefore, the evaluation can show that learning took place, but that learning may no longer be relevant to the new job. This is even more important when there is a time lag between the end of the learning and the placement. The personnel records may show that the employee completed the required learning program, but may not indicate that there had been significant changes in the job itself.

An evaluation on the job, after placement, may not be an indication of an inadequacy in the education program as much as the need for some immediate training.

Development

In the absence of job relatedness, as defined earlier, development is much more difficult to evaluate. To avoid vituperation, all the parties concerned should agree, beforehand, on just what is going to be evaluated and when.

The most obvious point of evaluation is at the end of the learning experience. Even development should have objectives, so it is possible to determine if the learning took place. What cannot be evaluated is how the learning changed present or future job performance, as that is not the purpose of development. If an evaluation is done which indicates that job performance change was expected, it perverts the purpose of development, making it training or education, but after the fact.

This, once again, indicates why development is offered so infrequently and so unevenly. No direct job performance behavior is normally included in a development learning experience; therefore, there should not be any such evaluation.

CONCLUSION

Evaluation is important and necessary. Without evaluation, the manager does not have the basis for making decisions about HRD programs in the future as well as in the present.

The evaluation process starts before the learning actually begins, and continues (except in the case of development) after the learning ends. It is a process which involves more than just the HRD people and should be carefully coordinated with the needs and priorities of the manager.

7 Organizational Support for HRD

HRD is not the concern of only the HRD people, although it too often seems that way. The major reason for an organization to provide HRD is to assist managers in solving human resource related problems. If HRD is not integrated into the whole fabric of the organization, it becomes less useful and, generally, begins to disappear. When a human resource problem surfaces, there will then be hectic efforts made to revive the dormant activity. The result is a high-cost HRD operation, utilized only for putting out fires, and not generally seen as part of the necessary elements in an organization.

There are many reasons why the HRD unit can find itself isolated. If the general tenor of the organization is that HRD is a non-productive activity, then few people in the organization will want to be associated with it. If management utilizes the HRD unit as a place to send people until the organization can figure out where to place them, then this organizational Siberia cannot function.

At times, the isolation is due to the HRD people. They see themselves as offering a service nobody wants. They then engage in self-perpetuating programs which justify their existence, but at a bare subsistence level.

Earlier, we discussed the need that some physical and financial resources should specifically be identified as being for the use of HRD. This indicates support. There are often practices within an organization which communicate support for an activity, and these practices should be extended to the HRD function. They can take the form of participating in certain staff meetings, being involved in certain functions or negotiations, or just having appropriate office space.

CONCEPT OF SUPPORT SYSTEMS

The need for support systems is not new, but you would have difficulty finding very much in the literature about this aspect of HRD. My own interest was not particularly piqued until a seemingly unrelated incident. In late 1960, I was asked by the *Harvard Business Review* to take a look at programs being offered by the private sector for the "hard core disadvantaged." This was a term used to identify those who had not been in the workforce on a regular basis, but who wanted to be. At the time, the federal government supported this effort through a variety of programs under the Manpower Training and Development Administration of the Department of Labor.

I looked at a number of organizations and the results of my study were published in the March–April 1970 issue of *HBR*. From this evolved a model. It was possible to identify that successful programs had some common elements and that these were related to the systems they had developed for supporting this unique HRD program.

As the study was reviewed and discussed by my colleagues and myself, the question constantly arose: "Don't we do the same things for all our HRD programs?" Since then, I have been able to identify similarities, and there is a study currently underway. The preliminary findings indicate that the basic model described here is relevant.

The HRD Concept

A word of caution: The support system approach being examined in this chapter applies only to *training!* It is possible that there are systems which support education and development, but they have not yet been identified adequately enough to allow for a discussion at this time.

In the following discussion, there will be frequent references to training, and the reader should note that *only* training programs are looked at here.

The support system consists of five elements:

1. Organization involvement
2. Pre-training
3. Training
4. Job linkage
5. Follow-up

Each of these will be discussed with examples and suggestions. It is more important for each manager to look into specific organization policies and practices to identify how HRD is supported. There are some generalities, but there are also many specifics which would apply only to certain managers and their organizations.

ORGANIZATION INVOLVEMENT

Here we go into definitions, rather than semantics. Previously, this was referred to as "organization commitment."

The difference between commitment and involvement is the difference between a promise and an act. Commitment merely means that you support something, though it is stronger than just being "in favor." It implies that you have made a promise—but the act has not yet been performed.

Involvement is acting out that promise in front of others. The acting out (behavior) signifies a stronger affirmation than commitment. This has been observed in many places; for example, in guerilla warfare. (There is no implication here that the organization is a battlefield or a desirable site for guerilla warfare!) When obtaining new recruits, the guerilla band will have a swearing-in ceremony so that others can see that a commitment has been made. The real joining does not take place until there is some kind of overt action by the group, when the new recruits become involved by engaging in an action that stamps them as being part of the group. This can be a raid, a riot, or some other obvious action which signifies to outsiders that they are from part of the group.

Within an organization, the behavior need not be so violent, but it should be equally observable. General statements by managers are not sufficient. There must be observable behavior which indicates support of the HRD function.

Time

There should be definite periods of time allocated for HRD. The amount and use will vary, depending upon the nature of the training and the duration of the program. The time may range from one hour to one year, but whatever it is, there should be a specific policy which sets aside time for training.

A major decision involves "on-the-clock" or "off-the-clock." That is, should the training take place on company time, or after hours on the employee's time? Generally, "on-the-clock" is most desirable, particularly for training. A different argument might be prepared for education and development.

Training is job related, and the company should provide time for such learning. In some rare cases, it is not possible to allow employees to take time during shifts, public contact hours, or other times when it is essential they be on the job. In such instances, it is possible to utilize other arrangements, such as compensatory time (giving other time off when it will not interfere with production or the work of the organization).

Providing time for training is observable. This is a way management communicates to all within the organization that the training is beneficial to the employee and the organization. If the manager has to squeeze the time out of other activities, or the employee must be restricted to learning on personal time, the communication to all is that HRD is not that important.

We will deal with time further under other elements of the support system, but if there is no specific policy covering on-the-clock time, it cannot be expected that HRD will be seen as having management support.

Financial Resources

HRD costs money—it requires financial allocations. Of course, the organization intends to get back more in increased performance than it has paid out for the training. This is desirable, but it is not always possible, particularly where performance is not currently measured in dollars and cents.

The most obvious support is in providing adequate financial resources for the physical resources. If the HRD unit is housed in an undesirable part of the building, this communicates a lack of involvement by management, no matter what policy statements are issued, or speeches made, on behalf of HRD. The involvement (observable) far outweighs the commitment (promise).

In addition to the usual financial support, there are some areas unique to HRD which managers should consider. One of these is commonly called "tuition refund." The practice is spreading rapidly, with many variations. In Europe, it is commonly called "Educational Leave," and under the laws of some countries, it is education and development. It is not to be job related. In the U.S., it is more customary to provide tuition refund for job related learning.

There are many variations. One is that the employee can take any learning experience, outside the company, which has been approved. This can be a course in a university or community college. It can also be a seminar or workshop, offered by a private company or a public seminar. The key is that it usually requires prior approval and then some other minor restrictions. For example, the amount of refund might be tied to the grade achieved by the student. (This contributes more to grade inflation than it does to increased learning.) The refund might only be for tuition or might include all expenses, including travel.

In some companies, the supervisor can approve tuition refund, while in other companies, it may require approval of a committee. The variations in administering a tuition refund program are innumerable. Of greater importance is a clear statement on the part of the company as to its policy about tuition refund. Any statement must have financial backing. It is dangerous for an executive to announce that tuition refund is available, and then in a smaller voice add that it is subject to the availability of funds in each department. The policy and the availability of financial resources must match if there is to be involvement.

There are other kinds of financial arrangements that can be made available. For long-term training, there could be a fund to advance money to the trainees, or to provide for no-interest company loans.

Earlier, we discussed the ways in which the HRD unit can be organized: budget, cost center, and profit center. Despite a decision, managers may have to build in some flexibility for new training needs which might arise but cannot be met within the normal financial struction of HRD. This does not mean giving the HRD unit a blank check. It does mean considering other financial arrangements for HRD when the need arises.

Participation

It is customary, in some organizations, to have an important group learning experience opened by a ranking official. You, as a manager, may have been asked many times by the HRD people to officiate at such an opening. You probably considered it a chore and a waste of time, and you may have been right. In the eyes of the trainees, however, if the higher officials in the organization are giving their time to be at the opening, the training is important. A few minutes of your time at the opening of the program can produce benefits far beyond the time invested. It is concrete evidence of involvement and it is highly observable.

There are social customs associated with such participation. In the U.S., the tendency has been to limit such official openings and even ignore the higher levels of the organization in many training programs. In most of the rest of the world, it is rare to find a program which does not have some official opening with a statement by a very high official. In some cases, the statement may be read by a lower official, but not by the instructor. As we become more interdependent, and as there are more foreign companies operating in the U.S., American officials will find their presence at the opening of a training session an obligatory part of their jobs.

Once the training program has begun, there may still be the need for a manager to attend. Usually this will be in the role of a resource person to provide some information or experience which is unique to that manager. It is easy for a manager to delegate this to somebody else, but that very delegation can signify lack of involvement. If the manager does not feel it is important to attend, this is readily communicated to the learners. The present of the manager at one or more sessions, as appropriate, is observable evidence of involvement and can significantly contribute to the success of a training program. The next time you are asked to participate, weigh your response against what you have already allocated in the way of financial resources, as well as the benefits you expect the organization to get from the training.

Many training programs conclude with some kind of ceremony. It may be a simple one, in which certificates are given to the trainees, or it may be more elaborate, with a banquet or some other formal activity. This is another time when participation by a manager signifies involvement.

Training Committee

A common practice, in large organizations, is to have a special committee related to training. The functions and responsibilities of such a committee can vary greatly. It is generally advisory, but it can also be involved in decision-making. (Note the example earlier of a training committee to approve tuition refund.)

Managers are members of many committees, and you can easily see that the HRD (or training) committee may not be one of your highest priorities. This is understandable, but it would also depend to a great degree on the function of the committee. If it is merely to pass on tuition refund or similar matters, then the presence of a manager may not be crucial. Where there is policy involved, the presence of managers is essential. Attending such committee meetings is important, for HRD units should be relating to the needs and problems of the managers. If a manager sends a lesser level person, delegating attendance to somebody down the line, this readily signifies a lack of involvement and even raises a question of commitment.

There is no easy recommendation to make about the role of managers *vis a vis* HRD committees. The role will vary, depending upon the particular committee, but it would be disastrous if managers were to be absent from all such committees. If none of them seem appropriate, there could be something wrong with the HRD committees, and this too is something the manager should investigate.

PRE-TRAINING

Training, like the proverbial iceberg, only exposes a small part of itself. What you, as a manager, may see is only that a learning experience is being offered. Unless you have been in HRD as part of your assignment in an organization, you probably have little idea of how a program gets put together and what it means.

Since a significant amount of training is conducted in a classroom, many managers view the organization's training classroom as similar to the college classrooms they knew in the past. The physical facility may bear some resemblance, but what occurs is usually quite different.

In a college classroom, the professor has almost complete control over what is taught, under the banner of "academic freedom." In a training classroom, there is no such freedom and none is expected or needed. The training experience must bear directly on what the organization wants the trainee to learn in order to be more efficient on the job. There are very few who would argue that there is any ethical or moral principal involved here. In fact, if the learner does not approve of what is being taught, perhaps a change in job would be more appropriate.

To make the learning as relevant as possible, there is a great deal of up-front work which must be done by the HRD people. If they are forced to do this in isolation because managers choose not to be part of the process, then the HRD people can hardly be blamed if the training is less than relevant to the needs of management. During this pre-training phase, while the training program is being designed and developed, it is essential that management be involved. If your HRD people are conducting training programs and have not involved you before the program begins, you should be questioning their approach to providing HRD in your organization.

There are a variety of specific actions which indicate the involvement of management.

Selection of Trainees

One of the most crucial decisions to be made is "Who should go to a training program?" The obvious answer is, "Those who need it." But how is this determined?

If the manager must rely on a printed announcement (sometimes a multi-color advertising brochure) from the HRD unit as the basis for this decision-making, it is highly probable that the wrong people will be sent to the program.

You, the manager, should know the objectives and the content. This can then be matched against the needs of the employees as you know them. If you don't know the needs, perhaps this tells you something about your style of management.

A much too common practice is to send people to training who can be spared. That is, their absence will cause the least amount of disruption of the normal functioning of your unit. The other side is, of course, that their learning will also contribute the least to improving the functioning of your unit! When the training is conducted on the job site, poor selection is less likely to occur. Most informal training occurs at the job site, but the formal training is more often conducted away from the job site.

The manager should be directly involved in selecting the prospective trainees. The process might involve interviewing (and probably counseling) those who could benefit from the training. This involvement by the manager will indicate that the training is part of the managerial responsibility.

Determining Objectives

A manager should ask to see the objectives of the training before they have been finalized. This means entering the picture very early in the design stage.

When the training is being done specifically at the request of the manager, and for his subordinates, this involvement is automatic. The HRD people cannot possibly design and develop the program without direct contact with the manager they are serving.

In large organizations, there are usually general offerings which are available to large numbers of employees from throughout the organization. The HRD unit, in effect, conducts a school. Some of the lists of offerings, with descriptions, bear a marked resemblance to college catalogues.

There is nothing wrong with this—*if* the managers have been involved early enough in determining the objectives. This means giving the time and energy needed to refine the objectives so that everybody understands them.

Where training courses are repeated, the manager should be constantly questioning whether the objectives should remain the same. It is the responsibility of the HRD unit to fine-tune the objectives relative to the particular learners who are in the training program at the time. It is the responsibility of the manager to periodically review the objectives to determine if they are still relevant to the policy, practices, and procedures in the unit.

Evaluation

In Chapter 6 we discussed evaluation and the role of the manager in that process. It need not be repeated in detail here, but some points can bear emphasis.

Planning for evaluation must take place early in the training process, and that means during the pre-training phase. This is the time for the manager to do those things we have discussed earlier.

If the manager is not involved in planning the evaluation during this pre-training phase, it will be too late to do much about it later. The clock will have run and there is no way of pushing it back without adding additional cost.

Confer with Prospective Trainees

It was noted, during the section on selection of trainees, that there could be the need for some interviewing and counseling. Now we must go beyond that.

In conferring with the *prospective* (note the emphasis on this word) trainee, the manager should be seeking to identify many points. The discussion will focus around the planned training program, but the subordinate and the manager should not start the process by agreeing that training is necessary.

If the training is solving a problem, then this is the time for you the manager, to do some problem exploration with your subordinate. Do not discard the possibility that out of this discussion will come the decision that training, or that a particular training program, is not the appropriate response. There should be no commitment that the conferring process will result in a training program, or in that subordinate going to the training.

Training is a response, and the conference at this point should be concerned with *what* needs to responded *to*. This is a time when the mutual perceptions of the manager and the subordinate should surface. The subordinate may have some suggestions for improvement. These are more likely to arise when the manager is discussing the need for training with the person who is doing the job, or with the person who is supervising the job.

Arrange for Work Coverage

When an employee is off the job for training, there are many ways to handle arrangements for work coverage. One is for the other employees to do the work of the missing employee. This may seem like an easy way to handle the situation, but it inevitably brings up the question of, "Who owes whom?" If at all possible, the coverage should not be accomplished by making the other employees do extra work. Such a practice might cause employees to avoid taking necessary training for fear that they will then have to deal with possible hostility from those who had to do the covering.

If the training is of a very brief duration—just a few hours—it may be possible to cover that job just as the unit does when somebody is out for sickness or some similar short absence. If the training is longer, going over several days, coverage may be accomplished by the same mechanism as when somebody is on vacation.

It is most important that the coverage be planned and approved by the supervisors and managers involved. Training time should not be squeezed out of what can be made available, but should be seen as a regular and recurring event for which management has planned.

Review Material and Course Content

Agreeing with the objectives is an important task of a manager. It is equally important to review the material and course content, which should be carefully examined to be sure that they reflect the current as well as the planned policies and procedures.

In one manufacturing plant, this was done by having the managers go through a one day version of the week long training being offered to some of their personnel. During this one day, the managers were encouraged to suggest changes in content (not methodology) to be sure it conformed to their expectations.

In some organizations, it is the practice to have the concerned managers actually sign off on the course. No training can be offered to their employees until the managers have actually reviewed the course and indicated their approval or made specific suggestions.

If this practice is followed, it should be made clear to all personnel involved that this is being done. The trainees should know that their managers have seen the course and concur.

Notification of Trainees

Coverage is important, as indicated earlier, and related to it is the need for ample notification of the prospective trainees. While still on the job, the trainees can make suggestions as to how their jobs could be covered. Where production is involved, the method of coverage is fairly easy. For a service job, this can be much more difficult. In such a position, there are many personal elements involved, and the employees have more control over the flow of work. Ample notification is not only important but is an absolute necessity if the work is to get done and the training is to be accomplished with a minimum of disruption of the work of all concerned.

In addition to the job, there is the private life of the trainee. A prospective trainee may be part of a car pool, which management may be encouraging. When the trainee is notified to appear at a different site or is told to work different hours during the training program, all the carefully planned schedules relating to the car pool are wiped out. It is not suggested that employees in a car pool be deprived of training opportunites, but that they will need sufficient time to make the arrangements that will allow them to participate in the training without the punishment which can result when they do not carry their fair load in the car pool.

If the training is off-site, and away from the city where the employee usually works, this can be even more complicated. The trainee may have to make arrangements for other responsibilities, such as family events, community responsibilities, bowling league, and visits from friends and family. To ignore this aspect is to risk having a good training program engender hostility because of inadequate notification.

TRAINING

During this phase, most of the activity will be taking place away from the job and away from the manager. If there has been adequate involvement during the pre-training phase, there will not be too much for the manager to do at this time.

Avoid Interruption

It is demoralizing and disruptive to all concerned to suddenly ask a trainee to leave the class and report back because of a job crisis. If there really is a crisis, and the presence of the employee is absolutely essential, nothing can be done. But too often, the interruption is the result of poor planning. If so, the manager must assume the major portion of the blame and try to do everything possible to meet the needs of the situation, short of withdrawing the trainee from the learning experience.

In many HRD facilities, there is provision for receiving phone calls which can be answered later, during breaks. Even this approach should be used sparingly. The breaks (even the meals) are frequently part of the total learning environment. To deprive the trainee of the opportunity to take part in these activities is to cause him to lose some of the value of the training program.

Maintain Contact

The employee who goes to training should not feel as if attendance at the training program is akin to being in a penal institution, with limited contacts with "home." Too often, the employee leaves the job feeling that a sentence has been imposed. While there should be no interruption during the training, this does not mean the employee should be deprived of all contact with his job and the rest of the organization.

If you do not make any provision for some kind of continual contact, do not be surprised if the employee shows initiative by creating contact. This can take the form of coming into the office each day before a session, quickly running over during coffee breaks or lunch, or even going back to the office in the evenings, when this is possible. For production line people, this is not as easily done, but there will be substitutes: the employee may engage in lengthy phone conversations, in the evening, with other line workers. Another possibility, for longer training periods, will be weekend visits to other workers to keep posted on what is happening.

Short-term programs (several hours a day for several days, or one full day) do not cause this anxiety. But despite all the technology and complaints about lost time on the job, we are still experiencing pressure for training of several days duration. So, rather than force the employee himself to create a network or a process in order to keep related to the job, why not build one for him? This will be more effective and less time-consuming in the long run.

When it is a short program, a day or two, a phone call in the evening between the days may suffice. This could come from another employee, but with the understanding that this is being done at the request of the manager.

For longer training programs, other techniques can be used. When the

ORGANIZATIONAL SUPPORT FOR HRD   135

trainee is nearby, the manager can arrange for an occasional lunch. Although the trainee might miss one lunch with the other trainees, it is more than compensated for by being able to tell other trainees that "my manager took the trouble of coming over here to have lunch with me and keep me posted on what's going on back home." The effect of this can be extremely benficial, unless your trainee is hearing it from another whose manager had come when you had made no such provision!

As long as you are "in the neighborhood" (on a planned visit), why not sit in on some of the training? This should be prearranged with the HRD people, and if they hesitate or do not make any such provision, you should have some questions. In a few cases, such as a sensitivity group or a similar high-impact program, a visit may not only be inappropriate but may be damaging to the flow of the learning. This is readily determined beforehand, and the trainee would not feel neglected. However, there are very few cases where this would apply.

If the HRD people are less than enthusiastic about your appearance, there could be a fundamental problem. It might be that the HRD people feel that once a trainee comes into their territory, the manager should keep hands off. As a manager you could resent this, but more important, you should explore the reason. Are the HRD people (over)reacting? What is *your* policy regarding the HRD people and the work situation? Do you welcome them in? Are they invited for a follow-up (which we will discuss further below) or do you have the policy that once the trainee has returned to you, the HRD people should stay away? There should be an open street, with no protective barriers or walls at either end.

There are times when the trainee will be away for a long time (more than one week) and at a place distant from home. In larger companies, where there are elaborate HRD facilities, this is common, and companies bring their employees in from different parts of the U.S. and perhaps other parts of the world. In such a case, a physical intervention by the manager may not be feasible and probably would be overly expensive. Technology offers us many alternatives. The simplest is a "letter from home." There could be one written by the manager, and though it need not be long, it should be informative and not just social. Peers could be encouraged to write so the employee has information from other sources about what is happening back home. Letters from the trainee (which should be encouraged) might be reproduced (the technology is readily available in most organizations—even small ones) or placed on a departmental bulletin board if this seems more appropriate. Of course, the trainee should be forewarned that the letters may not be treated as personal communications, but will be shared. This will influence what and how the trainee writes.

Where other technology exists within the organization, why not use it? A tape recorder can be easily used, but first verify that the trainee has similar equipment at the other end. Even videotape might be useful, particularly if there have been some physical changes in the work site which would be of interest to the trainee.

If the trainee is in a different city, what provision has been made so the family is kept informed? Are there any family situations (such as the wife expecting a child) which the manager should know about? Are there birthdays or other family events? The trainee might not be able to return, but a manager might serve as a link and show real human relations in action.

Longer training periods, no matter where the training is located, might also include some kind of written report to the manager, to which the manager must react. There should be a full communication, with feedback.

Participate in Selected Sessions

If your HRD people are not calling on you to take part in at least some sessions in which you have trainees, you need to prod them. Most training, to be effective, should utilize the resources of the operating managers. You should be prepared to conduct sessions, as needed and as appropriate, within your area of experience and concern. Such an arrangement should be planned long before the HRD staff actually wants you at a session. You need to clear your calendar and make such other provisions as are necessary when you are to be away from your job site.

Obviously, most managers are not trainers—though all managers should have some training in how to conduct learning experiences, both formal and informal. It may have been a while since you last conducted a session; you may need to update some of your material. You should even check it out with the HRD people to see how it relates to the course content and flow. You may have developed your material, at some earlier time, with the help of the HRD people. There is the possibility, however, that they have made some changes with which you are not familiar. There are instances where HRD people have used a manager with full cooperation and understanding on both sides, then realized that some of what the manager had presented should either have been in a different part of the training program or should have been expanded because it was much more important than they had first realized. The manager may not have been informed (even some HRD people are poor communicators!). You would not want to be surprised while giving your favorite well-planned, well-rehearsed session, by being told that this material has already been covered. Even worse is to be going through your material, presenting your session, and having that uncomfortable feeling that all is not well. Only later, after the session, do you discover the awful truth—you were repeating material already presented.

Check with the HRD people before you do your preparation. Do not be disgruntled if they ask you to change something you have done successfully in the past. Your previous participation may have been a learning experience for the HRD people as well as for the trainees, and they may now have made it a more important part of the program. They still want you, but you should seek clarification as to the exact topic, time, place, etc.

There may be times when you participation is coupled with that of other managers. You may find yourself having the unique experience of meeting others with whom you have had little or no contact. This is merely another benefit which can accrue from participating in training sessions.

Attend Closing Ceremonies

Some training programs close with a whimper, and if so, it is essentially the problem of the HRD people. If, however, it has been designed well, a training program's closing should be marked by some highlight event. The trainees should not meekly fade away. There are some training programs where the end is in doubt—there has been a session in no way different from the others, and the trainees are not even sure the program has concluded.

Let us be more concerned about those programs which have some kind of obvious conclusion, for that is where you are more likely to be invited. If you have one or more college degrees and have attended many HRD programs, then another certificate may have little meaning. But the certificate and the closing ceremony are not for you; these formalities are for the trainees. As part of the program, you should be involved and visible. Even for some high-level officials, the ceremony and certificate can have significance. In 1968, I conducted a program and the sponsor requested a certificate signed by me and the internal HRD person. Then, in 1979, when I had occasion to be called back into the company and started with a visit to the office of the Assistant Director, almost immediately upon my entering his office he called attention to the certificate hanging on his wall!

There are essentially two parts to the closing: the ceremony and the certificate. The ceremony may be a small one with just the participants, some HRD people, and a few managers. It might follow immediately after the close of the program and be very informal. Another possibility is a closing banquet, with a high-level company speaker—and that could be you! Or, you might want to be sure to be there because the speaker is your boss! Generally, the higher the level of the trainees, the more likely there is to be a formal closing, with banquet, speakers, and other program activities.

The certificate can be a simple signed letter or a beautifully embossed or engraved document that suggests it might be appropriately deposited in the National Archives. The HRD people will have developed or purchased the certificate most fitting, so you need not worry about that. Fairly early you should determine if you are expected to sign the certificate, and how many there are. If you are one of these people whose hand shakes after the first drink, be sure to meet your signing obligation before imbibing.

The certificate may be distributed during the banquet or at some other public time. If you are to hand them out—a strong possibility—be sure you have seen the names so you can pronounce them correctly. It is assumed that you know all of your employees personally, but there can be good reasons why this is not possible. Also, given the multi-cultural nature of our country, there may be names which are indeed "foreign" to you.

The closing ceremony and/or certificate are part of the training and serve the function of providing recognition to the trainees—your employees. If you have not been asked to be part of any closing ceremony, perhaps you should investigate to see if your non-participation is appropriate.

With the increased emphasis on self-directed and individual learning, there could be trainees who complete a planned phase, but not as part of a group. They should not be left out. Your HRD unit should make some provision for these trainees to likewise receive public recognition from a status person. An easy way is to occasionally hold a "closing" ceremony for those who have completed an assigned learning program at some point in the last month, or the last three months, or other specified period of time.

In addition to the formal closing, a manager should seek other ways to link the trainee back to the job. The next section will deal with job linkage, but there are some activities which occur as part of the training; there must be an overlap.

You could meet with your trainee at the end of the training program and prior to his return to the job. Your interview with the trainee will be seen as part of the training program and the focus will be on that activity, so it will not be confused with performance appraisal or similar activities.

If you have several trainees, avoid having a group meeting. Of course, the individual meetings will take more time, but if you wish to obtain the maximum benefit from the time you are devoting, plan for individual meetings. There need not be very long at this time, as you will be having more meetings in the future.

JOB LINKAGE

As indicated above, there is some overlap between this element and training. If there is no overlap, you should question the process. Some of what you do during the training can also influence what you will do during job linkage. You will probably identify much more you should specifically be doing than can be covered in these pages.

Re-Entry Ritual

When a trainee returns to the job site there is always some kind of "ritual." The longer the trainee is away from the site, the more complicated and lengthy the ritual may be. Some aspects of the ritual behavior are productive, but others can be damaging.

First let us look at damaging rituals. The trainee (we will use the term even though that phase is now completed, since "trainee" is less complicated than alumnus or returned trainee) may be expected to do additional work or compensate for having been away from the job.

If the trainee went to a company learning facility, there will probably be some teasing about having fun at the country club while the rest of the group had to cover for him. If it is good-natured kidding, this is expected. However, there is a fine line between good-natured remarks and vindictiveness, so this ritual must be carefully watched.

The re-entry ritual can be used in an effective and positive manner. A manager can make the re-entry a ritual which all look forward to for sharing and reinforcement. The trainee should not be slinking back to the job; he should be seen as a winner returning home in triumph.

The returning employee has a great deal to offer as a result of the training, if it has been successful. This can and should be exploited. Sharing of the new learning is the least and most obvious that can be done. Other approaches can be developed as appropriate to the situation and the learner.

Review Goals

Before the trainee went off to the learning program there should have been clear goals and objectives. Once the program has ended, it is time to once again meet with the employee and review how those goals were reached. The focus is not on evaluation (though this will obviously enter into any such discussion) but on how the learner intends to use the learning.

While reviewing goals, the learner will be making linkages between the learning situation and the back home situation. This can also serve to assure that the learner has been kept up-to-date on any changes that have occurred in the interim.

The review of goals will actually go in several directions. For example, now that the training is completed, were the original goals realistic and meaningful? Although nothing can be done now that the training is completed, the experience can be helpful to the manager in planning for the next goal-setting experience with future trainees. The goal discussion may also lead to identifying other valid needs that could not have been foreseen.

Provide for Evaluation

In addition to any general review, there should be a specific evaluation once the trainee has returned. The initial evaluation will have taken place while the trainee was completing training, and there were probably several opportunities for evaluation during the training. For some programs, the various evaluations can discourage the trainee from experimenting with new behaviors and risking the possibility of making mistakes—and, without mistakes, it is likely that less learning will take place.

If evaluations have been shared, this might be an opportunity to review the results with the trainee. Your HRD people have presumably shared the data with the trainee during the course of the training program, but while they were looking at the data from the aspect of the learning, your focus will be on getting the work done in the manner you expect. If all has gone well, there would be no difference between these two objectives, but there could be. Rather than punishing the trainee, this could be another check-point to assure congruency.

If the evaluation of job performance is to be accomplished, the trainee should be aware of it, as well as your expectations. When the trainee uses the new behaviors on the job, you must first verify his performance. If it is as expected, perhaps little else need to done with the evaluation at this time. The learner has learned and is able to use the new behavior on the job. This is what you expected from the training program, and, as the manager, you've got it. You do have a responsibility to share this with the HRD people, to let them know their efforts have been fruitful.

If the job performance does not meet the standards which have been set, and which should have been reached in the training program, this is the time for you to know it and take some action. The trainee may have performed very well during the final stages of the training program and performed well enough to satisfy the HRD people—yet, after returning to the job, you may find that the performance is not acceptable. Do not start by blaming either the HRD people or the trainees. Do not even blame yourself. This is the time for some serious exploration, which should be undertaken as soon after the training program as possible, to avoid loss through fade-out (forgetting what has been learned because of lack of reinforcement).

Some trainees can perform up to standard in a protected environment, which is essentially what should be the norm in many training programs. The trainee can make mistakes which are not irrevocable or damaging to the trainee or the organization. When faced with the reality of the work situation, the trainee may "freeze up" or exhibit other manifestations of inability to transfer the training to the job site. More training is probably not the answer. As the manager, there are actions you must take—or you must call in the personnel utilization people to help you identify the nature of the problem and explore possible responses. The HRD people should also be involved in this process. There may be many reasons for the lack of acceptable performance, and a discussion with your HRD people is necessary. If they have not had any feedback from you, how can you expect them to make the necessary changes to avoid such a situation in the future?

You might call in your HRD people to be part of the evaluation process, but at this point, the essential responsibility for the evaluation is yours. You may need help, and this is perfectly understandable, as designing an evaluation may not be one of your skills.

Provide the Opportunity for Trainee to Apply New Learning

Training is job related, but the trainee may be returning with new skills which are not needed at just that moment. The ideal, of course, is that the trainee can move right from the learning situation into the job situation and apply the new learning immediately. This is not always possible. Unless there is some specific effort on the part of the manager, much time could elapse between the learning situation and the time when the trainee can utilize the new learning.

Within the limits of meeting the goals of the entire unit, a manager should endeavor to provide opportunities for immediate on-the-job application of the new learning. This may require some shifting of personnel for job assignments. If so, care should be taken so this does not punish those who have not been to the training. The trainee should be given opportunities; he should not be the recipient of unwarranted favoritism.

If there are some special arrangements so the trainee can apply the learning, the manager should inform others who might be affected, explaining why the changes have been made. This can have a positive effect on future trainees. There will be the expectation that upon returning from training, all trainees must be prepared to exhibit the new behaviors as soon as possible.

Provide for Sharing with Peers

This was discussed briefly earlier in this section, but now let us be more specific. There are times when only one individual can be sent to training—but why shouldn't the benefits be shared with others? This returned trainee can now be assigned to teach others what was learned about the new process or regulations.

Do not force this if it is not appropriate. If the learning was just for that particular trainee because he was not performing up to standard, then why force the others to share what they do not need? The goal of the training will indicate its possible application to others. Where the application does exist, the manager must provide for the sharing.

Planning for this beforehand is crucial, for it might indicate which trainee should be selected for the particular program. If the sharing is important, then you want to choose a trainee who can instruct others, is willing to share and is respected by his peers. The trainee should be apprised upon selection that there is the specific intent to have sharing upon his return. This could have an influence upon how the trainee collects and stores material, and even upon how the learning takes place.

The peers should also be prepared for the experience. The manager should take the lead so the other employees realize that the sharing is at the direction of the manager and not just an "ego trip" for the trainee. In some cases, the manager should sit in on the sharing.

Provide Compensation

Usually, training is not directly related to compensation (pay and other benefits). Compensation is more often a factor of job performance, seniority, or factors other than training. There are situations, however, where training might be coordinated with compensation, although it is not possible to provide any specifics, since even the question of pay is strictly an in-house, secret matter in many organizations.

Where there is a union, compensation is negotiated, but a manager might raise the question of how this could or should be related to training. Given the suspicion in most unions regarding training, one would not expect that training and compensation would be too closely related in an organization functioning under a labor agreement.

Where there is more flexibility, a manager should explore the possibilities. The more that some (not all) training can be seen as related to rewards on the job, the more it is likely to contribute to behavioral change. And one factor (reward) is that of compensation. If there is any way to link training and compensation, this should be explored by a manager.

FOLLOW-UP

This is not just another name for evaluation. Follow-up occurs much later in the support system model. By the time a manager is doing follow-up, evaluation is less significant. Time has passed and it would be almost impossible to assess which behavioral changes are attributable to learning, and which are the result of other factors.

The purpose of follow-up is to build on the training experience so that is not an isolated period in the employee's life with the organization. It is partially reinforcement (of the past) and partially prediction (for the future). It deals with helping the trainee (though he is now out of the training) to recall the experience and to build on it. It helps the trainee, with the manager, to identify other learning needs.

Reports from Trainees

Where appropriate, a manager could ask a trainee for a periodic report for some designated period after the training. If the employee is not particularly articulate or well-versed in communication skills, the reports could be oral rather than written. Where distance is a factor, reliance on written reports may be the only viable alternative. There is other technology, such as tapes or the telephone, but a written report is generally easier to deal with.

The report should not just be a random sharing. The trainee and the manager should have agreed beforehand on what the manager is looking for from the employee. The focus should be on specific examples of application of the training to the job.

There should be a terminal point, in order to avoid having the reports fall into the category of meaningless exercises which nobody knows how to discontinue. This is an example of effective use of the sunset or self-destruct approach. The manager and the employee should agree on the duration of this requirement. It could be for a few weeks, or even a few months. Beyond that time, the utility is questionable.

If a manager asks for such reports, there must be feedback. The employee should know, not just assume (or hope), that the reports are being read and considered. The feedback may be a note or call from the manager, indicating that the report has been received and read. It could be a brief meeting to discuss some point in the report. A thank-you note might be appropriate. The choice of feedback relates to the style of the manager and the culture of the organization.

Identification of New Needs

Any good learning experience helps the learner identify new needs. The major purpose of the organization, however, is not to provide learning to its employees, but to manufacture a product or provide a service. Training is important and can help the organization reach its goals, but we must realize that during the period of training, the employee is not available to contribute to reaching organizational goals.

Another outcome of training can be an improved self-image of the learner. Many adult learners are hindered from future learning because of a negative learning experience or lack of success in former learning situations. After a successful learning experience, the adult learner may become a convert. Learning suddenly seems to be the response to all problems. The learner actively seeks additional learning experiences.

Although this is a healthy approach, some of the learning needs the employee is now willing to consider may be outside the scope of the employing organization. This does not mean these are not legitimate learning needs—they are just needs the organization is not willing to meet with its resources. The employee can be encouraged to continue to learn even though the organization will not provide time, money, or other resources.

There will be some needs which are directly related to the job, but there may be a requirement that the employee cannot be released for another learning situation until a specific period of time has passed. This should be discussed with the employee so there is no confusion. The manager should recognize that the need to learn still exists, even though it cannot be met at this time.

This is another area where the HRD people can be very helpful. If they know of the need, they might be able to present some other alternatives whereby the need can be met. The expressed need might even suggest changes they should make in their training programs.

Additional Materials

There is so much available today in the way of materials to reinforce learning, it is difficult to see why more use is not made of the vast resources and technology.

One technique utilized by HRD units is to have a regular newsletter which is a follow-up for former trainees. This can include information about how some trainees are using the new learning on their jobs, thus encouraging others to do the same. Or, it could begin to respond to some of the questions the trainees had after they had returned to their jobs. In many fields, magazines and other printed material are readily available. A training program might include a one year subscription to a relevant publication. It might include some other printed materials, too, such as books or pamphlets.

The materials will likely come through the HRD unit, but the initiative should come from the manager. What should your employees be receiving in the way of additional materials, after completion of the program? For how long? As a manager, what do you want? Which of these materials do you also want to see? Some of this could also serve to keep you up to date.

CONCLUSION

A properly organized and delineated support system is essential if a manager is to receive an adequate return on the resources expended for training. The support system cannot possibly function without the active support and involvement of the manager.

There is much to be done in this area, and there is still a good deal we do not know about support systems. If, however, more organizations focus on building a sound support system for training, it is likely that they will improve the whole training operation, with subsequent benefits to the manager. But this cannot be done alone: the HRD unit must be involved. If the HRD unit is not interested in building a support system, a manager should raise questions about the relationship of the HRD program to organizational objectives.

8   HRD and the Organization

As HRD is part of the organization, it receives from the organization and gives to it. If HRD is used effectively by the managers in the organization, it produces more than just learning programs. It produces change! Any HRD program is designed to produce change, but some may produce more change than originally intended.

Once employees start to learn, at any level in the organization, there will be fewer limits to what they can learn or what they want to learn in the future. Learning can become power.

HRD AND POWER

There are different approaches to the concept of power, so we need to start with some definitions. A frequently used term which is confused with power is authority. This may help to clarify:

- *Authority* is the *right* to influence the behavior of another.
- *Power* is the *ability* to influence the behavior of another.

Learning programs do not usually bestow authority, for this usually comes from other sources. There is one form of authority which does change with learning. That is the authority which comes from knowing more about a particular subject than other people do, and, therefore, those others "grant" authority to the individual because of his knowledge.

Power exists because one individual thinks or believes that another individual has the capacity to offer rewards or punishments. Some of us wonder why the police are so ineffective (powerless) in relation to some criminals even though the police have the authority. If the prospect of capture and incarceration is not seen as punishment by the criminal, then the police have no power.

There are many kinds of power, and any manager who has been to learning programs has heard a great deal about this aspect of organizational behavior. Communications, for example, can be used as power. The person who has the information and does not share it is using a power strategy. When one individual knows something another does not, it constitutes power.

This works in all directions in an organization. The most obvious is from the top down, where withholding information from subordinates forces them to continually come to the manager rather than function on their own. In those situations, information is power. It can also work from the bottom up. The subordinate who does not share information with the manager is exercising power. True, it is a dangerous game, but some managers force subordinates into that practice; withholding information becomes a way to react to the manager's power plays.

Any HRD program can contain power elements. They will not carry that label, but by their very existence they deal with power. One way a manager can cope with this is to avoid the situation, by not supporting HRD programs nor making them available to subordinates. A more positive posture is to recognize the power possibilities of an HRD program and use them to everyone's profit.

Programs of Skills and Knowledge

As indicated earlier, HRD programs are usually concerned with skills, attitude, and knowledge. We will focus on skills and knowledge and their implications for power in the organization.

A skills program, at first, may not seem to have elements of power, but let us look more closely. A skilled worker can return from an HRD program (either training or education) with skills far beyond those possessed prior to the program. All concerned should applaud this, for that was why the employee was sent to the HRD program. Why should anybody feel threatened?

Let us suppose that a person who is a skilled worker is then promoted into supervision. If that new supervisor is comfortable in the new role, the power challenge will probably not emerge. If, on the other hand, this new supervisor has not separated himself from the previous skilled job, there is the possibility of a dangerous situation. The new supervisor may feel more secure being the one who is the leader by virtue of possessing the greatest technical skills rather than the best supervisory skills.

Fifty years ago, technical skill was a major criterion for selecting an employee to become a supervisor. But supervision has changed. Generally, the supervisor is no longer expected to be the person who is most skilled in production. The skills of the supervisor are in getting the work done through the efforts of others, planning, and all the other behaviors which do not relate to the specific job skills of the subordinates.

A supervisor who is comfortable in this new role seeks subordinates who have the requisite skills. Subordinates who are more skilled than he is do not pose a threat to the power of the supervisor. Quite the contrary, in fact. This stems from the self-image of the supervisor; he realizes that he will still retain all the power needed, for the increased skills of the employees do not relate to a power shift. If the contrary situation arises, and the new supervisor does feel threatened, the proper response is *not* less training and education for the subordinates, but more training for the supervisor!

A similar situation applies to the acquisition of knowledge. The trainee who returns from a learning program with increased knowledge may pose a threat to the power of the supervisor or manager. The employee may now know something which the manager never knew, or has forgotten. How many times have you heard that "knowledge is power"? This is not always the case, but it can happen frequently enough so that the manager should be aware of the implications. The response should not be to withhold HRD opportunities from employees, but to be sure the knowledge is shared. If the manager does some of the things indicated in the previous chapter on support systems, it is less probable that knowledge will become a part of the power conflict which exists in all organizations.

Programs for Minorities

Since 1960, the private sector of our economy has been involved in HRD programs for various minority groups. This is in addition to the vast number of government programs (see Chapter 9). There have been many problems with these programs, only some attributable to the HRD aspects. A more pervasive problem has been the lack of sufficient jobs to absorb the various minorities subsequent to an appropriate education program. As this book is concerned with HRD, we will limit the discussion to only that aspect of this complicated problem.

Providing minorities with HRD programs also provides them with the possibilities of power. When a minority group has been outside the mainstream, it has usually been because the group lacked power. After power was obtained through political intervention, the minority group also sought to share in economic power. This meant jobs, and much of this job need came at a time in our history when we were having the first significant economic difficulties since the 1930 Depression.

In 1968, several factors came together which introduced stress into the labor market. One was the emergence, at one time, of the largest group of 18-year-olds that had ever expected to enter the labor market. (Youth constitutes a minority group.) The first programs, related to civil rights and the Equal Employment Opportunity legislation, were producing minorities seeking employment. At the same time, there were cutbacks in the aerospace industry, which had been one of the fastest growing industries, and which had been, up to that time, a prime employer. In general, the economy slowed down and so did the availability of jobs.

Meanwhile, HRD programs continued to produce minority people with appropriate levels of competence but no place to go. Minorities began to learn much more about power and how to influence the system. This did not necessarily have to produce a confrontation, but it did, as expressed in the "white backlash" and the significant reduction in programs for minorities in the Nixon administration. The words used to describe this change were "benign neglect."

Fortunately, despite the recession of 1973-1975, U.S. companies have generally continued to offer programs and opportunities for minorities, even though it has meant dealing with power conflicts.

OD and Power

Organization development (OD) lacks any hard-and-fast definition, but most people do agree that it is concerned with change—and almost any change means a shift in power.

There are two major concepts of power, or two schools of thought about power. One suggests that power in an organization is limited. When one groups is to receive more power, somebody must be prepared to give up some power and retain less. The other school of thought proposes that power is not finite and that it is possible for a group to obtain power without somebody else having to give up any power.

The latter concept is inviting and humanistic. But it signifies an ideal rather than a reality. It would be wonderful if a group could get what it wants, with nobody else having to lose anything. A win-win situation is usually the most desirable! Reluctantly, one must admit that it is unlikely to reflect any substantial reality for all set actions. It is a wish, strongly to be desired, but until we are able to make it a reality, we must deal with the world as it is.

Where OD contains a learning element, even though it may be conducted by a unit designated by some other title, HRD is involved. As the purpose of such a program is organizational change through individual and group learning, it carries with it the need for shifts in power. It is almost impossible to identify an organizational change which would not involve some kind of power shift. To ignore the implications of such a learning program is to proceed naively and dangerously.

Confront Power Implications

The discussions above have one main purpose, to caution the manager not to avoid the implications of power which arise from HRD programs. There are managers who purposely withhold support from HRD programs because they understand the implications of power. A manager may have had a negative personal experience which colors all relationships with HRD. Some managers might place the blame on the HRD unit for the power conflict which emerged after an employee had been to a learning program.

When a manager lacks the skills to deal with power situations, that may indicate a learning need of the manager. The goal should not be to increase the ability of the manager to manipulate, but instead to deal with the implications of change and power as they arise from learning situations.

PLACEMENT OF HRD

The physical placement of HRD in the organization is a vital issue. Some people who believe that physical placement is immaterial either do not recognize the unique functions of HRD or have already made a decision as to its significance or lack of significance. Physical placement is a form of non-verbal communication, and where a unit is placed within the organization communicates a great deal to those inside and outside the organization who have business with that unit.

The placement of HRD should not be trapped by history. In earlier times, it was within the personnel function, and perhaps that was as good a place as any. Given the changes in the field, if it is still under personnel, that placement should be questioned. If the reader reviews the chapter on staffing (Chapter 3), it will become evident that the competencies required of an HRD person are not the same as those expected of people in personnel. Likewise, competencies in personnel will do little to enable an individual to function effectively in HRD. It is not a matter of which is better or worse: they are only *different*.

To Whom Should HRD Report?

The question of placement in the organization is more sharply focused when we raise the issue of reporting and responsibility. It is too easy to say that HRD serves the entire organization, and therefore it does not make any difference where HRD is placed. Is the organization prepared to apply the same criterion to other units that serve the entire organization, such as accounting, personnel, industrial relations, etc.?

When HRD is under the personnel office, it is more likely to be concerned with the usual goals of personnel and to respond to evaluation of papers processed rather than problems solved. This is not meant to disparage the personnel operation. The criteria for evaluation of performance of the unit are different for HRD and for personnel. When under personnel, the HRD unit will be evaluated by the wrong criteria.

A conflict can also arise in terms of career lines. When under personnel, the HRD people will see their advancement as going to higher levels—in personnel. This encourages HRD people to develop competencies in the personnel field rather than in the field of HRD, and the result is that the organization is likely to get a lower level of performance from the HRD unit than it would if the unit was outside of the personnel function.

Once we leave the confines of the personnel unit, the question can be addressed more directly in terms of effective placement. This must be related to the purpose of HRD in the specific organization. There is no one general statement which can determine where the HRD function should be placed. It is necessary to explore a variety of alternatives. The choice of alternatives will be directly related to the organizational thinking about HRD, as well as the staffing decision discussed in earlier chapters. Another factor is where the organization has placed its other human resource functions—that is, personnel (utilization), environment, industrial relations, etc.

As a generalization, HRD should be reporting to that corporate official who is directly concerned with human resources. The titles vary, but they include Vice-President for Human Resources and Manager of Human Resources. (Note that this category does not include titles arising from the organization's merely changing the name of its personnel unit to "human resources unit.")

If there is no such position and no intention to create one, perhaps the HRD unit should report to that corporate officer who is most concerned with planning or overall administration. But let us not get tangled up in titles, for that is not helpful. Instead, think freely and place the HRD unit in that part of the organization where it can be most effective. Obviously, if placed too low or too deep within the organization, it is less likely to make the contribution of which it is capable.

Centralized or Decentralized

There has been an earlier discussion of the various factors to be considered in having either a centralized or decentralized HRD unit. Here, let us look at this issue as related to the total organization.

If decentralized, the HRD unit will consist of multiple units with different units in different parts of the organization. If the organization contains many specialized units (production, shipping, sales, etc.), this may be desirable. The HRD competencies required may be different enough to require staffing by people with some specialized knowledge, or even with competency in the functions they are servicing.

This occurs very frequently where the line people are suspicious of anybody who does not have line experience. It is possible that the HRD people will have line experience, but if this is all they have, they will be in Category II (as discussed in Chapter 3). As was noted in the analysis of this category, such an HRD unit can lack the specialized competencies required in HRD (and which take years to acquire).

If there are decentralized units throughout the organization, there should still be a central unit, highly placed, so as to provide a broad organizational perspective to HRD planning. This organization-wide unit may only consist of one person (preferably a Category I person), but there must be some kind of constant and direct contact with those who are planning the future directions of the total organization.

When there are decentralized units, who will evaluate the performance of the HRD people? Presumably, this would be the unit manager to whom the HRD people report. There is nothing wrong with this, but the unit manager must have been provided with sufficient direction, perhaps even training, to be able to evaluate a function so different from the functions of most of the employees in his part of the organization. This must be coupled with a careful examination of the expectations of the unit manager: What is really expected in the way of performance by the HRD people?

In some production systems, the supervisor is provided with an extra person frequently called a "utility" person or some similar title. This person does a variety of things, such as acting for the supervisor when he is absent, training new employees, and helping in on-the-job training of existing employees. Generally, this should *not* be the position the HRD person is filling.

The usual expectation is that the utility person is a potential line supervisor, and this generally is not the appropriate direction of growth for the HRD person. Combining the utility and HRD function also carries the danger of encouraging the HRD person to develop production skills rather than HRD skills. When the HRD person is functioning with a line unit, the expectation of performance should be spelled out very carefully—probably more carefully than for most employees.

Such placement again raises the question of movement through the organization. If the HRD person is not to remain permanently buried, who is looking at his performance and career growth? Within a centralized unit, there are probably several levels, and the possibilities of movement are known or can at least be identified. When the HRD people are decentralized, the possibilities of growth may be obscure. Who counsels this HRD person in terms of career growth?

One of the big problems with a centralized unit is that it can easily become isolated from the rest of the organization. The people in the unit can tend to relate effecitvely to one another but may exclude others in the organization. These conditions are easily handled, if it is recognized that they can occur.

A centralized unit has some advantages which managers might want to consider. It can avoid overlap, since the sharing of resources and personnel are much more easily accomplished. The whole HRD operation becomes more visible and can achieve more status. It is one of the realities of organizational life, as now practiced in most organizations, that being a large unit commands more respect and attention.

There are good reasons for both alternatives—centralization and decentralization—or some combination of both. Managers should look at the situation carefully, and then propose the best arrangement for that organization at that particular time. As conditions change, the decision should be re-examined.

ETHICS AND RESPONSIBILITY

When an organization offers HRD to its employees, as most large organizations must, it becomes necessary to step into the area of ethics and corporate responsibility. By definition, HRD deals with people and behavioral change. This coupling raises many questions which may not have been previously considered by managers.

Do We Have the Right?

One way of phrasing the problem is to ask, "Just because we may know how to change behavior, does that give us the right to do it?" As our technology and our understanding of human behavior have increased, we have begun to create many techniques which allow us to shape human behavior. At this point, we are not considering what is commonly called "brainwashing," but other, more humanistic techniques which still impact directly on behavior.

One can argue logically that as long as the company is paying salaries/wages for the HRD program, it has the right to call the tune. The employee can always, at least in the U.S., exercise the option of leaving the organization and getting a job someplace else. In a democratic country, this is an option available to any worker. Our courts have ruled that a contract that forces somebody to work (called a "yellow dog contract") is not enforceable, as it would constitute peonage, which is unconstitutional.

Within a work situation, the choices are not always that clearly spelled out. One of the visible controversial areas has been "sensitivity training," under a variety of labels (encounter groups, mirror groups, etc.). These are not all the same, but we can group them together for purposes of this discussion. If an organization has decreed that all managers are to go to such a learning experience, how does one exercise the right to refuse to attend? In what subtle ways does the organization, through its people, punish the individual who wishes to exercise such a right?

Do not look for answers here, for there are few to present. However, each organization which offers such learning programs must be prepared with answers even before the questions are asked.

There are other learning programs which raise similar issues, but perhaps not so dramatically. What about those programs of positive reinforcement, which reward for "appropriate" behavior only? The learner may feel as if he is a pigeon or a monkey, but he must go through the motions or risk the penalties imposed by lack of conformity.

Responsibility

The issue here may not be so directly in the ethical realm, but it does include some of the same aspects. That is, various kinds of punishment are imposed when the learner is not prepared to give up something to be part of the learning group.

In your organization, who pays for HRD? The answers can range from "We pay it all" to "We pay nothing." This management decision may reflect economic conditions, or may only be a reationalization for the decision not to pay for HRD.

Some organizations still contend that the employees should come to them fully prepared and never need any other learning experience. This is both naive and incorrect, for it assumes that all organizations are the same and that change does not occur. Obviously, both assumptions lack validity. An organization which does not wish to pay for HRD for its employees should openly admit this and then stand by its decision. Such an organization, however, should not be surprised if there is a high turnover rate. Employees will tend to leave the organization, rather than leave the real world, which is full of change. Unless jobs are extremely scarce, employees will look for organizations where there are chances for growth and movement—both of which require learning programs.

If the HRD program is for the benefit of the organization, then the organization should be making the expense or investment required to deliver the program. Of course, this also allows the organization to have control over what is taught, how it is taught, and the expected behaviors. Strictly from a decision-making point of view, there is no question about this: the company has the responsibility.

From the viewpoint of good adult learning, the adult learner should also be included in the process and have some responsibility. This shared responsibility will assure that both the learner and the organization will want to get the most out of the learning situation for the benefit of both. This does not mean the employee should be asked to share the financial responsibility, unless the employee is also going to share in the benefits of the learning experience. Such is rarely the case.

Although the responsibility for payment is essentially in the hands of the organization, it may be legitimate to share the figures regarding costs with the employees. This should not be used to coerce behavior from the employees; nor should it be presented as a fringe benefit for those who receive it. HRD should be solving problems, and if the solution is fringe benefits, there are other activities which are much more pertinent.

Considering the free labor market in the U.S., what is the manager's responsibility to provide a learning experience when the employee can leave so freely? Perhaps this is one of the costs an organization must contemplate when it operates in a free labor market.

Some organizations have attempted to have a policy of "2 for 1," or some similar arrangement. If an employee is given time (money is not usually included here) from the job for learning, it is expected that the employee will "pay back" two weeks for every week off the job. Or it could be two months for each one month. If the employee chooses to leave (and there is nothing that can force an employee to remain), then it is expected that the employee will repay the cost of the learning experience. This may be enforceable if the manager has approved an expenditure for the learning experience and there is a written policy or agreement between the organization and the employee. But although it is enforceable, it can involve the organization in undesirable litigation. Most organizations prefer not to have these agreements and to avoid getting involved in such problems related to HRD.

One approach is to provide only minimal kinds of learning for employees. If they leave, it would be without the benefits one might get from HRD programs. This extremely conservative approach can backfire on the organization, for it communicates that the organization is not preparing employees for internal movement.

This whole question of responsibility poses many dilemmas which are not readily surfaced. Managers should constantly be examining the implications of all HRD decisions as they relate to ethics and responsibility.

UNIONS

Although only a comparatively small part of our workforce is unionized, unions are more prevalent in the larger companies. As indicated earlier, it is the larger companies which tend to have HRD programs, so we need to examine the relationships of managers to their unions, as they relate to HRD.

What will be discussed here is essentially the past, but there are new and exciting trends on the horizon. Perhaps an understanding, on the part of the manager, of past relationships between managers and unions will be helpful for the future, as unions become more interested and involved in HRD.

The first major union efforts in the U.S., in the latter part of the last century, were focused on craftsmen. There were workers who had high levels of skills. Some of these went through an apprenticeship and journeyman program leading to specific certification. Other programs were less well-delineated but were still generally agreed upon.

The underlying premise of such unions was that their members were skilled and therefore did not need training programs. Promotions were granted for a variety of reasons, stipulated by the union contract, and the policy was to promote and train rather than to educate and promote.

It was not until 1936, with the advent of the CIO (originally part of the AFL and rejoined with it in 1955), that industrial or non-craft employees were recruited into unions in any mass numbers.

From the earliest times, then, the unions could see no need for HRD programs for employees in the bargaining unit. Of course, they did not take any stand on those employees, usually managers, who were outside the bargaining unit. Although there are many unions today whose leaderships were not part of that earlier concept, there are still some remnants of this reflected in their cultural behavior. This is changing and can be expected to change even further under the impact of "industrial democracy."

There are many myths in the area of union attitudes toward HRD, though there is also probably a kernel of truth to them. In speaking to union leaders about HRD, you will find that the older ones will tell you stories similar to the following.

"We had a good man—he was a shop steward. The other workers trusted him and followed him. He was a real power in his shop. If somebody had a grievance, he knew just what to do, so they [the managers] did not make a monkey out of the worker and a scrap of paper out of the contract. What happened? They sent him to a learning program and then promoted him to a supervisory position—out of the bargaining unit. They bought him off!"

The manager, giving his version, would say: "We had a good worker who everbody looked up to and followed. We knew he was the shop steward, but he was not like those hotheads who use that position to gain favor and privileges. He was a natural leader—the men trusted him. If there was a grievance, he was able to see that it got settled at the floor level without having to exhaust the whole grievance machinery and even go to arbitration. Naturally, this was the kind of man we saw as a good supervisory prospect and managerial material. So we sent him to our usual learning program to see if he really wanted the job and had the ability. He worked out fine in the learning program, so we promoted him. We saw this as having a strong union man involved in supervision, and as a benefit to both sides."

There is a postscript to this, in many cases, as told by the union leaders. Once the man was out of the bargaining unit, and out from under the protection of the union—he was fired! There probably have been cases like this, and it would convince nobody to provide statistical data either pro or con. The unions still become worried when a leader (shop steward or other) is sent to an HRD program which might result in that employee leaving the bargaining unit and then the union. Some unions see the HRD programs as management techniques for identifying union leaders, isolating them by promotion, and then firing them.

Another technique, criticized by unions, is that of upgrading workers. At first it might seem that this is contradictory; usually, the more a worker earns, the higher the union dues. To understand this, one must recognize the variety of union contracts which exist. Some have plantwide seniority, so that if there is a cutback, the last employee hired is the first fired, no matter where he is positioned in the company. There is a regular "bumping" procedure, and those with longevity (more seniority) are the least likely to be laid off. Other contracts have seniority within certain classification groups or within units of the organization. Under such a contract, when an employee moves into a different classification or unit, this employee now has the least seniority. There are obviously some good reasons for contracts like this.

An employee may be sent to a learning program to prepare for another job, probably at higher pay. Then this worker is promoted. If there is a lay-off, and this new worker with years in another part of the plant is the lowest in seniority in that new unit or classification, the ax falls. There are unionists who will tell you stories of how management identified strong union employees, sent them to HRD programs to prepare for promotion, and promoted them. Very soon thereafter came the lay-offs—which the unionists contend management knew about all along—and out goes the strong union member. Another example, they say, of how HRD was used to weaken the union.

Whether these stories are true or not, there are still union leaders whose behavior is guided by the tales they have heard and perhaps even witnessed. Is it any wonder that some view HRD as a management tool to weaken the union?

Linkages

It is not an entirely gloomy picture. There are activities, even now, in which management and unions work together.

An apprentice program which is officially organized will have the joint concurrence of the management, union, and usually some agency of the government. In such programs, management and union sit side by side as equal partners in the HRD effort designed to produce the necessary skilled workers. They negotiate jointly the kinds of learning programs, work experiences, and levels of pay that will be involved.

In many of the so-called "manpower programs" of the past two decades, there were significant numbers of instances where both the unions and management cooperated.

There are probably other areas, related to HRD, where one could find examples of union and management cooperation. Unfortunately, they are too seldom written up, studied, or in some other way made part of the data bank related to union/management joint efforts in HRD.

Creating a Dialogue

There are too many managements that are still either anti-union or suspicious of unions. There may be some justification for this point of view, based on their own history regarding unions and HRD. However, if we continue to live in the past, neither side will benefit from the HRD activities available; and these are benefits that can accrue to both sides, as well as to the employees.

Managers of unionized companies should make it a point to include the union in HRD planning. This will take some of the mystery out of the operation and will keep the union from being either overtly or covertly opposed to HRD for its members. It is not suggested that the unions control the situation. Unless there are vast changes, the responsibility for HRD sits squarely in the court occupied by management.

Management/union conflict is another example of the misunderstanding that arises when one group seeks to influence and the other perceives this as a battle for control.

The history of our campus riots provides many examples of this, and the same can be expected to be replicated in the world of work, if both sides do not engage in the necessary dialogue.

Frequently, what workers seek is to influence what is going on in their employing organization. Only infrequently do they want to control the organization—they realize the high-risk implications of that. What the workers seek is some kind of influence. When this is denied them, we should not be surprised if they join together in some way so they can be heard. This joining usually means some kind of union—local, national, or international.

At that point the battle becomes joined. If managers see the search for influence as a search for control, they react by shutting off all possibilities. Every action becomes a legal one which requires solution by collective bargaining or arbitration. Less formal approaches are no longer possible.

During the usual period of negotiations, issues are raised in the areas of pay, fringe benefits, working conditions, etc. Rarely is HRD a bargaining issue, and perhaps it is better that way. But when a union does try to introduce HRD into a bargaining session, to influence what is being offered, some managements respond by saying that is not a negotiable issue. HRD is strictly the prerogative of management. Is it any wonder that some unions still view HRD as a management tool to weaken unions?

I have sat on many national committees and work groups which contained members of both management and unions. It is amazing to find how close they are in their thinking, as long as it is not their employees or members who are involved!

Managers should be sitting down with their unions to discuss the use and implications of HRD programs. Of course, the HRD people should be included in such discussions. HRD offers inestimable benefits for all sides.

HRD FOR NON-EMPLOYEES

Most of this book focuses on HRD for employees, but there is also a vast area of HRD for non-employees. What is obvious and has been referred to before is where the organization provides learning experiences for members (as in the American Red Cross or similar organizations) or for some of its consumers (as in the case of the Inernal Revenue Service). Let us focus more closely on this area, for managers must make some decisions regarding the use of HRD for non-employees.

Prior to Hire

There are companies that have developed a practice which is of interest and even of benefit to others. HRD (essentially education) is provided for people who are *potential* employees.

In two cases, this has been used to good advantage. The first is the case of planning to employ people who have not usually been in the workforce. These potential employees do not have the basis for making decisions about the kind of work they wish to do and may even have difficulty understanding what will be expected in the workforce. The company can agree to provide education for them to prepare them to enter the workforce. Sometimes this is done in conjunction with some government program, but that is not required.

During the education, there can be some form of reimbursement for the potential employee. It is generally limited to cover transportation and food—a minimal amount. The period is usually only a week or two, during which the potential employee is receiving an orientation to the organization and an understanding of the possible placement available within it. Upon completion of this experience, there must be a mutual decision. The potential employee must want to work for the company, and the company must be prepared to offer a job. If either side refuses, there is no relationship joined. This type of education program can reduce turnover and its attendant costs and trauma. This tecnique has been used effectively by several companies, though it has not yet been adequately studied.

One pharmaceutical company uses this kind of program with the sales personnel (called medical detailers). A prospective employee will be recruited and screened by the personnel utilization unit, but not placed on payroll. The individual will be told that there is a pre-employment phase which has mutual benefits. (If the prospective employee chooses not to join the company, there is no record of employment, and the prospective employee does not get a reputation as a "job hopper.") In the pre-employment phase, the prospective employee is referred to the HRD unit for a program in which the first phase is a commercial course (purchased by the HRD unit), organized into a programmed instruction format so the prospective employee can study at home in a self-directed manner. After the prospective employee has completed the course and successfully passed the final examination, he notifies the HRD unit and they arrange for the next phase.

If the prospective employee wishes to continue the program, there is a brief orientation to the company, the product line, and the expectations of performance. If the person wants to continue further, and the HRD and personnel units agree, the "prospective" is dropped and we now have a new employee. There is still a probation period. The new employee will first work alongside a carefully selected, experienced employee, who will serve as a mentor. From this point on, there will be some of the usual training that is provided for all new employees.

Note the elaborate pre-employment phases with carefully designed HRD experiences. The organization using this approach has reported significant reduction in the turnover of new employees, as well as higher performance levels of new employees than in the past. This could not possibly have been done by the HRD unit alone. Various managers had to participate in the program and coordinate their needs and schedules so that the program could be successful.

There is a fine line here which awaits further clarification from the Internal Revenue Service and other government agencies. Can the prospective employer still maintain that the prospective employee is not a full employee? If it is ruled that there is full employee status, then there are questions related to unemployment compensation, minimum wages, etc. Nobody has ruled the practice illegal—but then, nobody has ruled. It is hoped that there will be clarification, for the prior-to-hire practice can go far to meet the needs of both citizens and organizations.

Meetings

One of the fastest growing activity areas of organizational behavior appears to be meetings. This trend started in about 1976 and is increasing with amazing rapidity.*

Companies conduct a variety of meetings for a wide range of reasons. One of the most common is the stockholders meeting, which in most states is

---

*More details can be found in Leonard Nadler and Zeace Nadler, *The Conference Book*, Gulf Publishing Co., Houston, Texas, 1977.

required by law to be held annually. There can also be meetings (as opposed to training, education, or development) for information, foreign visitors, families, people who work for the company in distant cities, incentives awards, etc. This has become such a significant field that new organizations have emerged composed of people who do a great deal of meeting work. Graduate courses are offered in designing and implementing meetings. Hotels have started to advertise that they are staffing their conference units with professional conference planners rather than merely sales or banquet personnel.

Many of the same competencies needed by HRD people are needed by meeting planners. Caution: They are not *exactly* the same. For some meetings, however, managers should consider using their HRD people as a resource. This does not mean just having them make the flight arrangements, or the hotel and food plans, or even the entertainment plans. The HRD unit can create a *total design* of those elements of a meeting which can make for success or failure.

Your company may have good in-house HRD capability that could be used effectively for meetings for which you have responsibility. It could even cost you less to use your in-house HRD people than to contract out to others. Not all HRD units have the competencies or even the interest in meeting work, so do not be surprised if they do advise you to seek other resources. You will not know this until after you have checked it out with them.

Customers

In addition to meetings for customers, many companies have to provide either training or education for customers. The training would be for those people who are already customers (already using the product or service). Their use of your product might be improved through an appropriate training program, even though they are not employees.

Some of the large computer companies do this continually, but do not see it as an HRD function. For working with customers, you will often hear the terms Service Representative or Customer Representative. When you look at the duties, you will find they are to instruct the customer personnel in the use of products or services. Particularly with products subject to change and improvement, there may be a contract stipulating that training will be provided as part of the regular purchase agreement.

For prospective customers, education may be offered as a way of encouraging them to purchase the product or service. This is not strictly selling, but involves instruction of customer personnel prior to the sale.

These are learning activities and, as such, are related to HRD people. The actual personnel doing them may be in service or sales and they should probably remain there. Your HRD unit can be useful, however, in reviewing the learning materials and helping to improve the competency of those employees who will be instructing.

CONCLUSION

Where an organization has an HRD unit, it should be seen as an important part of organization life. Managers should make sure that the HRD people are included in the discussions about HRD related to power, placement, ethics, responsibility, and the union (where one exists).

The closer that HRD is tied into organization life, the more it can contribute to the success of the organization. There is no question that an organization with an active HRD program raises issues which might otherwise not exist. The effective managerial response should *not* be to eliminate or overlook the HRD unit, but to openly explore the issues raised when managers decide to offer HRD.

9 Social Issues and HRD

There have been many discussions about the function of private organizations in the U.S. and whether or not they should be involved in social issues. By now, this discussion should have moved onto a higher plane. There really is no choice. As has been said, the business of business is business! A business must make a profit if it is to continue to function. If, however, the only purpose of a company is to make a profit, it should expect to have a negative image and to receive abuse from the community in which it operates. Many companies have found this out, and perhaps too late. Why wait?

Managers have been involved, and should be involved, in many areas of social issues. In this chapter, we shall look at some of these, within the purview of the HRD function.

DISADVANTAGED

The term "disadvantaged" is misleading, confusing, undefined, but almost generally accepted. It arose in the early 1960's and, unfortunately, has stayed with us. It was meant to convey a group of citizens outside the mainstream of our society and therefore not having the advantages of most of the population. This "disadvantaged" state could be the result of race, color, religion, sex, language, etc. The term has slowly been legislated to the point where specific disadvantaged groups have become legally defined. As expected, these definitions change, and it would be foolhardy to state what they are at this time—for even now there is legislation including some groups and dropping others. Right now, the newest group of disadvantaged are people over 70 years of age.

Legislation

Each of us may view the disadvantaged person differently, but we are bound by the law to act in specific ways. Managers have found, to their woe, that determining who is disadvantaged at any point of time is not done by sociologists, psychologists, social workers, or any other such experts, but by legislators. Of course, these legislators do rely to some degree on the advice of professionals, but as legislators they are also subject to the influence exerted by their constituencies.

One of the first groups we officially recognized was the group of workers being displaced by the onrush of automation. This was in the late 1950's and (more significantly) early 1960's. The Area Redevelopment Act was designed to help those who had been put out of jobs by encroaching technology; it was superseded by the Manpower Development and Training Act of 1962. Two years later, the Manpower Development and Training Act was swept into the War on Poverty, and with the Economic Opportunity Act of 1964, it became part of major pieces of legislation designed to help the disadvantaged. There was additional legislation, and the interested reader should examine the writings of Sar Levitan, who has studied this area more closely than almost any other individual.

One common factor can be found within the cited, and subsequent, legislation. Learning (training and education) was the core of those programs. The ultimate goal was job placement in the private sector, and frequently the private sector was involved in providing HRD experiences for the disadvantaged. Without doubt, some of the managers reading this book were very directly involved, and may still be.

Corporate Actions

The record of what the private sector has offered in the way of HRD support for the disadvantaged has never been adequately identified. Those programs which relied on federal funds have found their way into the computer, and various researchers will probably write more about them in future years. Right now, we are still too close.

One example is the National Alliance of Businessmen. It started out in the late 1950's as the Alliance for Progress, whereby companies volunteered to provide HRD and help the disadvantaged get jobs. This was replaced by the

National Alliance of Businessmen, which was operated by the private sector (though it did use some federal funds). When it started in the middle 1960's, some of our largest companies detailed top personnel to various parts of the country to get the program moving. In each of the offices in the operating cities, there was an HRD advisor—usually a top HRD person from one or our leading corporate giants. This practice continued for many years, and remains an outstanding example of how managers were loaned by their companies, with HRD assistants, to help in programs that were essentially social in content and objectives. There could not possibly be any direct return to those companies who provided these skilled personnel.

This social activity on the part of many of our organizations should be continued, and there should be more recognition of those managers and HRD people who are assigned to this activity. Such assignments should be seen as positive events in the careers of these people, rather than as sacrifices or as a way to put people "out to pasture." Without support from all managerial levels, it is not possible to recruit top-level people for these strenuous and difficult assignments.

CHANGING WORKFORCE

Our workforce in the U.S. has been changing over the past decade or two. There is nothing a manager can or should do about this—except react to the changes. It is important for managers to recognize that there are changes and not to continue to manage as though this was 1950. This may sound simplistic, but we still do find people yearning for the return of the "good old days"—whatever they were! Perhaps some things will go back to what they were, though this is doubtful. There is no question, however, that at least into the early days of the twenty-first century, we will have a workforce quite different than the one we have known. This means that the HRD decisions required of a manager will be quite different, so let us explore some of these differences.

Workforce Projections

In dealing with the future, there are some things which are predictable, though still subject to major and unforeseen calamities. It is fairly easy to predict that our workforce will be getting older, at least until the end of this century. The reasoning behind this is that there would have to be a major change in the birth rate to have any influence on the age make-up. Such a change as a significant increase in the number of births would result in individuals who would not enter the workforce until at least 18 years after they are born. That is why the prediction is so easy to make. The new members of the workforce will have to have been around for at least 16 years, and more likely 18, before they join the workforce. At present, it does not look as if there will be such a change.

For some 30 years, in the U.S., it was easy to make predictions, as most workers who reached the age of 65 retired at that time. This pattern may still hold, but we are in the throes of changes which were unforeseen a few years ago. There is now legislation which makes the over-65 group one of the minorities which cannot be discriminated against. Except for some legislated exceptions, most people can now work until age 70. There is talk of eliminating the mandatory retirement completely, and it would be no surprise if this change should occur.

This will produce many significant changes in managerial decisions in various areas, but we will focus on HRD. For one thing, we have research to show that adults can continue to learn until they die, or have some kind of brain damage, so there is no end to the possibilities of learning. There *are* differences in *how* adults learn, based on age. The research is inadequate at present, but as the workforce (and the general population) grows older, we can expect these differences to be the focus of study by various groups concerned with adult learning.

At this time, we do know that the older person in a learning situation tends to focus more on quality than quantity. The younger person's function is just the reverse. This means that the evaluation of learning, as well as the process, will have to reflect this difference.

The usual pyramid picture of the workforce, based on age, will appear more like a trapezoid. The base will be shorter, in comparison with the top, than has previously been the case. This could mean fewer promotional opportunities, and therefore the nature of the HRD programs will change—though it is not possible to make any specific predictions on what these changes will be. There are still too many variables to be considered, but the need for a different way of looking at careers and HRD related learning activities will have to be considered. Managers should be working with their HRD units right now to plan for the possible changes that will have to take place as the average age of the workforce creeps higher.

Non-Americans

Since the first Spanish settlements in the North American continent, we have had "non-Americans" in the workforce. The native Americans (a generic term for the various nations we refer to as Indian) may well regard us as the foreigners, but the general designation of "non-Americans" is applied to those who have immigrated or been brought into this country, while their children are considered Americans. What does this mean?

After we became a nation, most of the immigrants we received were at the lower end of the economic scale, and perhaps even the social scale, in the countries from which they emigrated. From time to time, we received people with skills who were displaced because they were on the wrong side of a rebellion (such as in Europe in 1848 and again in 1870). Generally, the immigrants were highly motivated people—not just the cast-offs. (The reader who wishes to pursue this further is encouraged to read the two books by Yale Historian Oscar Handlin: *The Uprooted* and *Children of the Uprooted*.)

With the closing down of our open immigration policy in the early 1920's, the increase in our population reflected native births rather than immigration. After World War II, a slow trend of immigration emerged, supplemented by many illegal immigrants. By 1976, it was estimated that we had over eight million illegal immigrants in the U.S., though some contend that the true figure is considerably higher.

On the legal side, the make-up of our immigrant groups changed. With a more humanistic approach, we let down the barriers on "Oriental" immigration. With the collapse of Vietnam, our Congress authorized many special quotas for the Vietnamese. Each succeeding wave of immigration has brought with it many workers who have entered the workforce at the local levels and then worked their way up. To look at some organizations is to see a stratified relationship resembling a "tel". (This is a hill which has been occupied for many centuries. By taking a slice down through this hill—the actual translation of the word from several semitic languages—one is able to see different societies who occupied the same place in succession.)

In New England, for example, in one organization, it was possible to look at the organizational chart and see the flow of immigration from the top down: English, Irish, Portuguese, Black, Hispanic. Each of these groups, except for the English, started at the lowest levels and have been (or are) slowly working their ways up. Recently, with the application of the Equal Employment Opportunity legislation, the movement of these minorities within these companies has been accelerated.

There is another group—but they are not immigrants. They are foreigners, and this is a group that could present innumerable problems unless we recognize who and what they are. All the previous waves of immigration, referred to above, consisted of people who essentially remained in the U.S. Most came to become citizens; others came to "make their fortune" and then return home, and some have done this. Since the early 1970's, there is a new foreigner—a different kind of non-American. This can be a person from Japan, Sweden, Germany, and, more recently, any of the OPEC countries.

Having foreign *investment* in the U.S. is nothing new. Since the earliest settlements, there has always been foreign investment. Many Americans forget that the settlement in Amsterdam (now New York) was financed by a trading company and that for years the company governed New York through a series of company appointed governors.

For more than two centuries, however, though we had investment, we had very few foreign managers. But starting in the 1960's and accelerating in the 1970's, some foreign companies sent their managers over to protect their investments. This is a new kind of non-American, who is at the top of the economic and social strata. The numbers are increasing and they are becoming more observable. For probably the first time in our industrial history, Americans are finding themselves working under foreign managers in the U.S.! It is hoped that some of these managers will read this book and be able to identify the problems and concerns which are present but have yet to surface.

Minorities

Minorities have always been with us, and always will. The very nature and history of our country cries out against total conformity and the elimination of minorities. In some situations, we have done less than a satisfactory job in working with minorities. Since 1964, our record has been better, but it is a continual problem and one which we have to face.

It is difficult to find an all-encompassing definition for "minorities." Essentially, they are groups of people with some kind of common identity. Some of these minorities do very well, but here we are concerned with those for whom special action has been, or should be, taken. This does not make them any less of a minority but does assure that they will have an equal opportunity to share in the benefits of our country, while still remaining a minority.

In our past history, religious minorities were among the most identifiable. As we are one of the few major countries without an official religion or religious qualifications for office holding and other forms of sharing in our democracy, we have tended to attract those who were the subjects of religious persecution in other parts of the world. This is not a naive statement ignoring the fact that in some parts of our country, and among some of our citizens, there is still a strong trace of religious discrimination and even hatred. For the person on the receiving end, it is little solace to be told that this is no longer a major problem. We still do not have that perfect world for which we yearn.

Minorities today fall into three general areas. The first is still color and this includes all those generally classed as "non-white." The major identified groups are Blacks, Hispanics, and native Americans. Some would also include Orientals, which is an ambiguous term (most of this group have been in the U.S. for a long time, but are still outside the mainstream and generally lack the social and economic mobility which all of us seek). These groups are highly identifiable and few have the opportunity for "passing" (not being seen as part of that minority) even if they wanted to. And why should they? We pride ourselves on being a pluralistic society. In general, we have reached the stage where we can accept people as they are, but still more needs to be done to bring full equality for all. It is no easy matter, and organizations of all kinds have been, and will continue to be, involved in this.

A more recently identified minority is women, though females actually outnumber males in our society, and as of 1979 women made up about 50% of the workforce. It is true that studies indicate that women still do not have a "fair share" of the economic benefits, but this also depends upon the statistics and the criteria. There was a time when being a woman closed many areas of employment, particularly those at the upper levels of our economic structure. As the decades pass, it can be expected that the acceptance of women at all levels of the organization will become a fact of organizational life. There will still be those who discriminate against women, just as there are those who discriminate against others who do not eat the same food, dress the same way, or belong to their country clubs. There is no question but that the status of the female minority has changed considerably, and that more female managers are reading this book today than would have been possible in the early 1960's, when a female manager was still an oddity.

There is another minority, but a changing one. For a while, there was a youth minority, and the U.S. was even accused of being a youth-oriented society. It was said that fast food was an accommodation to the youth generation, and one can point to other symbols of our society which were presumably developed to satisfy the vast youth market.

As we entered the 1980's, this changed. The average age of our population took rapid jumps. One statistician, going back to the opening of the century, pointed out that at that time, only about 3 percent of our population was over 65. As we approach the end of this century, it is estimated that 20 percent of our population will be in that age bracket. Some may argue that it could not possibly get that high, but there are others who point to the year 2010 and make even higher predictions. This would be due to the significant increase in births after World War II, a group that will be entering the 65-year age group in 2010.

We are moving from a youth minority to an over-65 minority. We have already seen one effect of the Gray Panther movement in Congress' action of 1978, advancing the retirement age to 70 for some workers and eliminating it totally for others. A significant minority is currently evolving and perhaps we will do a better job with that group than we have done with some minorities in the past. The over-65 group, to be sure, will be a more affluent and influential minority than many we have had in the past.

Implications for HRD

What does all of this mean for HRD and for managers? Some of the implications are fairly obvious. But for managers who have not been involved with HRD, the obvious can easily be overlooked.

There will be a broader age range in the workforce, as well as a different distribution. This will require different learning programs, and managers should be involved in these. In addition, there will be implications for management behavior and the need for new kinds of programs to train managers (and perhaps to educate them).

As we become more sensitive to minorities, and as the possibility of international travel increases, managers may be called upon to include many other minorities in their workforce. It will not be sufficient to merely reintroduce previous programs. Different minorities require different kinds of learning programs. Cultural differences always require different learning approaches, and cultural differences among minorities are an important consideration.

The range of retirement ages for the workforce will be much broader than it was in the past, when the focus was usually on 65. We can expect that some workers will take advantage of the new legislation and opt to stay in the workforce longer. For them, a pre-retirement program may be at the age of 70 or 75.

As another approach, some organizations will seek ways of encouraging some workers (including managers) to retire earlier to make way for other workers. This too will require pre-retirement learning programs, but of a vastly different nature than for those at the upper end of the workforce. All of these HRD programs need to be coordinated and related to management plans and decisions regarding retirement.

COMMUNITY RELATIONS

Increasingly, organizations in the private sector have become involved in the communities in which they are located. It is no surpirse to find non-profit organizations being very active in the community, for that is the very purpose for which some of them were created; if they are not serving the community, they may not have any real function at all. For profit-making companies, a different type of decision is required.

The term "community" requires some discussion. Before we were such a mobile society, and before the growth of suburbia, it was easy to identify a community. It was usually a piece of geography with specific boundaries and an identified group of people who lived in that area. If somebody changed a job, it also meant a change in the community in which he lived, shopped, and did the other things that were part of his life.

After World War II, we saw increased mobility and the growth of "bedroom communities," or suburbia. Essentially, people then worked in one place and lived in another. Efforts were made to reverse, or at least to modify, this trend, but to date they have not been too successful. The experimental communities of Reston, Virginia, and Columbia, Maryland, are prime examples of specific efforts to provide a community where people could live and work at the same place.

Some companies have endeavored to provide a relationship to the communities in which they operate or from which they draw their employees or their customers. Community now can mean the entire country! There is a good example in the Exxon Education Foundation. In 1977, Exxon detailed a leading HRD person to work with the Foundation to make the managerial experience of Exxon available to the country's universities.

Whether or not a company should be involved in its community, defined in the broadest sense, is a managerial decision. For some of this involvement there is a place for HRD, and we will explore some of those possibilities.

Utilization of Facilities

Many of our large companies have extensive HRD facilities. The purpose, of course, is to service the HRD needs of the organization. There are times, however, when the facilities are not being used by the employees and when they could be made available to non-employees in the community. The most logical example is found in the office. At night, the offices of most of our companies are seldom used. Why not use these facilities to conduct classes in office functions? The equipment is there, and it certainly is the appropriate environment.

In 1978, the IBM Corporation sponsored some TV programs and, of course, had commercials. One of these showed exactly what we are discussing: the use of some of IBM's office space, at night, for conducting classes in basic office skills for people in the community who wanted to learn, wanted to earn, but lacked the necessary skills. In this instance, the teachers were IBM employees. During the late 1960's and early 1970's, Westinghouse likewise made its facilities in the populous areas of New Jersey available for learning programs for non-employees in office skills. There are probably many more examples, but there has been little effort to recapture or document them.

Some organizations that have large HRD facilities also make them available. It is sometimes possible for community groups to rent the facilities at a nominal charge, when they are not being used by the host organization. Of course, there are problems. The prime focus of the HRD staff and facility is to provide those programs required by the company, and this should remain the primary purpose. The availability of the HRD staff and facility merely presents another opportunity for those managers who are interested in promoting community relations with the community and serving the community.

If a manager decides to do this, it should be seen as a management decision, not as an HRD decision. If it is not clear to all that management has decided on this policy, the HRD people can be labeled as "do-gooders" (which, unfortunately, is too often viewed as negative behavior) and, as such, a part of the company which is no longer contributing to the goals of the company. Managers need to stand up and clearly state their community relations policy, and explain how the HRD unit is helping them reach their goals in this area.

Supporting Community Learning Programs

Communities frequently have learning programs which could use the support of the HRD unit of private companies. This is different from the discussion above, which focused much more on facilities.

One idea growing in the U.S. (though the direction of its growth is unclear) is "community education." It has received vast financial support from the Mott Foundation of Flint, Michigan, and is now a nation-wide effort, with centers funded by the Mott Foundation and the federal government. Unfortunately, there is confusion about whether it is community *education* or community *schools*. The community *school* program was designed to make the schools available not only to the children during school hours, but also to all citizens, of all ages, at all hours. The focus at that time was still on the school building.

Slowly, this began to change into the broader concept of how the adult learning groups in the community could be utilized to help solve community problems, or could increase the attractiveness of the community. This direction was somewhat stunted with the drop in enrollments in the public schools and the desires of some local school people to increase the utilization of their physical facilities. This tended to shift the emphasis from community *service* to utilizing the *schools*. It is hoped that this will change, and that there will be additional opportunities for non-profit organizations to be involved in broad programs of community education (using learning programs to improve communities).

Community education is not limited only to the poor or disadvantaged, but can be found in a wide variety of communities. Managers need to decide if their organizations should be involved, and they can look at some of the areas where HRD would have a role in such involvement.

Earlier, we mentioned the use of company facilities. Obviously, under the community *school* concept, this would not be welcome, but the broader community *education* concept would welcome this kind of specific assistance.

HRD people have had considerable experience in helping others learn how to teach. When a community needs more teachers of any subject, it is likely that the HRD staff can help prepare them. The HRD staff may also be able to share some equipment, such as projectors, etc., though there is often a sufficient number of these in the community. The videotape recorders (VTR) may be fewer in number, and a manager may want to consider making this kind of specialized equipment available from the HRD unit as needed by the community. Of course, it is expected that the manager will first have checked with the HRD unit, so that the staff is not deprived of this equipment for company programs, which are the first priority.

The two year community college (sometimes called junior college) is a unique U.S. institution. We have many of them spread throughout the U.S. Some of these are direct results of company help. For example, the Community College in Dearborn, Michigan was born out of a need the Ford Motor Company had for more technicians. Ford could easily have mounted its own program, but chose instead to use this opportunity to assist a local community institution. The Ford Company provided materials, instructors, equipment, and perhaps even funds (though this information is lacking). The result was that Ford got its technicians. Even more significant, they had made a "contribution" to the community by helping to establish an institution that did more than just meet the needs of the Ford Motor Company.

There are many more possibilities for supporting community learning programs, but the initiative should come from the company. This does not mean that the company should impose itself on the community, but that it should seek out those needs which are appropriate for some form of company contribution, intervention, or support.

Career Education

There is another concept—career education—which provides important opportunities in the community relations area. The term "education" is used here in the same sense as we have defined earlier: preparation of an individual for a future job. The only difference is that this individual will generally be a student still in high school, and the job could be many years in the future.

The essential impetus for career education arose from the efforts of Sidney Marland, who was Commissioner of Education. He saw the need for our schools to provide something concrete for those students who would not be going on to higher education, but would be entering the workforce immediately after graduation. They needed some specific skills to make them employable. This was a difficult task for the schools, and one reason was that the schools lacked the equipment and instructors. Despite the Vocational Education Act of 1968, there had been few exchanges of instructors between schools and the private sector. That Act provided funds for such exchanges, but was under-utilized.

The world of work had changed and was changing very rapidly. It was no longer possible to give a young person a specific skill, since it might be out of date by the time of graduation. This led to the idea of clusters, or groups of related skills which would enable a young person to seek and compete for jobs.

After Marland left the Office of Education, others in the field continued the work. Among the leaders in building the concept was Kenneth Hoyt, who served many terms (on leave from his university) with the Office of Education to develop the concept and actions. He has written extensively about career education and his books and articles are recommended to managers who want to know more about this activity.

The concept and practices of career education tend to change at the federal level, so we cannot predict what it might be in the future. The need will still remain, so let us look at what private companies can do to facilitate movement of young people from the world of school to the world of work.

Historically, some companies have been part of a "cooperative movement," which was based on the private sector cooperating with schools to provide real work experience for students still in school. Usually, these efforts have been directed to specific areas, such as engineering, and there are many companies that have cooperated for decades with selected schools of higher education. It is a similar concept and practice as career education, but the audience is different. In career education programs, the students are still in high school and the intent is to give them skills through placement in real companies with real jobs. Many of these young people do not have the slightest idea of what the world of work is. It is not their fault. It is one of the prices we pay for progress—or at least for change.

Prior to World War II, there was almost nothing of what we today call suburbia. Work place and living place were close together. Children, while they were growing up, were surrounded by adult role models from the world of work. Even in large urban areas, it was customary for the fathers to bring their sons (infrequently, their daughters) to their place of work on Saturdays or other holidays. With the advent of suburbia, and living places far removed from working places, children were deprived of the role models in action. What many saw was the father leaving very early in the morning to catch the suburban commuter train or driving off to combat the rush hour traffic. On returning, they would see an exhausted and weary traveler who did not evoke much in the way of enthusiasm for that kind of life. The ever-present TV programs did little to alleviate this. Can you recall a single TV program which depicted any reality in terms of factory or office jobs? Where have the role models gone? How can young people find answers to their questions about work, unless the private sector provides real life opportunities for the student before he makes some decisions about an economic role in our society?

Actually, without the help of the private sector, it is doubtful if any program of career education can work. The schools cannot possibly simulate the real. There is no way for the student to learn about the world of work if private companies do not make some efforts in this direction.

It is usually the personnel utilization departments that are part of this process, in the all too few cases where private companies have been involved. Perhaps they should have a role, but the major effort should involve the HRD unit. The placement of the student within an organization is for the purpose of learning—the basic HRD function. If the student is there to learn, then the HRD unit should be helping to plan and evaluate the learning. The HRD people should be the counterpart of the school.

Usually, the HRD people have not been involved, and for good reason. If a manager makes a decision to become part of a school-work effort, then the manger must also find ways to acknowledge the role of the HRD unit. The HRD unit is most often evaluated in terms of learning hours, problems solved, or some other criteria related to the goal of the organization. If community relations is part of the goal of the organization, this should be so stated, and the HRD unit given some responsibility for a career education program, as with any other program of the company.

ECONOMIC CONDITIONS

Organizations cannot control economic conditions. If the general economy is good, each company wants its share, but when conditions are bad, or declining, managers must make critical decisions in the fight for economic survival. HRD is part of this cyclical movement and decision-making.

When economic conditions are good, there are fewer questions posed about the role of HRD in the organization. HRD is accepted and expected, though of course it should be measured against some kind of criteria. There are many managers who still use HRD as a fringe benefit which their organizations can afford in good economic times. When times get rough, they cut the fringe benefits, including HRD. Such thinking is really counter-productive both for the manager and the organization.

If there are no distinctions made among training, education, and development, the whole HRD program can expect to take a cut when the economy goes down. If there is a difference, let us see what should happen (and, in many cases, did happen during the decline in 1973–1975).

Development is almost wiped out, since few organizations can afford that kind of high risk during tight budget times. This is logical and is to be expected. Education will probably be reduced, if not eliminated, as there will be fewer promotional opportunities. Also, with more people on the labor market (as with the more than 9 percent unemployment in 1975), organizations can hire people with needed skills without providing education. Of course, you must carefully consider such a management decision, because of the implications for your own employees. They will see their chances of advancement reduced, not because of insufficient positions, but because the positions are being filled by outsiders. This suggests that there should still be sufficient education to provide for internal mobility.

Expenditures for training tend to increase. Recall our definition: training is designed to improve efficiency on the present job. During a tight economy, a manager wants all the efficiency possible, and training is one way to get it. During this time, managers may have to consider becoming involved in some of the special programs the government sponsors to keep the economy going. Some of these will relate to HRD. Not all are government sponsored.

During the 1973-1975 recession-depression, there was an interesting example of how management and unions can cooperate. Both the United Auto Workers and some of the private auto companies recognized that there was a need for HRD for workers who were laid off. This was a unique understanding. It was realized that workers who were laid off could lose their skills. Jointly, the union and the companies agreed to conduct HRD programs during the lay-off to keep the skills at appropriate levels. Although no longer employees after the lay-offs, some of the workers still came to the plants and the HRD programs. Too little has been done to record this experience and to share it with others. It was unique, but it was (and is) certainly important.

During periods of economic decline, managers should be looking to their HRD units to identify programs which can assist in improving community action on the part of many organizations.

GOVERNMENT ROLE

There have been various and numerous references to the role of the federal government *vis a vis* private industry. This has been a growing role. We could discuss whether this is appropriate or not, but that would be less helpful to managers than to explore the real situation. The trend at this time, throughout the world, is increased governmental involvement in the private sector. In the U.S., it is slower than in many parts of the world, even though it is too fast from some U.S. companies.

Legislation

Earlier in this chapter, the legislation enacted from 1960-1975 was discussed. After 1975, there was a slow-down in legislation, but now it is on the increase again.

The earlier legislation was focused on the disadvantaged. There will likely be more legislation to help the people in that category, even as we redefine the category. There are broader movements in the wings which managers need to consider.

It is not inconceivable that we will see some kind of federal legislation aimed at finding ways to reward the private sector for providing HRD and jobs for special kinds of workers. Until some specific legislation is in the discussion stages in some committee, it would not be fruitful to discuss this too much. There are so many possibilities, but they all depend on having private companies accept increased responsibility in the communities in which they operate.

The most well-known piece of legislation in this regard is the Comprehensive Employment & Training Act (CETA). Of course, in the title of this act, they mean HRD—but that would not produce an easy acronym. Here again, a specific discussion would probably be non-productive. It is almost a certainty that there will be some legislation in the future, but the form can be expected to vary with the political winds. This has been the history of CETA and is a political reality. Managers should be sure their HRD units are keeping current with the changes and serving as a source of information and help. There will be many decisions to be made by managers regarding such legislation and the relationship with the communities where plants or services are located. The decisions are managerial ones, but the HRD units should be providing the necessary background on which sound managerial decisions can be based.

National Norms

We do not have any national norms related to HRD. As the government increases its role, this can change. To date, there have been several studies by government agencies seeking to identify or establish some norms. One series of studies was related to identifying the role of private industry in education for the work place. Others dealt with trying to clarify terminology, though they focused more on the broader field of adult education. HRD was included because it could not possibly be ignored. Attempts at glossaries have not yet been successful, but this is only a matter ot time.

The Department of Labor tried to study HRD, particularly training and education. What seemed to be a hallmark study was allowed to gather dust and there was no follow-up from the baselines the study had been able to establish. Sometime in the future, we can expect that the government will mount some kind of effort, for without agreed-upon terminology and concepts, we will never know what is really happening in the U.S. in the field of HRD. Without that knowledge, any government intervention will always be time-consuming and costly.

It is interesting that the closest attempt to influence the field came from the Internal Revenue Service. For many years, without saying so in exact words, they have allowed companies to deduct expenses for training, but not for education. Similarly, individual taxpayers could deduct expenses to improve their performance on their present jobs or fields (i.e., training) but could not deduct any expenditures for preparing to enter new fields (i.e., education). In 1978, the IRS made some movement toward collecting withholding tax on some of these expenditures and even tried to get most of HRD considered a fringe benefit and therefore taxable. Congress called a moratorium and legislated that there would be no changes until some later period. As a manager, you should be sure your HRD people keep up to date on the legislation and the IRS rulings related to HRD as a deductible item for your company on its tax return. Aside from the economic issue involved, it would not be helpful to your reputation with your community to be found guilty of evading federal tax statutes.

RECOGNITION FOR NON-COLLEGIATE STUDY

As a manager, you may think you are conduting a business for profit (or whatever the good of your organization may be). If you are employed by a large company, you are also housing a school within your organization, no matter what you label it.

There has been increased pressure for degrees, and with it, the need for some system of recognizing the learning experiences provided by non-school organizations through HRD programs. This has led to some significant movements in the U.S. for recognition of HRD programs by the academic world.

What is Academic?

The purpose of HRD is not to provide degrees or anything similar to that. Certificates are frequently awarded, but nobody has suggested that these do more than provide some kind of recognition within the organization.

As HRD programs have become more sophisticated, and are directed by more qualified professionals, they have begun to meet another need. We are a credentialed society, and to rant against this would do little to change it. Some companies have HRD programs which would meet the standards of any accredited institution of higher learning. Some of these programs are even taught by professors from accredited institutions.

In the mid-1970's, a grant was given to the American Council on Education to originate a project on credit for non-collegiate learning experiences. These were all within employing organizations. The aim was to provide some kind of equivalency data so that insitutions of higher learning could accept the HRD programs being conducted by non-school organizations. It is still too early to identify the impact of this work, though some colleges and universities have already granted credit for courses listed in the bulletins of the American Council on Education.

Cautions

This could be an exciting and rewarding approach to provide recognition of the quality programs one finds in many HRD operations. It is not an unmixed blessing.

If the movement grows, HRD people might be persuaded to change their programs to more closely resemble those offered by higher education institutions. This would not only be a duplication, but would deprive the in-company HRD programs of some of the flexibility they need. Instead of solving problems through learning, the HRD operation would become an in-house college.

The programs could easily be forced to be reported about in terms of clock-hours rather than company problems solved. We are still suffering from clock-hour (or head count) practices in HRD. We have been slowly moving away from that form of accountability. Undue emphasis on bestowing collegiate recognition for HRD programs could push the function back to the student-hour form of reporting.

Despite this caution, managers should be aware of the movement and have their HRD people explore it for the benefits which might accrue to the organization as well as to individuals.

CONCLUSION

More and more organizations are recognizing the need to be informed about and involved in social issues. There are many ways they can do this, and their HRD operations provide another resource.

A great many companies were part of the programs for the disadvantaged and minorities. The changing workforce also presents challenges to organizations, for which HRD can be an appropriate response. Community relations is always of concern, and HRD can provide a resource here as well.

Crucial to all this is the need to involve the HRD operation—a direct result of the managerial decision to become involved in the various communities related to the organization. When this is done, there must be ways to recognize the efforts of the HRD function which cannot be evaluated in the usual manner.

10 International and Multi-National Aspects of HRD

As our world shrinks, activities in one part of the world increasingly affect other parts of the world. Leadership shifts from one place to another in an unpredictable fashion. At one time, the U.S. held the leadership in many areas, including HRD. This is no longer the case and probably will not be again. It is not necessary for us to be the leader in all things, and we must to be open to learning from those who a short time before were the underdeveloped countries.

In this chapter, we focus on the international aspects of HRD. Some have been mentioned before—and we could not have avoided them even if we wanted to. Some of what was said before will appear again in this chapter, but with increased emphasis on the international focus. This material should be most helpful to those managers who are in any way involved in the international aspects of business and industry, but others will also find it helpful, for we shall indicate trends that can be expected to have their impact on the U.S.

For the skeptical manager who still will not accept that we are impacted upon by foreign activities, just take a look at flexi-time. The whole movement started in Germany, though there are still American managers who insist it was a U.S. development. It was not. We may have made some modifications as the practice spread in the U.S., but this is to be expected; given cultural differences, any movement will change as it goes from one country to another. This should not obscure the undeniable fact that flexitime stated in Germany (although there is debate as to exactly which company was first to implement it, with at least three different German companies credited as its innovator).

PAID STUDY LEAVE

There is a growing practice of providing funds to employees so that they can study outside the company. This is sometimes called "Educational Entitlement," and this could be a very apt title.

It *is* frequently "education," as most of the countries that have this as part of their national legislation insist that the employees should not study anything directly related to the job. "Entitlement" carries with it the assumption that it is a regular right to which workers (at all levels, including managers) are entitled.

Legislation

One of the earliest pieces of legislation was in France in 1957. This provided for up to two weeks each year when a worker could be off the job to study social and economic subjects. Later changes in the law extended this to housewives as well. Some studies have indicated that one difficulty with the law is that it is not adequately utilized by those who are eligible. In 1977, only about 7 percent of those qualified were using it in France, although no studies have yet determined the cause for such a low level of participation. We can rationalize by saying that, in any event, 7 percent more people were benefiting than would be the case without the legislation.

In the U.S., the impact has already been felt, since many union contracts now contain a similar provision. By 1978, some studies indicated much of the same pattern as seen in France of lack of use of this provision. (You should not confuse educational entitlement with tuition benefit programs, although you could be excused for being confused, since they appear almost the same in their administration. The purpose, however, is different—though there can be overlap.)

Educational entitlement was meant to focus on non-job related learning to which a person was entitled by virtue of being a citizen. It started with employees, and in some European countries has been expanded to include housewives and other dependents above the usual school age.

Tuition refund is usually for job related learning experiences. The trend to expand this in the U.S. has led to the Internal Revenue Service intervention discussed in Chapter 9. In some foreign countries with educational entitlement programs, this has not been a factor. Their legislation took the whole question out of the tax situation and put it squarely in the area of social issues.

In the U.S., we still have to deal with this and we should be studying more about what has happened in other countries. Your HRD people should be looking into this so they can provide managers with some basis for either taking a position or making decisions.

International Labor Organization

The ILO has been around for a long time and is regarded with much respect in many parts of the world. Unfortunately, for political reasons, the U.S. has chosen to withdraw from the ILO. But we can do little to influence the organization from the outside, and our stand is regarded as petulant and immature in many parts of the world, so it is almost a certainty that we will return to the ILO. As a manager, you should know more about it, particularly in relation to paid study leave.

The ILO is a UN agency, although its history began before the founding of the UN. It includes unions, employers, and government. It establishes general rules for improving the conditions of those three groups as they interface in the real world. They do a great deal of HRD work, but that is not why they are included here.

The ILO has recognized the significance of paid study leave and has taken a position on it which should be known by all managers. This does not mean you have to agree, but you should at least know about the ILO's position, which is accepted in many countries of the world.

Specified time. The ILO says that legislation related to paid study leave should specify certain time factors. One question is what the minimum requirement is for an employee to be considered eligible. The maximum period available should be stated in the appropriate legislation. It is not necessary for a person benefiting from the legislation to utilize the maximum time.

During work time. The paid study leave should be part of the regular work year. It would not put the job in jeopardy. Quite the contrary, the employer could not fire the worker because of using paid study leave. The paid study leave would be in addition to any vacation or similar leave currently authorized by the employer. This would avoid forcing employees to use their vacation for study. It would be additional time off the job, and this certainly has its impact on managerial decisions.

Adequate financial support. For the most part, these programs have been funded out of general revenues, but no matter how they are funded, there must be identified financial resources. The employer is not exptected to bear the financial burden for these programs, as contrasted with tuition benefits (which is an employer sponsored program). The term "adequate" needs further definition, but this would probably be decided upon on a country-by-country basis, depending on the historical and cultural factors that vary from country to country.

It Can Happen Here

For those who say they think this is just something for the socialist countries, they should recognize that the major thrust for paid study leave has come from a wide variety of countries with various economic systems.

Some years ago, a similar program was suggested in the U.S., though at that time it was suggested for those who were out of the workforce. The idea was labeled as "educaid," as it came on the heels of legislation for "medicaid." The idea was that each retired person could get up to a fixed sum each year to be spent on learning programs of any nature. That idea is still around, and with the changes in the retirement age, it just might be enacted—but without any age provision.

IFTDO

The initials which head this section stand for International Federation of Training and Development Organizations, which was founded in Geneva in 1972. By 1975, there were over 40 countries represented. In 1978, the 7th Annual Conference was held in Washington, D.C., with over 600 people from 55 different countries attending. (I was the designer and the Chairperson.)

IFTDO does not have individual members; the members are national societies. In the U.S., the American Society for Training and Development is a member of IFTDO. As Americans, we can take some credit for IFTDO. It was started by a grant from our Agency for International Development. That grant was terminated after the first four years, and the organization has continued and grown since that time.

IFTDO has many advantages for all organizations in the U.S. with HRD programs. It provides HRD people with direct lines into what is happening in other countries. If your corporation is multi-national, the IFTDO has possibly served as a place to bring your HRD people together from different countries without running the risk of labeling the meeting as another example of "Yankee Imperialism." All the countries have equal status. The Executive Committee contains only one American.

IFTDO is still a young organization. The exchanges that have occurred at the various international conferences have been of a high quality, though there has been some tendency toward nationalism. This can be expected, particularly considering the political nature of some countries which only allow certain people to attend such international conferences.

This short section is not meant to give an in-depth look at IFTDO, but rather to call it to the attention of managers. It is another resource, and you and your HRD people should be familiar with it.

LEVY SYSTEM

There is a system used in many countries of the world which is not practiced in the U.S. at this time. In general terms, it is a system whereby the government taxes employers and then uses the money for HRD programs. The practice is found in countries including Great Britain, Colombia, Brazil, Venezuela, Nigeria, and Fiji. It is amazing that so little has been done with it in the U.S., but managers should certainly know about it. If yours is a multi-national company operating in any of the countries of the world with a levy system, you are right in the middle of the picture, and may not have been informed about how it works.

The system varies from country to country, as is to be expected, but it generally works this way: the government taxes employers, and this money is then used to provide HRD programs. In some cases, the money is recovered by the employer if certain approved courses are conducted. In others, the government uses the money to support quasi-government HRD centers.

There will be no attempt here to cover all situations, but perhaps a few examples will be helpful. Nobody knows just where it started, but some credit Colombia with one of the first programs in 1958. Among the larger countries, the British Industrial Training Act of 1964 is seen as the basic legislation in the field.

Under the British system, the tax is imposed and then companies can get a return if they conduct approved programs. The mechanism is based on using industry boards that must approve the training. The Act can be credited with being the basis for increasing the vast numbers of HRD people that can be found in Great Britain.

In Venezuela, there is somewhat the same system, and perhaps a more detailed picture will help the reader understand how the program works. There is the Instituto Nacional de Cooperacíon Educativa (INCE), founded in 1959, a government agency which collects 2 percent from all payrolls. This is put into a fund which INCE uses to conduct courses and—more important—to encourage others to do so. Any company can conduct any course it wants, but the course must meet INCE standards if the company expects reimbursement.

In 1975, Venezuela nationalized the oil companies, and foreign control was eliminated. It soon became apparent that with this nationalization, they needed to replace the vast HRD capabilities which had been provided by the foreign oil companies. Therfore, on January 26, 1976, a new organization was formed: the Instituto de Adiestramiento Petrolero y Petroquímico (INAPET). It was established to supplement the HRD programs being conducted by the nationalized oil companies. It is funded by receiving 60 percent of the money collected by INCE from the operating oil companies.

There are many variations, but all indications are that the levy system is an effective way of having companies pay for HRD. It can help smaller companies which could not otherwise afford the expenditure, and it encourages larger companies to offer at least some HRD programs which are designed to meet the needs as established by the government for the general good.

In Brazil, the levy system is used differently. It starts with the tax. Then quasi-government agencies have been set up to provide education to prepare workers to enter the fields of business, industry, and rural work. One assessment of these programs can be found in job placements, for almost all of their graduates are immediately placed. One of their managers shared the complaint with me that they have trouble keeping the learners in their centers. As soon as they achieve some basic skills, they are recruited by companies who desperately need even minimally educated workers.

By no means does this discussion include all the possibilities or describe all the programs. The number of countries using the levy system is increasing as it is being found to be a meaningful way to encourage more employers to offer HRD.

OPERATING ABROAD

If your company has plants and/or offices in other countries, some of what is being said here may sound familiar. In many foreign countries, HRD decisions come to the attention of the manager more rapidly than in the U.S. because of the political and social implications involved.

There is even a problem with the heading of this section. We used to say "overseas" and assumed that the term included all foreign countries. But what about Canada and Mexico? They are foreign, but certainly not overseas. Our language keeps changing to reflect the fact that our neighbors to the north and south have their own particular restrictions. We need to be aware of them to function effectively even that close to home.

The term "host" country signifies that particular non-U.S. country in which an American company is operating. Among the many factors to be considered here are two which have important HRD implications and should be known by managers.

School Systems and Degrees

In each country, the school system is different—though the physical plants may bear some resemblance to those in the U.S. Avoid the mistake of looking for direct comparisons. You will hear terms such as high school, college, bachelor's degree, and institute, and frequently they do not have the same meaning as they do in the U.S. If your organization is seeking a person at a certain level of schooling, which we frequently do in the U.S., it is necessary to find out what that level means in the host country. There is no direct comparison for most of the schools and diplomas with our system in the U.S.

If your HRD people are sending host country people to the U.S. for either training or education in an institution of higher learning, be sure they have checked it out first. If a degree is being sought in the U.S., you have to be sure that the receiving institution will accept the credentials of the learner from the host country. Your HRD people can easily check this out with the Cultural Attache at the American Embassy in the host country. The Visa Section of our Consulate is also an important source to be sure that all the legalities have been taken care of. They are not complicated and are for the benefit of all concerned, even though sometimes the host country people do not feel that way.

Degrees from higher education institutions are viewed differently in many parts of the world than they are in the U.S. Before sending a host country employee to the U.S. for a degree, have your HRD people verify expectations. In some places, once a person has a degree—particularly from a foreign university—he expects certain amenities. These are not specifically stated, but are certainly understood.

In the U.S., if an employee is assisted by the company while getting a degree, this is a wonderful extra. In many countries, once the employee returns with the degree, it is expected that there will be an increase in salary at least and also many of the perks (perquisites) which come with a degree, such as housing, an automobile and driver, a larger office, etc. Earning the degree automatically earns the perks, even before there is performance on the job. This does not apply to all countries, but it is best to have your HRD people check this out before you become involved in any program of sending employees to the U.S. for degree programs.

In developed countries, this might not be the same. They have had institutions of higher learning for a long time—in some cases, longer than we have. The title of the degree can be very important; frequently, the individual is addressed with the degree title (for example, terms which would be equivalent to Lawyer Jones or Engineer Brown). In England, name cards tend to list all the various degrees to which an individual is entitled. (In Germany, I was addressed as Herr Doctor Professor Nadler.) Your HRD people should be verifying the appropriate way to use the host country learning institutions, although there is still a great deal of prestige in obtaining a degree from an American university.

Expectations of Host countries

If you are going to establish a plant in a host country, you should realize that you will probably have to provide at least a training program, and perhaps an education program as well, for your employees. How about non-employees? Some of the developing countries have recognized the significance of HRD and have allowed a variety of plans to have foreign companies assist in developing the human resources of the whole country.

In some countries, your company will be faced with the demand from the host government that for each employee you train or educate you must also provide learning for one non-employee (who will go to work for a local company). You may have to double your HRD capacity to meet both your needs and the requirements of the host government.

In addition to job related HRD programs, you can also expect to be involved in other HRD programs. (This is more prevalent in developing countries, where they face the twin problems of illiteracy and exploding population.)

For your own purposes, you may have to include literacy as part of regular HRD programs. There is no generally accepted international definition for literacy, as much as the UN has tried to get agreement on one. There are various approaches to the problem, and one is to deal with "functional literacy." That is, the literacy level an individual needs to function in a particular country at a particular time. This is a realistic definition but does not help too much when the host country asks you to conduct literacy programs for employees. You may need some specialized HRD people who can identify the specific literacy needs and can assist in designing the appropriate learning experiences.

Programs related to population are frequently referred to as "family planning." Avoid the words "birth control," as they are taboo for religious reasons in many of the developing countries. "Family planning," as a term, has been generally accepted because it still leaves options open as to the size of the family. Of course, in some orthodox countries (both Catholic and Muslim), even the term family planning can provide difficulties. In the Philippines, such programs are called "responsible parenthood."

You may think that such programs are outside the realm of what the employer should be concerned with, but this is not always the case. In Malaysia, there was a joint program between the Malaysian Trade Union Congress and four large employers. The union conducted a learning program for employees and it was coordinated with the clinics the companies maintained. In that country, and in some others, many large companies have their own fully staffed clinics (actually small hospitals) right in the company compound. The learning program was funded by the ILO and one objective was to help the young workers learn about controlling family size.

The union was interested, since the birth rate was growing so rapidly that the population could be expected to double in 17 years. The union recognized that such growth could not be matched by economic growth, and there was the strong possibility that the end result would be an extremely high rate of unemployment. That condition is not conducive to union growth.

The employers were also interested, for unemployment would mean that there would be unrest, lower per capita purchasing power, and similar factors which are detrimental to employers in the private sector. They joined the union in this mutual HRD program. The employers, several of which were foreign companies, recognized the expectations of the government and the people and received warm praise for their efforts.

Another expectation is to respect the minority problems in the country. Our minority problems have been discussed earlier—and difficult as they have been, and perhaps still are, they do not have the long and bitter history which can be found in other countries.

In Malaysia, I was asked to help a major multi-national company in what they were calling an OD effort. The majority of the company's managers was Chinese. The government had issued a decree, which, in essence, said that 40 percent of the workforce had to be Malays. The Chinese, in many cases, had been on the peninsula now known as Malaysia for longer than some of the Malays, who had come across the Malacca Strait from Indonesia. It is easy to argue: Who is the real Malay? But that is not the point. The government issued a degree, and as a foreign employer you either conform or get out.

The Chinese family system is based on a high level of mutual support. Chinese managers, for example, are expected to educate other Chinese from their family to be their replacements, and this has been going on for a long time. If I had been a consultatnt to the Malaysian Government on this task, there were many avenues we could have explored. As a consultant to a multi-national company, there were fewer options. To force the Chinese managers to educate Malays as replacements was impossible. It had been suggested that I conduct a "sensitivity session" with the Chinese to help them see the point. I informed my client that in my judgment this would accomplish nothing. We had to explore alternatives which would allow the Chinese to at least mofify their behavior without violating their centuries-old family responsibilities. Also, the government had to be involved, as there were other alternatives depending on how the decree was interpreted. (As a P.S.—the client and I agreed to disengage on this one. They did hold sensitivity groups, which accomplished nothing toward solving the problem. A lack of enforcement by the government, at that time, gave them some breathing space.)

GOING AND COMING

Any company involved in the international scene has a constant flow of people who are leaving the U.S. and returning. There are two particular kinds of traffic which relate to HRD.

Job Assignment

There are those employees, frequently managers, who go abroad for just a brief period. These employees need HRD prior to departure, even if their stay is to be a short one. Unfortunately, there does not appear to be a sufficient recognition of this need. The attitude seems to be that it is not worth the investment to have an HRD program when the employee is only going for a short period of time.

Quite the contrary, it is possible to do a great deal of damage in a short period of time if the employee is not sensitive cross-culturally. For some countries, it is important to know about certain specific behaviors and customs, some of which are completely unacceptable, and others which are expected.

For longer job assignments, there is also controversy. There are those who say that there should be an extensive education program prior to departure. Others argue, equally strongly, that the real learning can only take place when the employee reaches the new country and receives training there. A middle position is that some things are best learned prior to departure from the U.S., while others are best learned after arriving at the new country of assignment. The learning program, as prepared by your HRD people, should also reflect the kinds of logistic support that the employee can expect to receive in the new country.

It is not possible to make any overall statements except to point out that a decision concerning whether or not training and education will be offered should be the result of a *management decision*—not the absence of a decision. Harris and Moran have discussed this in a book directed to making managers cross-culturally sensitive.

How about the family of the employee? Should they participate in any special learning program? The general feeling is that they should, either before departure or on arrival in the new country. In the U.S., the spouse may be involved in the work life, but not the children. It is an unusual situation where the children are expected to be part of any company activities.

For an employee working outside the U.S., it is generally very different. The involvement of the spouse is essential and the children can be a help or a detriment. The questions of schooling, playmates, social activities for teenagers, etc., can all be part of the problem of adjustment to a foreign assignment. If the employed spouse has to be concerned with family problems which were not previously present, this will naturally affect his job performance.

There is a great deal we know about preparing individuals and families for work outside the U.S. There are individuals and organizations who offer such HRD services, and some who specialize in different parts of the world. Large employers will probably have a person or unit with special responsibility for employees with such job assignments. It is hoped that these units do more than just the necessary processing. HRD is an essential element for any employee who will be working in a foreign country.

Less noticeable, but equally important, is the return. Too little attention has been given to this aspect. It is assumed that returning to one's own country does not present any problems, and this is simply not true. Returning does present two distinct problems. The following case study will indicate one of them.

The employee returned to the U.S. after six years in the Far East and Africa. After several days, the employee (let's use Mr. X) found that he was having trouble at lunchtime. Mr. X worked in an office situation, and people went to lunch at various times, particularly on the executive side. He noticed that it was often 2:00 or 3:00 PM before he went to lunch, and he felt his behavior was causing comment. Mr. X finally realized that in his previous foreign assignments he had not had to make any decisions about lunch. At noon the offices were closed and everybody left. The decision about lunchtime had been made for him for six years, and now he had to do it for himself. The decision was not difficult, but the recognition that such a decision was necessary took a little time to surface.

Then Mr. X had trouble finding a restaurant. There were many available, but for the past six years he had not had to decide about where to eat. If he had a business luncheon, the restaurant and meal were decided upon by the host. If he was the host, his host country employees made the decision for him; they knew how to handle such situations. If he did not have any business luncheon—an unusual situation in countries where a good deal of business is done in conjunction with eating—he just went home and had lunch with his wife, if she was at home. Now he had to decide on a restaurant and he found himself wandering around. (One day he stopped into a supermarket and bought some crackers as an easy way around that decision.)

Once he reached the point where he could choose a restaurant, he was faced with decision-making about what to order. As indicated above, the choice of where to eat usually included what would be eaten. He had not really had to make too many menu decisions for six years. He found himself eating hamburgers, milk, and cheese cake—American food which he had not had very much of in the past six years. Imagine, two whole weeks of the same lunch menu! Finally he adjusted back to the U.S. norms and behaved as would be expected of any white collar worker in a major city. In the interim, he experienced some discomfort which affected his productivity.

This case study may sound contrived, but in checking with many who have returned, the same story was repeated with only minor variations. As for this case study, I can vouch for it—for I was Mr. X! A very basic HRD program to prepare an employee for returning can do much to alleviate the re-entry problem and make the employee efficient much more quickly than if he is left to adjust without some learning help.

The second problem is less dramatic but more traumatic. The returning employee is coming back to a world which has changed quite a bit in the interim. If there has been constant communication and even frequent "home leaves," the adjustment may not be as difficult. The employee often stays in the host country for several years, with only occasional visitors from stateside. The employee hears of changes back home—in the company and in the country—but these are only vague and difficult to internalize. When the employee returns, he is faced with entering a different culture. He may bring back some words and phrases which have not become part of the normal vocabulary (for example, "honcho" or "jefe" for boss) and he can easily be perceived as being exotic, if not peculiar. Those who have not been abroad may begin looking for signs of strange behavior—and even strange diseases! During this period, the job performance of the employee cannot be expected to be up to standard. We need to explore ways to help the employee and his fellow employees to capitalize on the foreign experience. Instead of being forced to forget the experience as soon as possible and "become an American again," why not use the returned employee as a learning resource? Being part of a mutual learning experience can help a returned employee integrate the new learning into the existing situation, and help those who did not go abroad understand more about other cultures, other people, and themselves.

International Meetings

Despite changes in the tax laws, more meetings are being held outside the U.S. than were previously. At present, only two such meetings can be deducted as a business expense in one year, so there has been a slow-down in the growth of the international meetings—for some. Others are still doing it, within the law, in a variety of ways. There is pressure for the law, a recent one, to be repealed. If so, the international meeting business may explode!

If your company has international meetings, there are many benefits to be gained. There are still companies which will hold meetings in far-away places, for good reason, but then restrict most of the activity to the airport hotel or the conference site. If your international meeting is held in a place where your people frequently do not go, then make use of this foreign site. This is not to suggest that you provide for a great deal of sight-seeing—although some should certainly be on the agenda.

You could arrange in the host country for informal meetings or socials with counterparts. If you have good HRD people, they should be able to arrange for some learning situations which are not available in the back home situation.

International meetings should be an opportunity for growth for your people. In addition to the regular agenda, there should be other activities of a cross-cultural nature. The foreign country can serve as a resource for some development activities—general growth, though not related to the job. Some might see this as a perk, and perhaps it is, but the use of a cross-cultural environment for development can be significant for managers (and others) who are ethnocentric (i.e., culture bound). They should not just be dropped into a foreign country. Some HRD preparation is advisable so that they can get the most from the experience.

CONCLUSION

Times have changed since the post-World War II period, when the U.S. was the major innovator and exporter of HRD ideas and programs. There is much that can be learned from other countries and from their HRD programs.

The practices of paid study leave and levy system are two areas where other countries are doing some new things. We should learn more about these to see how they can be of help in our human resource situations.

There are many ways for this learning to take place and your HRD people should be attending international meetings such as the annual conferences of IFTDO and meetings sponsored by your company.

We are truly becoming one world, and your organization must be part of it. One activity area which must be involved is your activity in the area of human resource development.

Bibliography

Disincentives to Effective Employee Training and Development. Bureau of Training, U.S. Civil Service Commission, 1973. (Principal Researcher: Ruth Salinger).

Gardner, John. *Self Renewal.* New York: Harper Colophon Books, 1964.

Harris, Phil and Robert Moran, *Managing Cultural Differences.* Houston: Gulf Publishing, 1979.

Kepner, Charles H. and Benjamin B. Tregoe. *The Rational Manager.* New York: McGraw Hill, 1965.

Knowles, Malcolm. *Self Directed Learning.* New York: Association Press, 1975.

Lippitt, Gordon. *Organization Renewal.* New York: Appleton Century Crofts, 1969.

Nadler, Leonard. *Developing Human Resources.* Austin: Learning Concepts, 1979. Second Edition.

Tough, Allen. *The Adult's Learning Projects.* Austin: Learning Concepts, 1979. Second Edition.

Index

Index

accountability, 74, 81
administrator, 43, 55, 56, 57, 60, 65, 70, 71
adult learning theories, 44, 97
advocate, 52
Agency for International Development, 182
Alliance for Progress, 163
American Airlines, 69, 104
American Council on Education, 177
American Oil Company, 36
American Red Cross, 27, 158
American Society of Association Executives, 27
American Society for Personnel Administration, 64
American Society for Training and Development, 4, 43, 64, 68
andragogy, 97
apprentice, 29, 155, 156
Area Redevelopment Act, 163
Arranger of Facilities and Finance, 49
assessment center, 104, 105
audio-visual materials, 46, 69
authority, 145

behavior modeling, 105, 106
behavioral objectives, 113, 114

behavioral science, 1, 101, 102
Berne, Eric, 102
blue collar blues, 18
bottom line, 31, 91
British Industrial Training Act, 183
budget, 13, 50, 73, 74, 75, 81, 86

career development, 4, 17, 52, 53
career education, 172-174
career planning, 35
case study, 45, 69, 70, 99, 104
Categories of HRD people, 60
    collateral duties, 61, 63, 64
    organizationally identified, 61, 62, 63, 64
    professionally identified, 61, 63, 71, 151
change agent, 54
Civil Service Commission, 10, 75
classrooms, 12, 13, 79, 98, 121, 129, 130
client, 51
coaching, 100, 101
college, 68, 69, 70, 84, 177
community college, 29, 47, 84, 127, 172
community organization, 68
community relations, 169
compensation, 142

Comprehensive Employment and Training Act, 176
Conference Board, The, 12
conference center, 83
conglomerates, 33
consultant, 43, 51, 52, 53, 54, 55, 56, 57, 60, 64, 70, 71
consulting, 7
Continuing Education Unit, 67
cooperative programs, 29, 173
Corning Glass, 21
cost accounting, 91
cost center, 75, 76, 77, 78
cost data, 91
counseling, 3, 53
curriculum, 96, 97, 99
curriculum builder, 44, 45, 65, 68, 69
customers, 26, 160

decisions, managers, 8, 11, 12, 13, 17, 19, 20, 31, 32, 33, 34, 35, 36, 48, 52, 54, 56, 57, 58, 78, 86, 92, 95, 104, 120, 128, 130, 153, 158, 165, 170, 171, 176, 188
Department of Commerce, 8
Department of Labor, 176
Developer of HRD Personnel, 46, 66, 70
development, 2, 23, 25, 26, 30, 37, 38, 39, 87, 92, 113, 123, 125, 126, 127, 160, 174
disadvantaged, 33, 125, 162, 163, 171, 175
Drucker, Peter, 35
DuPont, 77

Economic Opportunity Act, 163
education, 2, 23, 24, 25, 26, 28, 29, 34, 35, 36, 67, 87, 89, 90, 92, 112, 113, 121, 122, 123, 125, 126, 127, 146, 147, 158, 160, 163, 174, 176, 180, 186, 188
educational entitlement, 180
educational technology, 44, 113
employees, families, 29
Equal Employment Opportunity, 19, 33, 88, 148, 166
equipment, 79, 80
ethics, 153, 154
Etzioni, Amitai, 25
evaluation, 108, 109, 110, 112, 113, 114, 118, 119, 120, 121, 122, 123, 131, 139, 140, 142, 150, 151
expense, 23, 24, 89, 91, 153
expert, 52
exercises, 99, 104
Exxon, 57
Exxon Education Foundation, 170

Facilitator of Learning, 43, 66, 67
facilities, 78, 81, 82, 83, 84, 85, 86, 170
finances, 50
financial aid, 29. (*See also* tuition refund)

financial resources, 23, 30, 72, 78, 86, 98, 127, 128, 129, 181
Finkel, Coleman, 83
flexitime, 20, 179, 180
Ford Motor Company, 172
fringe benefit, 154
future, 25, 34, 37, 39

Gardner, John, 25
General Electric, 81, 105
goals
    individual, 18
    organizational, 18, 19
Government Employees Training Act, 34
graduate degrees, 60, 61

Handlin, Oscar, 166
Harrison Houses, 83
Harvard Business Review, 125
Havelock, Mary, 118
Havelock, Ronald, 118
Holiday Inn, 81
Hoyt, Kenneth, 173
Human Resource Accounting, 88, 89
Human Resource Administration, 4
Human Resource Environment, 2, 3, 17, 19
Human Resource Management, 2, 4
Human Resource Utilization, 2, 3, 16, 17, 19, 30

in-basket, 104
industrial relations, 4
instructional strategies, 94, 95, 96, 98, 100, 101, 103
Instructional Strategies Developer, 45, 46, 69
instructor, 13, 14, 44, 45
Internal Revenue Service, 27, 158, 159, 176, 177, 180
international, 15, 179
International Federation of Training and Development Organizations, 182, 183
International Labor Organization, 181, 186
interpersonal relations, 30
investment, 23, 24, 26, 90, 91, 153

Japan, 12, 16
job linkage, 138
job satisfaction, 17, 18, 42

Kellog Centers, 84
Kepner-Tregoe, 30
Knowles, Malcolm, 5, 106

lay offs, 21
learning, 5, 6, 7, 9, 10, 19, 22, 23, 26, 27, 28, 37, 38, 43, 44, 45, 50, 53, 54, 55, 70, 82, 89, 90, 94, 95, 96, 98, 99, 100, 101, 105, 109, 110, 111, 112, 113, 114, 117, 118, 120, 122, 130, 134, 136, 139, 141, 145, 147, 148, 153, 154, 156, 160, 165, 174, 190

learning specialist, 43, 46, 47, 55, 56, 60, 64, 65, 68, 70, 71
lecture, 98
legislation, 88, 175, 180
Levitan, Sar, 163
Lippitt, Gordon, 25
Litton Learning Corp., 77

Mager, Robert, 114
maintainer of relations, 48, 71
management by objectives, 62
Manpower Development and Training Act, 163
manufacturing, 32
Marland, Sidney, 172
McDonalds, 28
meetings, 159, 160
mentor, 101
minority group members, 33, 51, 53, 68, 147, 148, 167, 168, 169
models, 95, 96
Mott Foundation, 171
Motorola, 81
multi-national, 10

National Alliance of Businessmen, 163
National Conference Center, 83, 101
National Training Laboratory, 83
native Americans, 165
needs, 8, 70, 143, 144
non-employees, 26, 30, 158, 170

objectives, 99, 108, 109, 111, 113, 114, 119, 130, 131, 139
organizational behavior, 1, 2, 102, 146
organization development, 42, 55, 57, 102, 148
organization involvement, 126
organization, non-profit, 34
overhead projector, 45

Pepsi-cola, 81
performance, 30, 116, 121, 123, 140, 190
personnel division, 10, 59
personnel function, 9, 53, 64, 140, 159
physical facilities and resources, 12, 72, 91, 98
plans for progress, 33
policy, 33
power, 145, 146, 147, 148, 149
product knowledge, 32
production, 31
productivity, 10, 14
profit center, 76, 77, 78
programmed instruction, 100
promotion, 24

quality of work life, 3, 19, 20

recognition, 138
research, 108, 109

retirement, 54
risk, 23, 24, 25
role play, 45, 104
roles, 43, 63, 64

sales, 32
Salinger, Ruth, 10
scholarships, 29
school system, 12, 29, 47, 84, 85, 184
secondary school, 29
self-instruction, 44
self-learning, 44, 58, 96, 106, 159
Skinner, B. F., 97
slides, 45
social issues, 162, 181
space, 13, 78, 79
staffing, 58, 59, 62, 64, 82
Standard Oil of Indiana, 45, 82
State Technical Assistance Act, 8
stimulator, 53
subject matter specialist, 45, 68, 69, 97
Supervisor of HRD Programs, 47, 48
supplies, 80, 81
support system, 125

Tough, Allen, 5, 106
training, 2, 23, 24, 25, 26, 27, 29, 30, 31, 32, 53, 67, 87, 89, 91, 92, 98, 105, 110, 112, 113, 118, 120, 121, 122, 123, 125, 126, 127, 128, 129, 130, 131, 132, 133, 134, 135, 136, 137, 138, 139, 140, 141, 142, 143, 144, 146, 147, 151, 155, 159, 160, 163, 174, 175, 176, 185, 188
transactional analysis, 102, 103, 104
turnover, 9, 16, 153
tuition benefit (*See* tuition refund)
tuition refund, 57, 88, 127, 128, 129, 180, 182

union, 14, 19, 27, 34, 36, 142, 154, 155, 156, 157, 158, 175, 180, 181, 186, 187
United Auto Workers, 175
university, 29, 67, 68, 69, 70, 84, 98, 127, 177

videotape, 45, 46, 49, 69, 80, 135, 171
Vocational Education Act, 172
voluntary associations, 34

Westinghouse, 170
Westinghouse Learning Corp., 77
white collar washouts, 18
work-study, 29
workforce, 16
workforce planning, 2, 3, 34, 35

Xerox, 12, 81

zero-based budgeting, 74